THE ART
OF DESKTOP PUBLISHING

*Using Personal Computers
to Publish It Yourself*

To Tony Bove

Cheryl Rhodes

Bantam Computer Books
Ask your bookseller for the books you have missed

THE ART
OF DESKTOP PUBLISHING

*Using Personal Computers
to Publish It Yourself*

Tony Bove, Cheryl Rhodes, and Wes Thomas
(the Editors of *Desktop Publishing*)

With Contributing Editors
August Mohr, Robert Purser, and Steve Rosenthal

BANTAM BOOKS
TORONTO • NEW YORK • LONDON • SYDNEY • AUCKLAND

ACKNOWLEDGMENTS

The authors gratefully acknowledge the research and contributions of Tim Bajarin, Hugh Daniel, Troy and Debbie Soult, Karen Thomas, Mick Wiggins and Paul Winternitz.

In addition, the authors wish to thank the crew of *Desktop Publishing* Magazine for their patience through the deadline crunch, especially Shannon Essa, Shaun Ralston, Kathy Slusser, and Julie and Paul Swanson.

We specially thank William Bates (Knowledge Engineering) for his help in learning to use JustText, John Scull and Martha Steffen (Apple Computer) for lending us a LaserWriter, and John Warnock (Adobe Systems) for PostScript. We also specially thank Ken Abbott (Manhattan Graphics), Liz Bond (Adobe Systems), Paul Brainerd (Aldus), Robert Doyle (Micro Cosmos), Royal Farros (T/Maker Graphics), Peter Hirshberg (Apple Computer), Guy Mariande (Tangent Technologies), Russ McCann (Boston Software), John Meyer (Ventura Software), Jim Rafferty (Cricket Software), Craig Slayter (SoftStyle), and Lian Zerafa (FTL Systems). Also thanks to Lenny Schafer (ImageSet) for his help in preparing this book.

The authors also express their gratitude to agent Bill Gladstone, and the editors at Bantam for shepherding this project through a very fast production cycle. Special thanks to Jono Hardjowirogo and Jim Walsh.

THE ART OF DESKTOP PUBLISHING
A Bantam Book / July 1986

Cover design by J. Caroff Associates.
Production by Bove & Rhodes Associates.
Coordination by Desktop Publishing Magazine.
Camera work by Production Resource (Menlo Park, CA).
Image setting by ImageSet (San Francisco, CA).

ISBN 0-553-34307-6

Published simultaneously in the United States and Canada.

PRINTED IN THE UNITED STATES OF AMERICA

B   0 9 8 7 6 5 4 3 2 1

TRADEMARKS

Macintosh is a trademark licensed to Apple Computer
Apple // is a trademark of Apple Computer
LaserWriter is a trademark of Apple Computer
AppleTalk is a trademark of Apple Computer
AppleWorks is a trademark of Apple Computer
LaserJet is a trademark of Hewlett-Packard
IBM is a trademark of International Business Machines Corp.
Laser CP is a trademark of Xerox Corp.
Art Grabber is a trademark of Hayden Software Company Inc.
Bernoulli Box is a trademark of IOMEGA Corp.
ClickArt is a trademark of T/Maker Company
ClickArt Effects is a trademark of T/Maker Company
Cordata LP300 is a trademark of Cordata
Cricket Graph is a trademark of Cricket Software
CtlLaser is a trademark of Rabar Systems
Do-It is a trademark of Studio Software
Document Compare is a trademark of The Model Office Co.
FONTastic is a trademark of Altsys Corp.
FTLTEX is a trademark of FTL Systems Inc.
Factfinder is a trademark of Forethought, Inc.
Fancy Font is a trademark of Softcraft Inc.
Fancy Word is a trademark of Softcraft Inc.
Filevision is a trademark of Telos Software Products
Font Explorer is a trademark of Heizer Software
Fontasy is a trademark of ProSoft
Fontrix is a trademark of Data Transforms Inc.
GEM Collection is a trademark of Digital Research
MacSpell+ is a trademark of Creighton Development
MacTablet is a trademark of Summagraphics Corp.
MacTerminal is a trademark of Apple Computer Inc.
MacVision is a trademark of Koala Technologies
MacViz is a trademark of Microvision Company
Maccessories is a trademark of Kensington Microware Ltd.
Magic is a trademark of New Image Technology
MagnaType is a trademark of Magna Computer Systems Inc.
Mastercom is a trademark of The Software Store
McPic! is a trademark of Magnum Software
Micro Planner is a trademark of Micro Planning Software
MicroTeX is a trademark of Addison-Wesley Publishing Co.
Milestone is a trademark of Digital Marketing
WIPS is a trademark of Datacopy Corp.
Multimate is a trademark of Multimate International
PC MacBridge is a trademark of Tangent Technologies Ltd.
PC Paint Plus is a trademark of Mouse Systems
PC Paintbrush is a trademark of ZSoft Corporation
PC Scan is a trademark of Dest Corporation
PCLPak is a trademark of Hewlett-Packard
PCTeX is a trademark of Personal TeX Inc.
PageMaker is a trademark of Aldus Corporation
Paint Cutter is a trademark of Silicon Beach Software
Paper Airplane Construction trademark Simon & Schuster
Pattern Collection is a trademark of RoZet
PostScript is a trademark of Adobe Systems Inc.
PrintMerge is a trademark of Polaris Software
Printworks for Lasers is a trademark of SoftStyle
ProKey is a trademark of Rose Soft
ProPrint is a trademark of Creighton Development
Punctuation & Style is a trademark of Oasis Systems
Q-Art is a trademark of Queue Inc.
QuadLaser is a trademark of Quadram

GRIDS is a trademark of Soft Wares Inc.
Genesis is a trademark of Tegra Inc.
Graphics Expander is a trademark of Springboard Software Inc.
Graphwriter is a trademark of Graphics Communications Inc.
Hayden:Speller is a trademark of Hayden Software Company Inc.
Hercules is a trademark of Hercules
Imageware is a trademark of Quadram
InMotion is a trademark of Ann Arbor Softworks
Index is a trademark of Digital Marketing
Interleaf is a trademark of Interleaf Inc.
Jazz is a trademark of Lotus Development Corp.
JustText is a trademark of Knowledge Engineering
LaserControl is a trademark of Insight Development Corp.
LaserFonts is a trademark of Century Software
Laserstart is a trademark of SoftStyle Inc.
LaserTEN is a trademark of Qume/Hitachi
Lasergrafix is a trademark of QMS
Linotronic is a trademark of Allied Linotype
MITE is a trademark of Mycroft Labs, Inc.
Mac 10 is a trademark of Paradise Systems Inc.
Mac Spell Right is a trademark of Assimilation Inc.
Mac the Knife is a trademark of Miles Computing
Mac-Art Library is a trademark of CompuCRAFT
MacBottom is a trademark of Personal Computer Peripherals Inc
MacDraft is a trademark of Innovative Data Design
MacMemories is a trademark of ImageWorld Inc.
MacPublisher is a trademark of Boston Software Publishers Inc.
QuickPaint is a trademark of Enterset
ReadySetGo is a trademark of Manhattan Graphics Corporation
ScenicWriter is a trademark of ScenicSoft Inc.
SideKick is a trademark of Borland International
SmartCable is a trademark of IQ Technologies
SmartModem is a trademark of Hayes Microcomputer Products
SpectraFAX is a trademark of SpectraFAX Corp.
Spellbinder is a trademark of Lexisoft
StarJet is a trademark of Control-C Software Inc.
SuperKey is a trademark of Borland International
Superpage is a trademark of Bestinfo
TOPS is a trademark of Centram Systems West, Inc.
Text Pac Software is a trademark of Dest Corp.
The Mac Art Department is a trademark of Simon & Schuster
The Newsroom is a trademark of Springboard Software Inc.
The Print Shop is a trademark of Broderbund Software
ThunderScan is a trademark of Thunderware, Inc.
Turbo Lightning is a trademark of Borland Intl.
Type-Set-It is a trademark of Good Ideas
Ventura Publisher is a trademark of Ventura Software Inc.
VersaTerm is a trademark of Peripherals Computers & Supplies
VideoWorks is a trademark of Hayden Software Company Inc.
Mac the Ripper is a trademark of Miles Computing
Volkswriter 3 is a trademark of Lifetree Software
WX is a trademark of Tech Knowledge
Windows DRAW! is a trademark of MICROGRAFX
Word Finder is a trademark of Writing Consultants
Word Plus is a trademark of Oasis Systems
WordStar is a trademark of MicroPro Intl.
XyWrite is a trademark of XyQuest, Inc.
ZyINDEX is a trademark of ZyLAB Corporation
dBASE II is a trademark of Ashton-Tate
dMacIII is a trademark of Datalogica USA

Tony Bove and **Cheryl Rhodes** are the editors and publishers of *Desktop Publishing* Magazine. They also founded and edited *User's Guide* (a magazine for CP/M computer users) and *DataCast* Magazine (with Jim Warren). They are co-authors of several books on using personal computers: *Free Software* (Baen Books/Simon & Schuster), *CP/M User's Guide* (Baen Books/Simon & Schuster), *InfoWorld's Essential Guide to CP/M* (Harper & Row), and *WordStar Pocket Reference* (Addison-Wesley). All books were produced by the authors.

Tony Bove has over ten years experience in the world of microcomputers and publishing. He has contributed articles and reviews to a variety of magazines including *InfoWorld*, *PC World*, *The Whole Earth Software Catalog*, and *The Whole Earth Review*. Tony Bove also co-authored (with LeRoy Finkel) *The TRS-80 Model III User's Guide* (John Wiley & Sons), and co-wrote *The CP/M Handbook* (Sybex).

Cheryl Rhodes has over eleven years experience in computing and electronic data processing. Cheryl is a self-taught computer literacy instructor who has coordinated such projects as the Apple Van Project (Lawrence Hall of Science, Berkeley, CA) and Computertown USA! (People's Computer Company, Menlo Park, CA). Both Tony and Cheryl are hosts of the desktop publishing electronic conference on The Well (Sausalito, CA), and are frequent lecturers at industry trade shows.

Wes Thomas is President of Wes Thomas Public Relations, a PR firm specializing in desktop publishing and artificial intelligence. He has over 25 years experience in systems analysis, writing, editing, publishing, public relations, and advertising. Working from his home in East Northport, New York, he uses electronic mail to communicate with clients, writers, and editors around the U.S. and Canada.

CONTENTS

PREFACE

Happiness is owning the means of production.

— the unknown desktop publisher

This book was written and produced in less than three months. In those three months we researched and wrote all of the chapters, compiled the list of companies and products, generated the index and table of contents, printed proof pages on a laser printer, and produced the final typeset pages. In every step of the process we used personal computers and desktop publishing software.

Specifically, we used CP/M computers and PCs with WordStar (MicroPro) to write and edit the chapters, XyWrite (XyQuest) to produce the table of contents, and Index (Digital Marketing) to produce the index. We used dBASE II (Ashton-Tate) to produce the list of companies and products. On PCs we checked the spelling and punctuation using The Word Plus and Punctuation & Style (Oasis Systems). Finally we transferred the text to an Apple Macintosh in order to use JustText (Knowledge Engineering) and the Apple LaserWriter to produce pages. We then substituted an Allied Linotype Linotronic 100 typesetter for the LaserWriter, and ran JustText again (after making final changes) to produce the camera-ready typeset pages.

This process would have taken much longer and would not have been possible on personal computers without two major advances in personal computer technology:

- The Apple LaserWriter and Macintosh combination makes an excellent desktop typesetting system for producing complete pages. Without the Linotronic compatibility with the LaserWriter, we would not have been able to see proof pages in a manner of minutes, and go to the typesetter with final (final!) pages on disk that did not need any correcting or coding.

- Electronic mail services (specifically MCI Mail) made it possible to send chapters to co-authors on the East Coast, send revised chapters back to the West Coast, send review sections to reviewers in various parts of the country, and receive last-minute changes on the same day that we started typesetting the final pages.

With desktop publishing technology, we authors had control over production, and we were able to produce a book with up-to-date information. before printing the book. The editors at Bantam were not convinced that the low-cost methods would not be advanced enough or settled enough to be used to produce a first-rate, professional-looking book. By doing this book in this manner, we proved that the technology can be useful to large publishers as well as to entrepreneurs, small businesses, professional communicators, freelance graphic artists, professional writers, and even street poets!

The book is not just an example of desktop publishing — it is an attempt to cover the largest horizontal application ever to be found for personal computers. The topic encompasses word processing, graphics presentation, laser printing, typesetting, conventional production methods, page makeup, and design considerations. It informs those who are looking to buy systems to use for desktop publishing; it provides capsule reviews of products used in desktop publishing; it explains the concepts and terminology used in publishing production; and it provides examples of using the equipment to design and produce various types of publications.

The first chapter is an overview of desktop publishing equipment and applications. It introduces the hardware and software used for publishing and explains how we chose the systems we use to produce our magazine, *Desktop Publishing* (we use a similar setup to produce the magazine that we used to produce this book).

The second chapter shows you why you should "go electronic" with your words as soon as possible. Most desktop publishing projects start with word processing or scanning, to get the words into an electronic form so that they can be processed into typeset pages and archived for future use. This chapter explains word processing and text scanning with digitizers, and shows examples of typical word processors and how they can produce typeset pages on a laser printer or typesetter. It also shows you how to send text from one type of computer to another (for example, how to transfer text and data from a PC to a Macintosh).

The third chapter explains in detail the differences among various types of printers used with personal computers, from dot matrix to laser printers and typesetters. This chapter also provides an overview and examples of programs that prepare text for output on laser printers and typesetters, commonly called "printer utility" programs. Some of them provide typefonts that are not normally available on dot matrix and laser printers.

The fourth chapter shows you how to incorporate graphics with your text, using "painting" and "drawing" programs on PCs and Macintosh computers, and how to use image digitizers to scan graphic images into the computer. The ability to mix text and graphics on the page is an essential ingredient of desktop publishing.

The fifth chapter focuses on one of the major advances in desktop publishing: full-page makeup on personal computers. With the software described in this chapter running on Macintosh computers or PCs, you can move text and graphics around an imaginary page on the screen, draw lines and boxes, scale images to different sizes and prepare text for typesetting. You can then send completed pages to a laser printer or typesetter without doing paste-up by hand.

Having the tools is not enough — you must also learn how to use them properly. The sixth chapter explains the concepts and terminology used in conventional publications production and how they are affected by desktop publishing tools. The chapter is like a crash course in design, production and printing, with very specific tips on how to produce newsletter and magazine pages, books, advertisements, postcards, business cards, flyers and other types of pages, so that you don't have to go to design and production school to produce your own publications.

The seventh and last chapter describes the personal computer tools that professional graphic artists and typographers can use to do professional page composition. These tools are not for novices — they are very expensive compared to desktop publishing tools for beginners, but they are capable of producing professional-looking output that rivals the output from $50,000 to $500,000 systems. The desktop publishing revolution also applies to professional book and magazine production, and this chapter shows off the products that can do it.

The book ends with a glossary of typesetting and page makeup terminology, a list of companies and products, and a comprehensive index. The goal was to provide a resource for newcomers to desktop publishing as well as to professionals who are ready to use this equipment.

Producing this book has been an extremely rewarding experience, despite the drawbacks of using a technology that is barely proven and still percolated with bugs. We believe that the potential for individuals to do their own publishing will have an even greater impact on our society than the advent of personal computing. We hope our book will point the way toward a renaissance in individual publishing.

Tony Bove & Cheryl Rhodes
Woodside, CA

Wes Thomas
East Northport, NY

March 1, 1986

FOREWORD

Freedom of the press is guaranteed only to those who own one.

— A. J. Liebling

We have it in our power to begin the world again.

— Thomas Paine,
Common Sense

You may not think of yourself as a potential publisher, but you now have the ability to self-publish more than ever before. It has become cost-effective for almost anyone using a personal computer to prepare documents that appear professionally published. The new publishing tools put book making, newsletter publishing, magazine design, ad layout, documentation and promotional literature publishing into the hands of personal computer users who never before had the opportunity to do these things.

Publishing is a function that occurs in many different businesses and institutions. The inexpensive publishing tools not only make it easier for small businesses and small publishers to do their own work — these tools also reduce the bottom line of large corporations who spend thousands on in-house publishing systems.

The power of publishing has historically shaped our destiny. From religious pamphlets to political leaflets, from literature to comics, from newspapers and magazines to highly informative newsletters, the public has traditionally been informed by those who have knowledge of publishing methods and access to printing presses. No matter how much of the public's attention is captured by televised news and video entertainment, the print media remains the primary means of communication for conducting business and reporting news, and reading is still the most popular form of entertainment.

The power of computing has only recently changed our lives. For writers and small publishers, personal computers provide a means of self-expression through alternative, less-costly methods. Word processing programs introduced more people to computers, and spreadsheets made computers even more useful. While researchers argued over the possibilities of the "paperless office," personal computer users look for better ways to present their information in print.

We now know that the "paperless office" is a myth, that computers have not yet liberated us from all the drudge work, and in fact computers have created *more* work and *more paper*. We find ourselves spending nights "hacking" the word processing codes in our documents so that they'll print correctly, and spending more time trying to get our spreadsheets to print properly than devising the spreadsheet formulas that make them relevant.

The need for readable output has started a trend for using graphics and different typefonts and sizes to make documents more interesting and professional-looking. Meeting this need head-on was Apple Computer with the Macintosh computer and LaserWriter laser printer. The Mac is still one of the easiest computers to learn how to use for word processing and drawing graphics. The LaserWriter, awarded Product of the Year in 1985 by *InfoWorld* (a personal computer industry weekly), can mix different typefonts on the page with graphics, and provide near typeset-quality output.

Inexpensive page makeup software for laser printers first appeared on the Macintosh. Professional typesetting software first appeared on the IBM PC. These two approaches to publishing — the Macintosh-like "what you see is what you get" page makeup programs, and the PC-based professional typographer's typesetting programs — are competing in a market niche that includes corporate in-house publishing departments, communication firms (public relations, advertising, catalog publishers), newsletter publishers, book and magazine publishers, small newspapers, and thousands of small businesses that design and print their own flyers, brochures, reports and office paperwork.

Desktop publishing (coined by Paul Brainerd, who left a typesetter manufacturing company to form Aldus, makers of PageMaker) describes the application of personal computers to the production process of publishing. Desktop publishing is another major step in the evolution of human productivity tools. The personal computer with word processing, spreadsheet and data base software made computers useful for increasing individual productivity; now desktop publishing software, laser printers, and mass storage devices will bring us into the realm of everyday self-publishing.

What does desktop publishing do for you? Now you can do, cheaply, some of the tricks that make small businesses appear to be very large: improve your letterhead and business cards, put together marketing literature with typeset text, publish a newsletter to gain attention and get more business, and so forth.

Before desktop publishing became practical, you had to get typesetting done at a typesetting service. You had to spend time preparing the text for the service, then spend more time proofreading the result, as well as time and money dealing with a vendor. If you are not an artist, you wouldn't think of using graphics without hiring a graphic artist or using another vendor. Integrating the typesetting with the graphics (called "paste-up") was another chore, taken on by the highly-skilled (and highly-paid) vendor or someone you hired to wield an Exacto knife and a can of spray adhesive.

Newspapers and large magazines have been using computers for several years to do layout and paste-up, but these systems ranged in price from $50,000 to well over $500,000. The desktop publishing phenomenon is putting these sophisticated tools in the hands of personal computer users. There are thousands of marketing and service departments in large corporations that have to do some form of publishing, and to them desktop publishing is great news. Many small businesses see marketing opportunities in newsletters, self-produced brochures and flyers, and better control over office paperwork. Quite a few small publishers can now take advantage of computerized production.

Word processing was the most popular application of personal computers in the seventies because it gave people an efficient way to create, store and retrieve information for their businesses and professions. Spreadsheets and data base management became the most popular applications as people learned the power of processing and sorting their data to get results displayed on the screen and tabulated for reports.

The next step is to communicate those results clearly, *on paper*, and in the future, *electronically*. Desktop publishing holds the promise to be the most popular application in the eighties.

*   *   *

We are not strangers to the traditional methods of publishing. As assistants for the Appalachian Mountain Club's Boston Chapter newsletter and journal, we assembled typewritten text for typesetting and sent copies off to a graphics house in Vermont.

Four days later the typeset galleys arrived by Federal Express, and we did our first proofreading pass. Hours flew by as we cut and pasted xerographic copies of the galleys into a crudely marked-up and corrected layout, then Federal Expressed it back to the Vermont hills with typewritten corrections.

The Interleaf system running on a Sun Microsystems workstation is a complete desktop publishing system for around $48,000 (including laser printer).

Four working days later final xeroxes of the galleys reached us for final proofreading and layout by the editors. After two days of layout, the xeroxes were sent by Federal Express back to Vermont. Two more working days passed until the final camera-ready paste-up reached us, again by Federal Express. We did our "final final" proofreading, corrected any last-minute errors, and Federal Expressed the paste-up back to Vermont, where the graphics house made all final corrections and sent it off to the printer.

All told it took approximately thirteen days to prepare the newsletter from its final text stage (where everything is typewritten and edited) to the printer. We used Federal Express four times, and the graphics house used it three times. This was the state-of-the-art of newsletter publishing in 1975.

We moved on to computerized production methods soon thereafter, when we started jobs as writers of computer manuals. Our jobs quickly became more related to *producing* these manuals. The information was different then, but the goal was the same: describe how to use computers, how to type commands to start operations. This is hard to write about, or read, without some way to show words in different typefonts. The writer needed to use a different typefont for the computer command words than for ordinary text, and another different typefont for the messages displayed by the computer.

This typesetting problem was compounded by the need for total accuracy in computer manuals. The time spent proofreading and correcting the typesetter's output soon grew too much for writers, so copy editors were hired. With errors introduced at every step of this process, the writers who were familiar with computers began to see that quantum leaps could be made to shorten this process and make it more efficient.

One such quantum leap was the development of a standard interface between the word processing computers and the computers that were used to run typesetting machines. Text could be transferred directly from one computer to the other, eliminating the retyping.

The cost savings were not readily apparent to the managers of the in-house publishing departments of large corporations, even though large magazine and book publishers had already computerized. Computers were expensive at that time, and mostly used for running the business or doing research. Many editors felt threatened by this new technology — would it replace them as grammarians, punctuators, spelling checkers, even fact checkers?

The Apple Macintosh is a less-sophisticated desktop publishing system for under $11,000 (including Apple LaserWriter laser printer, hard disk, and PageMaker software from Aldus).

The writers felt differently — they saw that they would have *more control* over the appearance of their work, and they were very enthusiastic about having more to say about production schedules. In our writing department, the overwhelming majority of the writers voted to replace their typewriters with computer terminals and to use them to *both write* the manuals *and prepare them for typesetting*. This was in 1976, when personal computing was still viewed as a hobby.

Today we still see many publishers and corporate publishing departments using minicomputers (the kind we had in 1976) to do typesetting and image reproduction. Laser printers and typesetters, and advances in software, changed the cost of the minicomputer-based systems (they now range from $50,000 to $150,000). But the real quantum leap occurred in conjunction with personal computers.

We now use a desktop laser printer (Apple LaserWriter) to produce near-typeset-quality output, and a personal computer (Macintosh) to control the laser printer and to prepare text and graphics for output. The cost of the entire system including laser printer: $9,900.

To get real typesetting rather than laser printing, we take our Macintosh disk to a service that has an Allied Linotype Linotronic 100 typesetter, and we click the Print menu. The Linotype spews out full pages that look exactly like the laser printer pages, only with four times the resolution (1270 dots per inch rather than 300). The pages cost less than $2 each and there are no corrections needed, because we already proofed the pages on the LaserWriter. We used this system to produce this book.

We use different personal computers for word processing, and software to check spelling and punctuation, declare typefont settings and italic and bold words. Then we "pour" the electronic text into electronic pages displayed on a personal computer screen, where text can be moved and lined up with graphic elements to form complete pages. We can prepare electronic pages right up to the deadline, and use a laser printer to print page proofs.

The ability to transfer text and graphic information from one popular brand of personal computer to another, together with the proliferation of personal computers, has put typography and graphic design in the hands of anyone with access to a personal computer. Now the preparation of information is no longer a black art understood only by publishers, typographers, graphic designers and photographers. Self-publishing has become a general application of personal computers, performed in-house by most businesses.

Does this spell doom for professional typographers and graphic designers? Not at all, even for those whose sole expertise is in the use of older methods, which are still necessary for many publishing jobs. The tools are changing to make production go faster and easier. The artists are given inexpensive tools that enable them to create more freely. The word processing tools give writers the power to immediately record their thoughts as fast as their fingers can type them, and edit them later. The typesetting software gives typographers the chance to gain more business consulting for overall design without spending hours coding the text.

If you are a graphics designer, you can use a desktop publishing system to produce your jobs without having to rely on outside typesetting services. If you are a small business, you may want to hire a part-time graphic artist to use your desktop publishing system to produce your reports and marketing literature.

Do you still need a design and typography expert? Most people do not have the graphic arts experience or training in the methods used to present information on a page, and most publishers want the best results. You should use experts to design your publication and provide the specifications such as the typefont, size of the characters, lengths and widths of lines, and the look of the page. Then you can produce the material yourself, or hire a graphic artist to produce it on your equipment. You control the production schedule and save money.

*   *   *

Where do you jump in? That depends on your needs, and on your imagination. What could you do if you had the ability, without too much effort, to produce a good-looking newsletter, brochure, advertisement, piece of marketing literature, or even a business card? Are you a budding writer of self-help books who wants to impress a publisher by selling first edition laser-printed copies through mail order? Do you want to prepare first-rate children's books and educational materials, with less cost? Are your department's sales gains so impressive that you want to publish the charts and graphs to improve company morale?

Do you communicate with words and pictures? Do you want to set your words in a professional-looking typefont and combine them with pictures and graphics on the same page? Do you want more control over your work on documents or books, with less cost and more flexibility? You are ready for desktop publishing.

CHAPTER ONE

Overview of Desktop Publishing Tools

Production is not the application of tools to materials, but logic to work.
— Peter Drucker

Applications Remember the last time you prepared some text to be typeset? Did you spend a lot of time on the preparation and proofreading, and also a lot of money on a vendor's service, without much control over the schedule? Would you prefer to do the typesetting in your office, see the results immediately, and make corrections at no extra charge? Wouldn't you rather use an inexpensive personal computer so that you only have to type the text once, and have the computer do all the proofreading?

The essence of desktop publishing is this: saving time, gaining a measure of control, and ultimately saving money by doing it yourself. What makes it possible is that fantastic devices for processing words and pictures are now becoming affordable for personal computer users.

Laser printers costing over $50,000 have been in use for a few years. Today's desktop laser printers are in the $1,500-$24,000 range. They resemble office copiers, use regular copier paper, and are easy to maintain. They provide near typeset-quality output.

There are revolutionary advances in graphics production on personal computers. You can produce camera-ready art in an instant, and prepare color images for color separation and printing. Digitizing machines ($500-$5000, formerly $50,000) can convert an image into

1

digital information that can be edited on a personal computer screen and printed on a laser printer.

What can you do with all this equipment? Newsletters, brochures, flyers, advertisements, magazines, books, annual reports, community newspapers, catalogs, manuals... Almost anything that is typeset, and many things that are not yet typeset because the task is too difficult or costly, will benefit from using desktop publishing tools.

Some examples: an antique dealer we know bought a Macintosh to keep track of inventory and accounting, only to find that the software was harder to use than the original paper systems she was using. Then she realized that the Macintosh, equipped with MacPublisher (Boston Software), would be useful for producing a newsletter, and with data base software she could maintain a mailing list. She uses the Macintosh to produce a good-looking newsletter that draws in more sales. She also uses the Koala MacVision digitizer to scan images of antiques for publication and her archive.

Newsletter publishing is on the rise, and desktop publishing tools make newsletters easier to prepare and much less expensive than traditional methods. Tom Engleman of the *Dow Jones Newspaper Fund Newsletter* saved nearly $45 a page in typesetting and paste-up costs to produce the newsletter, by switching to self-publishing using the Apple Macintosh with ReadySetGo (Manhattan Graphics), a page makeup program, and the Apple LaserWriter.

Arthur Naiman, a book author, now produces all of his books using a Macintosh and LaserWriter, because he needs to have control over the manuscript and the ability to mix text and graphics on the same page, without anyone meddling with the pages before final printing.

We saved over $30 per page in the production of a bi-monthly magazine by switching from a typesetting service to in-house laser printing. Before the switch we were using PCs for word processing and preparation for typesetting, and saving money by not having the text retyped or coded by the typesetting service (we coded our own text, which is almost as complicated as programming). Switching to PageMaker (Aldus Corp.) saved us plenty of time formerly spent coding text files, with the added benefit of laser printing entire pages without doing manual paste-up. Typesetting the laser-printed and proofed pages amounted to an extra $1 per page, with no re-coding and no need for corrections.

Newspapers are getting into the act, even though they have large computerized composition systems already in place. The *San Fran-*

cisco Examiner uses a Macintosh and LaserWriter to produce bar charts and graphics. *USA Today* also uses the Macintosh for graphics, and PCs for estimating the layout. Small newspapers, like the *Source*, a twice-monthly newspaper for the University of Pittsburgh at Bradford that is put together using Microsoft Word, a Macintosh, and a LaserWriter, can be produced at a fraction of the cost it would take to produce them on professional typesetting equipment or through services.

The untold story is in the offices of Fortune 1000 companies, where work groups gather information for presentation to management and the work force, and especially in marketing communications departments. Managers could rally their division's sales staff to produce a weekly in-house newsletter that would broadcast their sales gains across the entire corporation. The newsletter might increase their visibility in the large corporation, boost morale in their department, and generally improve sales.

Countless agencies and services can save time and money producing brochures and printed information. Documentors can prepare manuals with graphics to enhance readability and the transfer of information. Managers can prepare good-looking progress reports for their executives.

In these times, if you run a small business, not many of your customers will have faith in your business if you do not use letterhead, business cards, and marketing literature for your products or services. All of these printed elements require some form of text preparation (such as typesetting or letter-quality printing), graphic presentation (page layout), production and printing.

Equipment Overview

The lesson we learn from the history of printing is that progress occurred first in the area of *typesetting*, which is the preparation of the information in a form we can readily read. The sudden improvement in the manner of preparing text made it possible to produce volumes in a short time and therefore at a reduced cost.

The focus of today's advances in presenting information is once again typesetting. Around 1975 we saw the first typesetting systems based on mainframe computers, and in 1980 they were controlled by minicomputers (mostly Digital Equipment Corp. minicomputers with exotic "front-end" systems such as Penta, Atex, AKI and others).

These typesetting systems could accept text from a variety of sources, opening up the possibility of incredibly fast publishing for mass communication.

By 1985 we had drawing and electronic "painting" software on personal computers, and the ability to merge typeset text and graphics on the same page, and see the page (and change it) on the screen before printing it. The Macintosh was the first computer to merge typesetting and graphics on the screen, and the LaserWriter was the first laser printer to take full advantage of its 300 dot-per-inch resolution to print graphics and words in different typefonts.

Publishing Solutions

We now have several solutions for doing publishing with personal computers:

- The "high road" (expensive, polished route for professional artists and typographers) includes $3000-$8000 page makeup programs for PCs that can send output to typesetting systems or control the typesetting equipment directly (that is, the PC acts as a "front end" to the typesetter). The typesetting equipment is usually over $20,000.

- The "middle road" (not so expensive, high quality) includes the Macintosh with PageMaker, or PC with Personal Publisher, Microsoft Word or similar package, along with the LaserWriter or other PostScript-driven laser printer.

- The "economy route" (least expensive, varying quality) includes the less expensive laser printers and dot matrix printers with PCs or Macs using word processing and graphics programs, and special programs that control printers.

Which route should you take? Start with the type of output you want for your application. The high road is the one for many advertising agencies, graphics houses and publishers. The middle road is very attractive for large and small businesses, and newsletter, magazine and book publishers. The "economy route" is perfectly appropriate for school newspapers, church and club bulletins, newsletters, reports and correspondence.

It is important to remember these routes as you investigate desktop publishing. You can go the "economy route" but you might find that your applications have grown beyond the limitations of the inexpensive laser and dot matrix printers.

The rest of the hardware and software you need depends on your application. Most writers and newsletter publishers need enough disk storage to accommodate a year's worth of text (a ten or twenty megabyte hard disk is usually appropriate). If you want to do page makeup on a PC screen, your PC or compatible needs enough memory (usually 640K) and a graphics card with a high-resolution monochrome (black and white) monitor. Software varies widely in price and in functionality.

Compatibility   Compatibility among computers is one of the least understood problems. The issue doesn't exist in the world of stereo equipment — you can put any record on any record player, or any cassette tape on any cassette player. But anyone who has looked into buying a personal computer knows already that there are several types of computers that are not compatible with each other — the same software and floppy disk doesn't "play" on all machines.

Standards have developed in the market as a result of consumer demand for compatibility. At first there were four "standard" types of personal computers: the Apple //, the Commodore, the Atari, and the CP/M-type computer (including Radio Shack). CP/M (Control Program/Microcomputers) was a generic piece of software called an "operating system" that acted as a compatibility layer between the programs you would buy for your computer and the hardware of the computer — so that you could buy standard programs that ran on a variety of machines.

Along came IBM, a company that is large enough to dictate compatibility in the U.S. market. IBM pitched its "PC" (personal computer) into the pool in 1982 and displaced a great deal of the CP/M market share, leaving CP/M and Apple with pint-sized portions of the business market. Commodore and Atari, always recognized as makers of decent "home computers," suffered the travails of the marketplace as its pundits predicted a dying home market.

Apple responded with its new icons-and-mouse environment based on the Macintosh; Atari has bounced back with its ST-520 computer that imitates the Macintosh, and Commodore is still alive and kicking with the new Amiga computer. However, the marketplace has changed, and nearly all these manufacturers are now addressing a common problem: compatibility with IBM.

It is theoretically possible to do desktop publishing on any type of computer, but the latest desktop publishing products fall into three distinct categories: products for the Apple Macintosh, products for the IBM PC, communication "bridge" products designed to give you the best of both worlds, and "high-end" system solutions that are priced more for corporate departments than for individuals. An example of the latter category is the Interleaf system ($50,000) that runs on Sun Workstations.

The Macintosh system with the LaserWriter printer and page makeup and typesetting software ($10,000) is a complete desktop publishing solution. You can put a similar system together on the IBM PC side, where there is no one distinct desktop publishing solution but a plethora of products that work with a variety of printers and typesetters, including the PostScript printers and typesetters on the "Mac side."

"Bridge" products (such as PC MacBridge) and networks try to provide the best of both worlds, either through the ability to connect a PC to a PostScript printer via the AppleTalk network, or directly through serial link; or through the sharing of files and resources over a local-area network. The goals are either to bring PC data to a PostScript device in the Mac world, or bring Mac data to the PC world.

The Macintosh setup is a complete desktop publishing system because the standard setup (with application software) can perform nearly all kinds of desktop publishing, from sophisticated typesetting to publishing an image data base. What's more, you can buy the entire setup from an authorized Apple dealer. The Macintosh was the first personal computer to break ground in desktop publishing, and many recently-designed systems imitate the Apple's functionality. You can learn a lot about desktop publishing by trying out Apple's setup, even if you intend to buy a PC-oriented system.

The predominance of Macintosh is due to its capabilities to mix text and graphics on the same page and show it on the screen. The Apple LaserWriter is the most functional laser printer on the market, outclassing the others by virtue of its PostScript software. The LaserWriter can produce near-typeset-quality output with a full range of typefonts and full-page graphics at 300 dots per inch; the only laser printers that can do all of these things are other printers driven also by PostScript.

The IBM PC is the predominant business computer, with a lot of programs for word processing and printing on various types of printers. The PC is not inherently a graphics machine, so in order to do graphics you have to add hardware to the machine.

The Commodore Amiga is a graphics-oriented machine, and there are software products becoming available to produce output on the Hewlett-Packard LaserJet and other PC equipment, and to produce output for PostScript printers and Apple equipment. The same is true of the Atari ST-520. Both computers hold promise of becoming cost-effective desktop publishing systems.

The Apple // family of computers has always been strong in graphics and weak in word processing. There are thousands of programs for Apple //+, Apple //e and Apple //c computers, but the most popular software is AppleWorks, an integrated package that combines word processing, spreadsheets and a data base.

We describe some Apple // software in this book, but the computer is not recommended for serious desktop publishing, although programs like the Newsroom (Springboard) make it possible to use the Apple // for producing high-school newspapers and club newsletters.

The generic CP/M computer also has thousands of programs for it, but most of the popular programs are now available on IBM PCs. Our coverage of PC word processing software mentions the CP/M counterparts, so you can use the information to do desktop publishing from CP/M computers (we use several CP/M computers as well as PCs and Macs). However, CP/M computers have no standard way to produce graphics, so the best you can do is advanced word processing, with paste-up by hand if you want to include graphics from another computer.

Nearly all computer hardware and software products fall into the categories of creating and entering data, processing data, storing and retrieving data, and getting output. The rest of this chapter is an over-view of the best products in these categories, along with our choices and setup for magazine production.

Creating and Entering Data

The act of typing has not changed in decades. The traditional keyboard of typewriters did not change too much when manufacturers put them on computers. The arrangement was designed to make it hard for fast typists to jam the mechanical typewriters, but most manufacturers did not change the arrangement even though computers didn't care how fast you could type.

The result is that most computers used as word processing tools still have the "QWERTYUIOP" arrangement that everybody knows. However, for those people who prefer an easier arrangement for typing faster (such as the "Dvorak" keyboard), it is possible to change the meaning of the keyboard keys with software that acts as a keyboard enhancer. SuperKey (Borland International, $69.95) is one example, Prokey (Rose Soft Inc., $130) is another.

Word Processing   Word processing software has evolved over the years to provide today's excellent writing tools. The ability to transmit your thoughts to the screen is limited only by the speed at which you type. You can save dozens of versions of a book chapter and edit the text any way you like, and still have on hand previous versions. The possibilities for experimenting with writing techniques are endless, and the programs for checking your spelling and grammar are impeccable.

Figure 1-1.   Quadram's Picture Computing System demonstrating the Imageware picture editing software.

Painting and Drawing

Software packages for drawing images are available for nearly every type of personal computer. The Macintosh started a trend in "paint" programs that let you click to black or to white each pixel of the screen to make subtle changes to an image. Other programs make it very easy to draw perfectly straight lines, boxes and shapes with precise angles. Once drawn, an image can be duplicated on the screen many times, and each copy can be enlarged, reduced, stretched or compressed. Images can be combined with text on the screen and stored together on disk for use in different documents or works of art.

Digitizers, Tablets, and OCR Devices

Various companies make drawing pads and tablets with light pens for tracing images or drawing images freehand for storage in the computer. Image digitizers are also available for personal computers, such as the MacVision digitizer from Koala Technologies, which takes images from a conventional video camera and reproduces them on the Macintosh screen.

Retyping already-printed material is now unnecessary, thanks to optical character recognition (OCR) devices that cost as little as $5000 (including graphics digitizer). With an OCR device you can scan pages of printed text and store them in computer files without retyping them. Entire books can be scanned into computers page by page without retyping. Information from mailing labels can be scanned into a data base and used for subsequent mailings.

These devices are new and their applications have only recently been made known to the world. Some of them have come under the scrutiny of the federal government for their possible use in counterfeiting. Image digitizers for personal computers are not good enough to reproduce dollar bills, and current laser printers are not capable of printing them, but the feds are watching this technology closely.

Getting Output

Digitizing the information and storing it on computer disks is only half of the process. The other half provides more price and performance flexibility. You have more choices with personal computers than with any other type of computer-based system.

For starters, there are many different kinds of printers, ranging from the least expensive dot matrix printers to the most expensive page printers. The dot matrix printers are capable of graphics as well as near-correspondence-quality text (daisy wheel and typewriter printers are considered correspondence quality). Laser printers are capable of emulating daisy wheel printers at much better resolution and print quality, and some laser printers are capable of full or partial-page graphics.

Typesetting vs. Laser Printing

Some laser printers are compatible with higher-resolution laser typesetters; for example, a PostScript-type laser printer such as the Apple LaserWriter is entirely compatible with the Allied Linotype Linotronic class of PostScript-type typesetters.

The LaserWriter and other laser printers provide near-typeset quality (close enough for most newsletters and some books and magazines). However, the power of the LaserWriter is in the flexibility you have to produce either laser-printed pages or actual typeset pages. The Macintosh computer can drive either the Laser-Writer or the Allied Linotype Linotronic typesetter. Both are available from services starting up everywhere.

This means that you can do your own typesetting and page makeup using a personal computer, and get output from your own laser printer or use a local copy center that offers a laser printing service. Some of the page makeup software works with inexpensive dot matrix printers, so you can "proof" your copy before using the more expensive laser printer.

The difference is largely resolution — at 300 dots per inch, laser printers print letters that have "the jaggies" (slightly jagged lines and edges). In newspaper printing the difference is not noticeable without a magnifying glass. Most people don't notice the difference when printed on plain paper or even high-gloss magazine paper.

Typesetters can produce output at 1270 dots per inch or more. The programs that drive typesetters can do more sophisticated typographic functions, such as *kerning* (adjusting the space between two letters). If you want the highest quality output, with kerned letters and precise control over line thickness, you may want to use the more sophis-ticated programs and a typesetter. You can save time and money by using a laser printer for proofing the page before typesetting it.

Choosing a Printer

Once you have decided what your publication should look like, you can decide which type of printer or typesetter you need by comparing output samples.

For example, if you want high-quality graphics and text on the same page with the best possible laser printer resolution and quality, you should consider the LaserWriter over the less expensive non-Post-Script laser printers. If you want mostly book-quality and manual-quality laser printing, with minimal graphics, you may want to use a lower-cost laser printer with your PC or Macintosh. The laser printer differences are described in detail in Chapter 3.

The choices for laser printers also depend on the word processing or page makeup programs you want to use. Some word processing programs for the PC and Macintosh can do enough typesetting and page makeup to handle office forms, newsletters and brochures. You can use most word processing programs with Epson or IBM-compatible graphics printers.

Putting Pages Together

Once you know your application (newsletter, book, marketing brochure, catalog, magazine), you can decide on the page makeup and typesetting software to go with your hardware. This choice alone may influence your buying decision. There are fantastic page makeup and typesetting programs for both Macintosh computers and IBM PC-compatible computers.

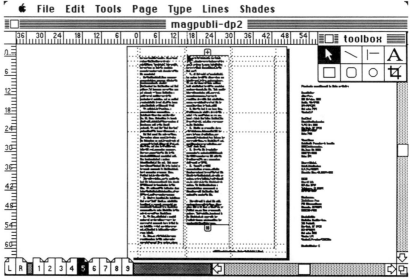

Figure 1-2.   PageMaker (Aldus) on the Macintosh can place graphics and flow text over many pages. You can then print the pages on a laser printer or typesetter without manual paste-up.

WYSIWYG and non-WYSIWYG The programs fall roughly into two categories: those that offer WYSIWYG (pronounced "whizz-ee-wig"), and those that are non-WYSIWYG. WYSIWYG means "what you see is what you get" and is used to describe page makeup systems — displays of pages where you can change the shape and size of columns and pictures and text, and see the results almost instantly on the display.

WYSIWYG software lends itself nicely to the "one page" concept. Using this kind of system you can change the elements of a page over and over until you "get it right", then send the page to the laser printer or typesetter. Most WYSIWYG software tries to match what you see on the screen to what you will get on paper as closely as possible. Some WYSIWYG programs can do multiple page documents, or offer automatic formatting of a document using a style sheet approach.

WYSIWYG is more economical because it doesn't waste printing time and paper, and it lets people draw straight lines where they have never been able to draw straight lines before.

Mistakes can creep onto your pages from using either method, but there are less possible mistakes with WYSIWYG because chances are that you'll see the mistake on the screen before printing or typesetting the page.

But that is not the whole story. WYSIWYG is a time-consuming process. It can take quite a few minutes to design a page with a WYSIWYG program, and once a page is designed and finished, what about the subsequent pages? The problem with most WYSIWYG systems is that it takes too long to design a multi-page document (such as a book), and the typesetting and page makeup process is not precise.

Non-WYSIWYG programs use a mathematical approach to typesetting, with mnemonic codes that perform typesetting functions. You need to get out your pica rulers, and with a combination of intuition and experience (and practice pages) you can get codes to work.

The non-WYSIWYG programs are designed for use by professional typographers who already know about typesetting features and are used to having more control over the space between letters and between lines of text. Some of the more sophisticated WYSIWYG programs (Ventura Publisher and PageMaker described in Chapter 5, and others in Chapter 7) can handle both single page documents and multiple pages, but the non-WYSIWYG typesetting programs in Chapter 7 are sometimes easier for producing large books and manuals, where the page design is the same for every page.

Choosing Page Makeup Methods

Using the non-WYSIWYG approach, with one set of codes you can prepare an infinite number of pages for typesetting; using WYSIWYG only, you can prepare a complete document, but you usually work on only one page at a time. This is the fundamental difference.

How can you tell whether the WYSIWYG program is better than the non-WYSIWYG program, or vice-versa, for a particular application? If you have more than thirty pages that are going to look the same, you might prefer to use a non-WYSIWYG method. Anything smaller, or more diverse, than thirty very similar pages could be handled by either method, whichever one you find more comfortable.

Most typesetting and page makeup software packages for personal computers give you one method or the other, but not both. PageMaker, for example, is all WYSIWYG, with the ability to copy "master pages" onto each page. It is a good implementation of WYSIWYG, but it does not lend itself to the non-WYSIWYG approach. However, Ventura Publisher for the PC provides both a style sheet approach (close to non-WYSIWYG) and a WYSIWYG approach (both are described in Chapter 5).

The professional composition packages, which are harder to learn but provide more typesetting control, are both WYSIWYG and non-WYSIWYG. JustText is a non-WYSIWYG program that provides professional typesetting from a Macintosh for only $195; the other professional packages are in the range $1000 (such as ScenicWriter) to over $45,000 (Interleaf). These are described in Chapter 7.

Producing Our Magazine

We jumped right into electronic page makeup on personal computers by publishing the first issue of our *Desktop Publishing* magazine using the desktop publishing products. It was an experience that has completely changed the way we do magazines.

What started as a search for an alternative typesetting method turned into a full-scale production overhaul. Our primary goal was to produce the magazine quickly and efficiently, with a secondary goal of using new desktop publishing products somewhere in the process.

The first issue was created by editing the articles on personal computers (mostly IBM PC-compatibles), transferring them to a Macintosh, and using PageMaker (Aldus) to prepare the pages. We printed the pages on an Apple LaserWriter for proofing, then finally output the pages on the Allied Linotype typesetter without having to do any recoding or reformatting.

The second issue was done mostly in PageMaker (Aldus), with some pages done with JustText (Knowledge Engineering). One advertisement was done on an Imagewriter with a digitized image. We used the LaserWriter for final output, to test if the web printing process would do it justice. The experiment worked, and we are able to produce this issue even less expensively, in a shorter timeframe without sacrificing quality.

The major benefit of using a laser printer was unrestricted access. We have never owned a typesetting system and had always relied on typesetters that could turn around our jobs in one or two days. With our own laser printer we can produce pages at any time of day or night, and make corrections instantly. The result was a much shorter production process, and a truly liberating feeling shared among us that we were really doing desktop publishing — and that anyone could do it!

Our System Choices   We chose the Apple Macintosh and LaserWriter because in the Fall of 1985 our choices were limited. We have many PC-compatible computers and CP/M computers, and when it came time to produce a magazine using the latest desktop publishing tools, we used them in conjunction with the Macintosh and LaserWriter setup. We found that the most useful (and least expensive) setup for page makeup on personal computers was the Apple Macintosh and LaserWriter.

We used CP/M and PC computers to write, edit, and prepare our text for production. These activities — including writing, editing, proofreading, and archiving the articles on PC-compatible disks — are germane to every publishing operation, and they usually take place on PCs, no matter what typesetting or page composition system you use to produce the final documents. Writers submit articles electronically via phone or in any of the many formats of floppy disk invented.

In short, we did on a PC-compatible computer nearly everything a typical knowledge worker would do before preparing for conventional typesetting and page makeup, or for the sophisticated dedicated composition systems from Compugraphic and the like.

We even used PCs to do some typesetting, although final formatting was done on the Mac. Using PCs we could type JustText typesetting codes into text files, then transport the text files to the Mac for the purpose of outputting them to the laser printer. JustText, which runs on the Mac, processes and prints the files.

Our choices for a desktop publishing system at that time (August, 1985) were roughly the following:

1. A dedicated composition system (with laser printer for proofing and typesetter) that can read PC disks. Cost: $38,000 and up, plus monthly maintenance fees.

2. A PC-driven typesetter or laser printer system. Most of these have a PC and typesetter bundled with the system (you are forced into buying another PC to dedicate to this system if you already have one). Cost: $18,000 and up, plus monthly maintenance fees on the typesetter, or service charges if you use a service for typeset output. Some systems are unbundled (you can use your PC); these are $7000 and up (professional typesetting software) and require output to specific typesetters.

3. PC software to work with the least expensive laser printer ($2500-$7000 for software alone, plus at least $2500 for a well-equipped PC or $5000 for an IBM AT, plus $4000 for a laser printer). Total cost: at least $9000 and possibly $16,000, plus toner cartridges ($60-$100) every 5000 copies.

4. An Apple Macintosh ($2400) and LaserWriter ($7000) with PageMaker software ($500) and JustText ($100) for sophisticated typesetting. Total cost: $10,000 plus toner cartridges ($60-$100) every 5000 copies.

The choices for PCs (option #2) were more limited at that time because the page makeup software was not yet available to integrate text and graphics with graphics editing tools. The scales have almost tipped to favor the PC approach, now that inexpensive PC page makeup programs are becoming available.

Option #1 was entirely too expensive, and option #2 meant buying a typesetter or using one service for output (we'd been using a service for years and didn't need to get new software just to use a service again).

The combination of PageMaker (for making pages on a Mac screen) and JustText (a conventional typesetting program with codes, not WYSIWYG like PageMaker but complementary) made the Mac-LaserWriter setup (option #4) very attractive — the LaserWriter is the best printer in its price range for preparing typesetting and graphics, and the Mac, even with software, costs less than some of the PC software by itself!

We chose option #4 with the knowledge that Allied Linotype's Linotronic 100 typesetter would be available at many services in the Bay Area, and that our final pages could be typeset in a single day without any errors at one of these services. However, we also knew that the LaserWriter would suffice for much of our production needs, and that the Linotronic was really only necessary for certain jobs that required the higher resolution of typesetting. Option #4 represented the best of both worlds (typesetting and laser printing) at the lowest cost.

What makes this possible is the Linotronic's compatibility with the Apple LaserWriter, thanks to PostScript. PostScript is a page description language common to the LaserWriter, Linotronic, and other high-resolution printed output devices. We used the lesser-quality Laser-Writer for proofing pages created on the Macintosh or in JustText, and when pages were correct, we took the disk over to the Macintosh connected to the Linotronic system, and used the same software to typeset rather than laser print the pages. There was no extra step in-between, so no errors could creep into the composition process.

The Macintosh and LaserWriter setup (option #4) used the least expensive application software for page makeup and typesetting, with excellent text and graphics integration, and a variety of real and potential output devices (which use the PostScript page description language). The word processing programs on the Mac (including JustText, which is both typesetting and word processing) had little trouble accepting our text files from PCs. The text was edited with either JustText or Microsoft Word, and PageMaker accepts Microsoft Word or MacWrite documents.

Thus we were able to use our PCs and CP/M computers to prepare articles for production, and still produce them with less cost than if we had used PCs for typesetting and composition.

Latest Developments

Some of the page makeup software available on PCs is still in the development phase, not yet ready for the public. Others, such as Personal Publisher (T/Maker Graphics) and Ventura Publisher (Ventura Software) are ready now, and provide excellent solutions for driving laser printers from PCs.

Our choices have also changed with the times. Today we use some PC programs, such as Microsoft Word, Personal Publisher, Ventura Publisher and XyWrite, to produce output on the LaserWriter (via PC MacBridge or directly), or the H-P LaserJet. We also use PageMaker, JustText, ReadySetGo and MacPublisher II on the Macintosh with the LaserWriter. The Corona PC and Laser Printer are used for office forms, letters and reports.

We use the ThunderScan digitizer with the Macintosh, and the Datacopy digitizer and OCR scanner for the PC. For hard disks we use the Apple HD-20 (twenty megabyte) with the Macintosh, and our PC has a built-in twenty megabyte hard disk.

The major concern of almost every personal computer buyer is compatibility. You may have at one time or another considered buying an Apple Macintosh, but decided not to for the simple reason that it is not compatible with the IBM Personal Computer (PC). The PC is now a standard among computers, and you don't want to stray too far from the standard.

However, the least expensive page makeup software has been available only for Macintosh computers, and the entire Mac and Laser-Writer setup described in the previous chapter was cheaper than anything you could set up for the PC with the same capabilities. This is still true, but the market is changing, as well as the nature of compatibility.

There's a saying among computer owners who are advising others about buying computers: "wait a while and the price will drop." Although Apple has a head start in the desktop publishing market, more people use IBM PCs than any other computer. The expensive programs that are now available for professional typesetting and page makeup (ranging from $2500 to over $8000) are being challenged from below: word processing enhancements, typesetting utilities, and complete page makeup programs are coming out, mostly in the $50-$500 range.

The Macintosh is also a viable solution for PC owners, now that Apple is supporting IBM networks and standard connections to PC-type devices. There are numerous "bridge" products that let you use the LaserWriter printer with PCs. Since the PostScript-driven Laser-Writer is a better graphics and typesetting printer than most non-PostScript printers, the bridge products represent real cost-effective solutions — simply slip the "bridge" card, such as PC MacBridge

(Tangent Technologies), into your PC, and get the LaserWriter.

Chapter 2 and 3 describe many of these alternatives — such as using a "bridge" product to share a LaserWriter among many PCs and Macintosh computers, or transferring to and from PCs and Macs (both in Chapter 2), or using a LaserWriter from a PC (Chapter 3).

CHAPTER TWO

Creating and Organizing Text

"Machines are built to serve men," I typed. I regretted it almost immediately.
— Kurt Vonnegut, *EPICAC*

**Going
Electronic**

It was an episode destined to be remembered in the annals of journalism management, a contributing factor to the most spectacular failure in magazine publishing history: Time Inc.'s *TV-Cable Week* (as reported in *Vanity Fair*, Jan. 86). The editorial effort to write reviews of over 16,000 movies and over 40,000 syndicated series episodes — every episode of every series ever seen on American TV — had to be assembled within six months and fed into the giant computerized composition system that would let Time Inc. publish thousands of local editions of the magazine at different regional printing centers.

Every show review had to be researched, written, edited, checked for facts, proofread, and then entered into the computer system. Many reviews were collected from freelancers and TV buffs, many more written by the staff. Time Inc. spent about $400,000 on the effort. But something important was overlooked.

The editorial project consisted of 56,000 scraps of paper piled up on an office floor. No one had been typing the information into the computer. "There's half a million dollars on the floor in here," shrieked the person who uncovered the mess.

"We'll have to hire more people" was the management response. They had no choice. There was no other way to turn 56,000 scraps of paper into electronic words to be processed by a computer.

You might suppose that if engineers can design an inexpensive machine that can read the bar code on a can of soup and turn the code into computer data, they ought to be able to design a machine that can read ordinary text and do the same thing. Such a machine has been designed and is used by large publishers and the government: the optical character recognition (OCR) device. Unfortunately the technology of typesetting had not caught up with the technology of character recognition, so Time, Inc. couldn't use such a device to both *read* the text *and prepare it* for typesetting.

That was a job only humans could do. The "rekeyboarding" of text into a composition system is done more often because the traditional intricate typesetting codes, barely understood by the keyboard operator and incomprehensible to most people, have to be typed along with the text.

This problem is solved by desktop publishing software for personal computers. Designed to work with popular word processing programs or to imitate them, desktop publishing software lets you print your word-processed text on popular laser printers, simulating real typesetting. Some programs let you transfer the text to a real typesetting system. Others let you control an expensive typesetter from your personal computer.

Text Scanning

Desktop publishing hardware is being developed to let you scan text into a computer without having to type it. As typesetting software becomes easier (the codes are easier to understand, and in some cases, the program displays the text on screen as you want it to appear on the printed page), it becomes cost-justifiable to scan text from a book or manuscript into a computer, and *then* have a typesetting operator prepare the text for typesetting, rather than rekeyboarding the text to accommodate the typesetting codes.

The technology of scanning text is known as OCR (optical character recognition), but the machines that could do it were limited to reading a few typefonts (the early machines read only the OCR typefont — the funny "computer letters" you see on bank checks, which has since become a designer typefont). Today's desktop text scanners can read more than one typefont, and they usually have no trouble with ordinary typewriter letters (such as Courier typefont).

Datacopy has the least expensive solution: text scanning software that works with a desktop image digitizer, combining image digitizing (described in Chapter 4) and text scanning in one machine.

The Datacopy Model 730 offers two levels of text scanning software. CIR-1 recognizes certain popular fonts like Courier and Elite (IBM typewriter fonts at 10 or 12 pitch), and other typefonts can be added for additional cost. CIR-2 recognizes the popular typefonts *and* has the ability to *learn new typefonts*. In an interactive session you can introduce the characters of a new typefont to the scanning software, which uses artificial intelligence techniques to remember them.

Figure 2-1. The Datacopy Model 730 Word Image Processing System (WIPS) can scan images at a resolution of 300 dots per inch. Equipped with CIR software, the Model 700 can scan text into a text file without need for retyping.

CIR-2 can also be used to "teach" the scanner how to read handwriting. The Smithsonian's National Air and Space Museum is conducting a project to digitize old airplane blueprints, where text and graphics are mixed on the same page. With the CIR software's ability to learn new fonts, the Smithsonian can digitize the text as a graphic image along with the other graphic elements on the page, then convert the text image to real text that can be typeset.

The Datacopy machine is easy to use as a digitizer or as a text scanner. It resembles a desktop copier, without the copier's paper path but with the glass platen normally found on copiers. You place the original document face down on the glass platen as if you were copying it. Then you start the CIR software and tell it to read a document.

CIR-1 and CIR-2 have two modes of operation: interactive, where each character is read and if the character is not recognized, the software asks you to type the correct character; and non-interactive, where the software reads through the document quickly, leaving a marking character in place of any unrecognized characters. You can assign any character on your keyboard as the marking character, and search for the marking character using any word processing program or spelling checker.

To learn new typefonts, CIR-2 in the interactive mode will remember the correct character you type in place of the unrecognized object, and substitute the correct character for that object from that point on. You can buy recognition modules for CIR-1 or CIR-2 from Datacopy's typefont recognition library.

When the conversion is finished, you can edit the resulting text file using any word processing program (as described later in this chapter). The text is useful as data for word processing or data processing. It is stored using the traditional ASCII set (American Standard Code for Information Interchange) that is recognized by all types of computers. ASCII is the standard data format for word processing and data processing on personal computers.

Many word processing programs use the ASCII "carriage return" and "line feed" codes at the end of each paragraph and not at the end of each line. The codes force the printer to move down one line (line feed) and over to the left margin (carriage return), just like you would do manually with a typewriter. Simple text files used with Lotus 1-2-3 or IBM's Personal Editor require the carriage return/line feed combination at the end of each line; however, a text file formatted this way is treated differently by a word processing program like WordStar — each line appears to be a separate paragraph.

Datacopy's CIR software handles this problem by giving you a choice. It will either store the scanned text with a carriage return/line feed at the end of each line, for use with programs like Lotus 1-2-3 or the Personal Editor, or store the text with the code combination at the end of each paragraph, for use with word processing programs. The CIR software recognizes a paragraph if it is followed by a blank line, or a line that is indented.

For documents containing both graphics and text, use the desktop scanner and WIPS (Word Image Processing System) software to scan each document page and save each graphic element as a separate image file, and the text as a separate image file. You can then use the CIR software to convert the text stored in the image file.

Text scanning works best with clean, crisp originals that were printed using a Selectric-style typing element or daisy wheel with carbon-film ribbons, or clean copies of the originals. If characters are broken, or you use a bad photocopy, the software can't automatically recognize the character. The text scanning process is fastest when you use a clean original and place it flat on the glass platen so that the lines of text are parallel to the top of the platen. The CIR software will read slanted text (resulting from the paper being placed askew on the platen) but will take longer than the usual scanning speed.

Both the Model 730 tabletop scanner ($4950) and the lower-resolution Model 720 ($3950) include an interface board for your PC that plugs into a half-card slot, and the WIPS text and image processing software (described in Chapter 4). The CIR-1 text scanning software is $695 (with additional typefont recognition modules for $195 each), and the CIR-2 character recognition and learning software is $1995.

Both the Model 720 and 730 machines require 640K RAM in your PC or compatible, a Hercules graphics card, and a high-resolution monitor (the Hercules is for high-resolution displays). You also need to have at least one empty half-card or full-card slot in your PC or compatible in order to plug in the Datacopy half-card.

Text scanning of typewritten pages is faster than the fastest typist and can continue at top speed all day long. According to Datacopy, the CIR software averages fewer mistakes than the most accurate typist, but this claim is nearly impossible to substantiate. In interactive mode you can make the scanning process more accurate than any other method.

It is possible to create pages on typewriters and scan the pages into the computer using the Datacopy. However, good typewriters are almost as expensive as personal computers. If you have a lot of typewriters and a lot of word processing to do, you can get it done on typewriters and position each page on the Datacopy scanner to feed the text into one computer. However, there is no substitute for writing and editing by computer if you are looking for the most efficient method. No matter how quickly inexpensive text scanners develop, they will probably not match the efficiency of creating the data electronically in the first place.

Text scanners are most useful for scanning pages from outside sources to be processed or filed by computer. For example, we find the Datacopy useful for scanning numerous press releases that come in the mail. The pages are meant to be used for new product information, and the text, once stored on the computer, can be searched quickly for references to specific products. Text search software is described later in this chapter.

Word Processing

The fundamental purpose of word processing is to develop your investment in your data — the words you use to describe your business or your profession. You need to use some form of word processing to produce any document or printed material. If you write anything for business or professional reasons, either someone is doing word processing for you, or you're doing it yourself. Either way, you have a considerable investment in the words already processed.

We write exclusively by computer, except when we are note-taking and our laptop portable computers are not convenient. The main reasons are that we can type the text once, change it as often as necessary, edit pieces from other documents into a new document, print the documents quickly, store them cheaply (floppy disks are less expensive than filing cabinets and reams of paper), and have them ready for typesetting without further typing.

Our reasons are not related strictly to the writer's application. All personal computer users need some form of word processing, and most need the type of word processing that lets writers create and edit text quickly and easily on a personal computer.

If you are considering buying a personal computer, it makes sense to start with the word processing task and get the right amount of equipment that is also sophisticated enough to tackle your word processing chores. Read this chapter to learn how word processing can lead to desktop publishing.

If you already have a computer and word processing software, read this chapter to learn how desktop publishing enhancements can work with your system to produce excellent output on laser printers, dot matrix printers, and typesetting systems. For many desktop publishing applications (church and club bulletins, some newsletters, school newspapers, resumes, office forms and stationery, manuscripts, reports), the use of the sophisticated printing commands in word processing programs, with the appropriate dot matrix printer, can yield excellent results from inexpensive equipment.

Word processing programs evolved slowly, and there has always been a need for "pretty-printing" on dot matrix printers from word processing programs. *Print formatting* (also called *text processing*) programs were created to handle, for example, the printing of text in various typefonts on the Epson class of dot matrix printers. One example is PrintMerge (Polaris Software), a program that interprets special printing codes you type into your WordStar text files. You use PrintMerge rather than WordStar to print the file, but you use WordStar to create and edit the file.

Other vendors take a different approach: Cordata (formerly Corona) supplies a special installation program to convert WordStar printing codes into the Cordata LP-300 laser printer codes, so that you can use WordStar ^P commands to change typefonts.

There are still other ways to print on a laser printer or graphics printer from your word processing program. *Utility programs* are available to control the downloading of typefonts into the laser printer's memory and change typefonts. There are also a host of programs, such as Fancy Font (SoftCraft, Inc., $180), that provide typefonts for laser printers and also dot matrix printers. Fancy Font (for use with any word processor on a PC or CP/M computer) and Fancy Word ($140, for use with Microsoft Word on a PC) provide a variety of typefonts for the H-P LaserJet and LaserJet Plus and Canon laser printers as well as Epson and Toshiba dot matrix printers (both are described in Chapter 3).

If you want to buy a new word processing program, you have many excellent programs to choose from. Most word processing programs for personal computers now have *drivers* for specific laser printers (software that controls the output of the text). For example, you can get Microsoft Word for the PC with a driver for the H-P LaserJet or LaserJet Plus, or a driver for Epson-compatible graphics printers, or a driver for PostScript devices. These are described in more detail in the next chapter.

All of these approaches are useful for preparing *galleys* of typeset or laser printed text — vertical strips of text that can be pasted by hand onto a page. If you are doing a two-column-per-page newsletter, you would be able to produce each column separately on the laser printer or typesetter and paste the output by hand onto a page. Some word processing programs offer codes for producing two-column or three-column pages without the need for manual paste-up, but in many cases the codes are too complex to understand, and the coding necessary to set aside areas where graphics displace text takes longer than doing the paste-up by hand.

To do actual page makeup on an IBM PC screen (in a WYSIWYG form — what you see on the screen is what you get in print), you have to spend more money on hardware than you would normally have to spend to do word processing. You would need at least a high-resolution monitor, hard disk, a monochrome graphics card, and 512K or 640K memory in your PC. On the other hand, Macintosh page makeup programs are much less expensive, require no extra hardware except an extra disk drive or hard disk (which you probably need anyway), and work well with Macintosh word processing programs.

You may want to stick with whatever computer you already have, and do desktop publishing using the least expensive route, but with high-quality laser printing. You can get excellent results using a low cost laser printer or dot matrix printer, and a word processing program equipped with the appropriate driver for the laser printer. However, you will not be able to merge text and graphics on the screen before printing it — which leaves some manual paste-up at the end, but solves the typesetting problem in a cost-effective manner.

Using a Macintosh

Although word processing software is generally more powerful on the IBM PC side of the personal computer market, using typefonts and doing typesetting from a word processing program is much easier (and usually less expensive) on the Apple Macintosh side.

There are also more page makeup programs available at this time for the Macintosh. This is largely due to the design of the Macintosh and its system software. The Macintosh has a high-resolution screen, standard connections for a mouse, and on-screen icons, pull-down menus and typefonts as part of the system. With all of these features built-in, software publishers can provide such features in their application programs easily and quickly. This is why a program like Microsoft Word, a program that can do sophisticated document typesetting as well as word processing, and PageMaker, a program that can do on-screen page makeup, came out first on the Macintosh. You have to buy extra hardware (high-resolution monitor, graphics card, and extra memory) to get the equivalent features on an IBM PC or compatible computer.

The Macintosh and Macintosh Plus come with a "software sampler" disk with demonstration versions of writing software (MacWrite), drawing and painting software (MacDraw and MacPaint), and project planning software (MacProject). Some dealers bundle the real versions of these programs with the computer package (not just demo versions that can't save data on disk). You can buy these products from your Apple Computer dealer, or substitute products from other vendors (we use Microsoft Word in place of MacWrite, but you can use either to typeset words).

MacWrite is a simple word processing program that lets you select different typefonts and produce single-column pages. MacDraw is primarily a drawing program you can use to do drafting, but it lets you integrate text with the line art. MacPaint and MacDraw are graphics tools (described in Chapter 4) that can also manipulate words, usually as captions or text used in the graphics. With MacDraw you can typeset text within a polygon or box, add captions to line art, or typeset very large letters as graphic elements.

One complaint heard often about the Macintosh is that its keyboard is not designed for intensive word processing. The Macintosh Plus comes with a keyboard that includes cursor arrow keys and a numeric keypad (two features lacking in the older Mac keyboard), but the slope and feel of the keys is the same. People who like the PC-style keyboard can still use a Macintosh and replace the Mac keyboard with one that resembles a PC keyboard — for example, Tangent Technologies offers the PC MacKey keyboard ($300) that resembles a PC AT keyboard complete with function keys and numeric keypad.

Hard Disks   The 512K Macintosh can do almost anything you want to do, but you may run into limitations related to the amount of disk storage you have. The older Macintosh single-sided disk drives can accommodate 400K bytes (roughly 400,000 characters of information); the newer Macintosh Plus disk drives are double-sided and can handle 800K bytes (800,000 characters). With two single-sided drives you can usually run any Macintosh program and prepare documents for printing or typesetting. The double-sided drives make it twice as easy. However, as your productivity increases, you will find yourself spending a lot of time changing disks and waiting for the Mac to identify new disks.

The answer to this problem is to get a *hard disk* for your Mac, which stores a large amount of information and loads data faster than a floppy. Apple offers the HD-20, which holds 20 megabytes — equivalent to 50 of the 400K single-sided floppy disks. Other hard disks include the MacBottom (Personal Computer Peripherals Corp.), the HyperDrive (General Computer Corp.), the MicahDrive from MICAH, Inc., the MAC-10 (Paradise Systems) and the Bernoulli Box (IOMEGA Corp.). The prices for hard disks vary according to the deal you can get from your supplier and according to the amount of storage space.

There are many benefits of having a hard disk, but it is important to realize that some applications *require* the capacity of a hard disk. For example, you need a lot of space to hold one digitized image. Programs like PageMaker need at least two 400K floppy disks to work properly, or one 800K disk, but this arrangement does not leave much room for your documents.

One major benefit of having a hard disk is that you can load as many typefonts as you want without fear of taking up too much disk space. Another is the organization that comes with using a hard disk — you can group files into different *directories* with descriptive names. Think of a directory as a labeled file drawer in a filing cabinet that contains a lot of folders — each folder is a *file* (with a label called a *file name*) and the entire drawer is a directory.

An investment in a hard disk is quickly repaid by the increase in your productivity, since you can store and retrieve documents, digitized images, and page layouts much more quickly. Programs load and run faster if they are stored on the hard disk. All of your documents and graphics are available to you without your having to switch floppies.

If you're trying to decide whether or not to have a hard disk or use floppies, imagine what it would be like to have all of your text files on floppies and all of your application programs on floppies. Now every time you want to use a text file with a different application program, you have to switch disks; every time you want a old text file, you have to find the disk and switch disks again. The solution to all this disk finding and switching is to use a hard disk that can hold *everything* all at once. Then, use floppy disks to hold *backup copies* of the programs and data files.

The backups are important for that time when your hard disk malfunctions. Nearly every hard disk has its "crash," due to power surges, static electricity, and other reasons, and the "mtbf" rate (mean time between failures, or the theoretical amount of time you can expect the disk to work properly between factory maintenance periods) is usually on the product specification sheet. If you keep data file backups, you can use the data on a floppy-only system, and you can restore the data to the hard disk after it is fixed (or to another hard disk).

The Apple HD-20 is a standard 20-megabyte hard disk for the Macintosh that is designed to sit underneath your Mac. The MacBottom hard disk also has 20 megabytes of storage space and sits underneath your Mac. Both disks are somewhat transportable because they have an automatic "park" feature — the disk recording heads retract to a safe area automatically when the power shuts off, so that the heads don't scrape against the disk while you are transporting it. Both disks automatically start the system so that you don't need a floppy disk.

The Apple HD-20 connects to the external disk drive port (connector on the back of the Mac), and if you have an external floppy disk drive, you can connect it to the hard disk (since the hard disk has taken over the external drive connector). The MacBottom, on the other hand, connects to either the modem or the printer port.

The Bernoulli Box is a cartridge-based system, similar to a removable hard disk, that comes in various configurations — from five-megabyte to 20-megabyte capacity. Although it is not usually faster than a hard disk, the Bernoulli Box is shock resistant, the cartridges are more reliable than either floppies or hard disks, and you can transfer large amounts (five megabytes) of data from one system with a Bernoulli Box to another (like a giant floppy). The Bernoulli Box Personal Server offers five-megabyte cartridges, and the Bernoulli Box for AppleTalk uses 10- or 20-megabyte cartridges. The cartridges are very rugged, inexpensive, and help make archiving (backing up) data easier.

The MicahDrive and the similar HyperDrive (10 or 20 megabyte versions) are the fastest hard disks for the Mac. Installed inside the Macintosh unit, both drives are also the most portable. Both drives automatically start the system without a floppy. However, both drives are not easily removable — if the drive fails, you have to open the Macintosh and disconnect the drive from the main board (not an easy task for a novice).

One difference between the two drives is that the HyperDrive Backup software can only write files to blank disks. If you try to backup data files onto an existing data disk, after a warning that the old data will be erased, Backup copies the new files on top of the old ones, renames your disk, and erases the old files. The data disks created with Backup cannot be read until you decode them with the Restore option in the Backup program.

Another major difference is between drives made before 1986 and drives made now: the older drives were not shipped with Apple's recently released *hierarchical file system* (HFS).

A 20-megabyte hard disk can store the equivalent of 50 400K floppy disks and thousands of files. Using the original Macintosh File System (MFS) software (which was specifically designed for floppy disks), it is hard to keep track of hundreds of files — imagine scrolling through hundreds of document names in a dialog box to find a specific file.

The method in disks made before 1986 was to let you partition (divide) the hard disk into "volumes." Volumes make the hard disk look like a collection of floppy disks. The problem with this method is that only a small number of volumes can be used ("mounted") at once, and switching between them is cumbersome, requiring the use of a desk accessory or even quitting an application and running the volume manager. This scheme also tends to use up large blocks of disk space for each file, resulting in a lot of wasted disk space.

Hard disks developed for sale in 1986 use the HFS software, in which folders are real directories for holding files (in the original file manager software, folders are graphic icons for keeping your desktop tidy — files in various folders were really all part of one single directory).

With HFS, folders can hold other folders, which can also hold folders, etc., down to any level. Choosing a folder in a dialog box gives you a list of that folder's documents, folders, and applications. You can use folders to logically group documents and applications — correspondence in one folder, MacPaint images in another, and so forth. HFS also lets you have thousands of files on one disk volume — no need to mount new volumes.

Since some existing Macintosh software is not compatible with HFS, make sure your hard disk has a utility to create MFS-compatible subvolumes to handle these older programs. The utility should allow Macintosh 512K users with "old" 64K ROMs to use an MFS subvolume on the hard disk as their boot volume (since an HFS volume cannot be directly booted by the old 64K ROMs). You should be able to "mount" and dismount subvolumes with a desk accessory and specify which subvolumes, if any, are to be automatically mounted on power-up.

MacWrite   MacWrite is a simple program for writing that almost anyone can learn quickly. The program does not have a lot of word processing functions, but it does have the basic ones, such as automatic word-wrapping to the next line, a global search/replace text function, and the general Macintosh features, including selecting different typefonts and a cut/paste function for moving text to and from the "clipboard" area of memory. It was bundled with the Macintosh but is not included with the new Macintosh Plus. You can buy MacWrite (in 128K and 512K versions) from Apple Computer Inc. for $125, but you might prefer Word for $195.

There have been three released versions of MacWrite. The first version 1.0 was replaced by 2.2 — both are memory-resident versions, therefore fast, but can handle only small files (no more than about five pages, depending on how much formatting and font changing you do).

The disk version, which is the most recent officially released 4.5, handles much larger files. Formatting rulers in 4.5 have a box you can check to force text to be printed at 6 lines per inch (12 point leading) and there are other improvements.

However, if you have a MacWrite document that was created with 2.2 and you try to edit it with MacWrite 4.5, any paragraph longer than 3000 characters must be shortened before 4.5 can read it. If you use a 128K Macintosh and you try to use MacWrite 4.5, you get the messages `Memory almost full` or `This operation can't be undone` when you try to change the fonts, or styles and sizes — even in a short document. Use MacWrite 2.2 if you use a 128K Macintosh, or upgrade both RAM (to 512K or greater) and your version of Mac-Write. Use newer versions for the Macintosh Plus.

MacWrite is designed to work properly with the Imagewriter printer. MacWrite uses instructions from the Imagewriter file, usually located in the system folder on your system startup disk, and the QuickDraw procedures built into the Mac's Toolbox ROM.

When you print MacWrite documents with the high quality print selection, the program actually substitutes double-size fonts for your fonts, and then prints the text at a 50% reduction. If your document was set at 10 point, MacWrite substitutes a 20 point font, scaled to 50% reduction. If you have embedded graphics, however, they will be printed as is, and not scaled up or down.

You can adjust your graphics to have better horizontal proportions by choosing "Page Setup" from the File menu and selecting Tall Adjusted printing, before you print your MacWrite document. The normal Tall orientation of graphics is stored at 80 dots per inch, but tall adjusted compresses it to 72 dots per inch, the same as MacPaint files. But, your text as well as graphics are adjusted, and you get expanded (and lower quality) letters.

MacWrite can print near-typeset-quality pages on the LaserWriter, but the ruler in MacWrite is not accurate with regard to the LaserWriter. The difference is due to the manner in which MacWrite displays text — at 72 pixels (dots) per inch. The print resolution of the LaserWriter is 300 dots per inch, not easily divisible by 72.

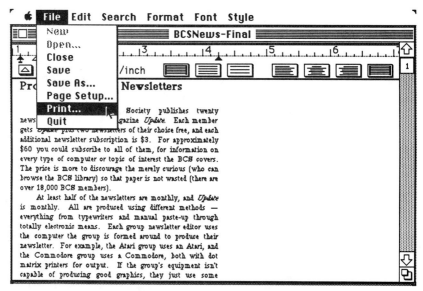

Figure 2-2. Although MacWrite's ruler is accurate for the Imagewriter but not for the LaserWriter, it can still print near-typeset-quality pages on the LaserWriter.

MacWrite does not give you *leading* control — the space between baselines of each line. MacWrite provides an automatic leading that you must live with if you use MacWrite. You can adjust it line by line manually, but it becomes a tedious operation for a long document. Type a space at the end of a line that you wish to move down from the line above, and "Select" the space (it will turn black), then pull down your "Style" menu and increase the point size until the spacing is correct. Although you could select the whole line of text as well, you would then increase the size of the letters rather than just the space above the letters.

The automatic leading feature is not acceptable to professional typographers who want more control over leading, but you might get by with automatic leading in your newsletter, correspondence, marketing literature, reports and documents. If you use MacWrite 4.5, you can force your document to have 12 point leading by checking the box in the ruler that forces 6 lines per inch vertically; 12 point leading looks best with 10 or 11 point size type. The automatic leading is somewhere between ½ and 1½ points more than the selected point size.

Also, with no automatic hyphenation feature, MacWrite's justified columns do not look as good as they should on the laser printer (they look fine on the Imagewriter). You may want to use ragged-right columns (justified to the left margin but not to the right) to bypass the lack of hyphenation (you may not need hyphenation in ragged-right columns). The only alternative is to hyphenate each line by hand or use a hyphenation utility program as needed to improve the appearance.

If you want to print MacWrite documents with a non-proportional look (to resemble typewriter printing), use the Monaco font.

Microsoft Word Microsoft Word ($195) is a far better program than MacWrite for word processing. Although it is not faster nor more powerful than most word processing programs for PCs, Microsoft Word on the Mac has several features that make it excellent for desktop publishing: "soft" hyphenation (you place "soft" hyphens in large words that are used as hyphens if the word falls at the end of a line), line leading control, variable tab space control, a wider range of point sizes for typefonts, and document specification to control the printing of multiple pages and columns.

For the most part, the page makeup programs described in Chapter 5 accept text from either Microsoft Word or MacWrite. You can do the text specifications in the page makeup programs if you want, or you can specify some of them (such as italic and bold words, and tab spaces for tables of numbers) in MacWrite or Microsoft Word and carry them over to the page makeup program.

We have encountered some problems with MacWrite if we specified many different typefonts in the same document, and used the same typefont for all of these words in the page makeup program. We had no problems with Microsoft Word documents. In fact, Word can handle a "foreign" file and convert it to Word format better than MacWrite. If you can afford Word, we suggest you use it rather than MacWrite. You can convert a MacWrite document to be edited by Word, but after you convert it, you will notice that the left margin is indented one-eight of an inch from the left, because MacWrite's rulers have a preset ruler indent of one-eighth of an inch that Word uses. You can easily change the left margin to zero once you have the document in a Word file.

As for printing text, you are all set if your LaserWriter is loaded with the appropriate typefonts and your system disk is properly installed for the LaserWriter. Just click on the Print selection in the pull-down File menu, and select Font Substitution in the LaserWriter menu — this selection tells the LaserWriter to substitute real PostScript fonts for the Macintosh fonts. If you don't select Font Substitution, your fonts will look exactly as they appear on the Macintosh screen (which has 72 dots-per-inch resolution).

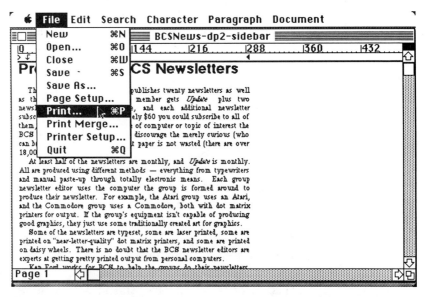

Figure 2-3. Microsoft Word's ruler is accurate for both the Imagewriter and the LaserWriter, and Word offers leading (line spacing) control and "soft" hyphenation.

With MacWrite or Microsoft Word and a LaserWriter you can do desktop typesetting. Microsoft Word's document style sheet provides a level of formatting control for all of the pages of a document, which makes Microsoft Word useful for typesetting books and large volumes of text as well as newsletters, brochures and short documents.

You can bring graphics into Microsoft Word or MacWrite documents and print them, but the graphics occupy entire lines — you can't place text next to graphics on the same line (use MacDraw for this). You can always leave room for the graphic elements, and typeset the text with MacWrite or Microsoft Word, then paste the graphics into place.

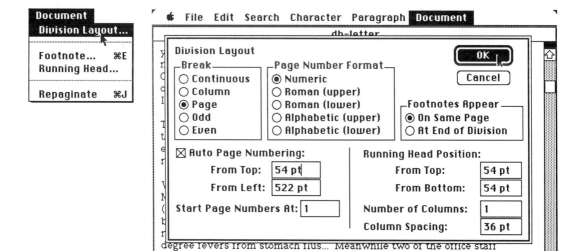

Figure 2-4.   The document style sheet features of Microsoft Word.

MacAuthor   MacAuthor (Icon Technology, around $200) surpasses both MacWrite and Microsoft Word, with both word processing and page makeup features. The program uses "frames," which are adjustable boxes (similar to MacDraw). To place a MacPaint graphic on a page of text, you create a frame where you want to place the graphic, and tell the program if you want the graphic scaled or clipped. The program then places the graphic in the frame, and automatically wraps text around the edges of the graphic.

Another use of frames is in creating *sidebars* (boxes of text next to main body of text). Put the box where you want it on the page, and load in your text file, and the program automatically wraps the words around to fit in the frame, and you can lengthen or widen it to fit the words. You can also embed frames within frames down to any level for special layouts.

Another interesting feature of MacAuthor is the ability to create and store "styles" for paragraphs, headings, and highlights. Using a Style Editor, you can specify margins, tabs, justification, font, font size, line, paragraph, letter spacing, and other parameters for a particular paragraph or heading. Once defined, the style shows up on the pull-down Styles menu for the particular document you're working on. You can then choose the style you've defined anywhere else in the document and any changes to the style take effect throughout the document.

Advanced features of MacAuthor include background printing; seven levels of superscripting and subscripting — for mathematical and chemical formulas, for example; overstriking of characters; strikeout; kerning; global changes of selected text to upper or lower case; and the ability to open four documents at once or four windows into the same document.

Using a PC or Compatible

The most popular personal computer is the IBM PC, yet it has many limitations. The PC was designed so that circuit cards (also called "boards") from third-party manufacturers could be added to it, and many companies have put out cards that overcome some of the PC's limitations. Some computer manufacturers have recognized the PC as a standard and have produced computers that are "PC clones" (near-exact duplicates of PCs, including the limitations) or "PC compatibles" (close enough to the PC but with more features, or faster).

One major limitation of the IBM PC and PC XT is the quality of screen graphic displays (the PC AT is not so limited). To improve the screen display of a PC or PC XT, you can add the Hercules monochrome (black and white) graphics card and a high-resolution monitor. Another method is to add the IBM Color Graphics card and a color monitor; however, text does not appear as sharp on color monitors as it does on monochrome monitors. High-resolution monochrome monitors can display text as it would look (near-

WYSIWYG) in different typefonts.

Nearly every page makeup program for the PC or PC XT requires some additional graphics card — either a Hercules-compatible card, an IBM Color Graphics card, or a similar graphics display enhancer. Many also require *extra memory* in your PC or compatible — up to 640K. The high cost of upgrading a standard PC or PC XT makes it unattractive compared to the lower-cost Mac and Mac Plus, which has lower-cost page makeup and graphics software. The PC AT, a high-performance model with a better graphics display and processing power for page makeup programs, is much more costly than a Macintosh.

However, most businesses already use PCs or compatibles, and PC programs like Ventura Publisher (described in Chapter 5) are setting new price and feature standards and making desktop publishing on PC XTs more economical. For word processing (if you are not doing graphics), you can get by with a standard 128K or 256K PC or compatible, which is less expensive than a standard Macintosh.

The basic IBM PC XT or compatible computer is usually sufficient for word processing applications. IBM bundles a 10-megabyte hard disk with the PC XT configuration, which can hold the equivalent of 26 floppy disks (or 10 million characters) of information. You can get external hard disks from other manufacturers for the PC, PC XT and PC AT that range from 10 megabytes to over 80 megabytes, with cartridge tape backup systems.

You may think you don't need ten megabytes of data storage, since a 380K floppy disk can hold around 380,000 characters. However, if you are doing a lot of work on your PC, you'll soon discover that one of its greatest limitations is speed, and the slowest part of the system is the floppy disk. The convenience of a hard disk far outweighs its cost, as long as you learn how to backup your files regularly.

The PC as shipped by IBM is not the best machine for writing. For one thing, it is slower than most of the PC-compatible computers from other manufacturers. For another, its keyboard is harder to use for touch-typists who are used to the standard Selectric keyboard. IBM makes both PCs and Selectrics, but failed to realize that PCs would be used mostly by people who do word processing.

There are many keyboard replacements for the PC that are designed for people who like the Selectric type of keyboard (the most popular type), or other types where the keys are arranged in Dvorak or foreign styles. IBM has also realized the need for a real word processing keyboard and offers one for the IBM PC AT model.

The most popular keyboard replacements are the Key Tronic KB 5151 (Key Tronic Corp., $200) and the "Key Tronic clone" keyboards such as the KS 8300 AT/AT (Key Solutions, $99). Both the KB 5151 and the KS 8300 AT/AT resemble the PC AT keyboard, which is preferred by touch typists.

Mouse devices are also available for PCs and compatibles, to work with Microsoft Windows, Word and other Microsoft programs, Digital Research's GEM (Graphics Environment Manager) and the GEM series of programs, and other programs that combine word processing and graphics processing. The Microsoft Mouse is one of the more popular ones, as is the Mouse Systems mouse for PCs. Graphics tablets (such as the Summagraphics Summasketch Tablet) are also available for PCs.

There are far more word processing programs for PCs than for any other type of computer. They range in price from $10 (PC Write) to over $1000. There are many that are not mentioned in this chapter, either because they are very much like the most popular ones, or they are not as useful (in our opinion) for desktop publishing.

WordStar   WordStar (MicroPro International) is the most popular word processing program for PCs and CP/M computers. There are no significant differences between the PC and CP/M versions. When you buy the "plain vanilla" version of WordStar, you can install it to run with almost any daisy wheel or dot matrix printer including Epson printers. You can then buy an inexpensive laser printer and modify WordStar to work with it. This is not hard to do; in fact, many laser printers are supplied with special "batch files" that automatically install WordStar for you.

For example, Cordata (formerly Corona) offers an inexpensive laser printer called the LP300 (which is described in detail later in this chapter in our laser printer comparison). With the LP300 package you get a WordStar installation "batch file" that installs your version of WordStar automatically — you don't have to know anything about the laser printer or WordStar. When the installation is finished, you can use WordStar's printing control codes to switch laser printer typefonts. You can then laser print all of your WordStar files.

Figure 2-5 shows sample WordStar text with the printing codes you would normally use to print the WordStar text on a daisy wheel or dot matrix printer. Figure 2-6 shows the result of printing the text in figure

2-5 on the Cordata LP300 laser printer, using typefonts downloaded from disk. For an office worker who uses WordStar to type correspondence and reports, what could possibly be easier? Most if not all existing WordStar files can be output to the laser printer without doing any page makeup or learning typesetting codes. All you need to buy is a laser printer, and you can re-install your WordStar program for the printer without spending money for a new program.

```
^AThe Magazine
For Hands-on Publishing^N
     ^QDesktop Publishing^W serves the needs of ^Qtoday's fastest
growing horizontal market^W to be interested in personal computers:
business professionals who work in non-publishing fields but want
to do in-house publishing.  It also informs those in the field --
newspaper, magazine and book publishers, electronic publishers,
writers, editors, graphic artists and production managers.
```

Figure 2-5.   WordStar text with printing codes for printing on dot matrix or daisy-wheel printers.

The Magazine
For Hands–on Publishing

Desktop Publishing serves the needs of **today's fastest**

growing horizontal market to be interested in personal computers:

business professionals who work in non-publishing fields but want

to do in-house publishing. It also informs those in the field --

newspaper, magazine and book publishers, electronic publishers,

writers, editors, graphic artists and production managers.

Figure 2-6.   The same WordStar text from figure 2-5 printed on the Cordata LP300 laser printer, using the same codes, but set with downloaded typefonts.

If the laser printer does not offer such a file, you can still use the printer with WordStar without buying another program if the laser printer emulates an Epson graphics printer or a Diablo daisy wheel printer. "Plain vanilla" WordStar can be installed for an Epson graphics printer to use the typefonts of the Epson, or it can be installed for a Diablo daisy wheel printer. All you need to do is put the laser printer into "Epson emulation mode" and use the Epson-installed ver-sion of WordStar, or "Diablo emulation mode" and use the Diablo-installed version.

There are limitations in this approach. Diablo daisy wheel printers have bold and double-strike characters, but no typefonts; therefore, most laser printers offer only one regular and one bold typefont while in Diablo emulation mode. Epson mode usually offers at least bold and italic typefonts depending on what you select as the startup typefont.

To support the H-P LaserJet printer from WordStar, you can use the PrintMerge program for PCs ($99, Polaris Software). PrintMerge operates entirely by adding a powerful new set of such commands to the WordStar lexicon. PrintMerge is not unique in using this approach, but its commands are by far the most complete among the utilities that are currently available.

For the H-P LaserJet and LaserJet Plus, the program provides a number of formatting commands that let you switch from one font to another within a document, and specify margins, page length, headings and footings, underlining, and superscripts. PrintMerge also lets you incorporate charts created by Microsoft Chart into WordStar documents. PrintMerge's LaserJet features are described in the next chapter.

You run PrintMerge in two steps. First you insert the appropriate dot and control commands within the WordStar document. Then, when you are ready to print the document, you leave WordStar (by typing **x** from the main WordStar menu) and enter PrintMerge. Once inside PrintMerge, a menu guides you through the process of configuring the printer.

PrintMerge is perfect for anyone who prefers the WordStar style of dot commands for formatting and Control-**P** for font switching. Some complain about the cluttered look the embedded commands give your document on screen, but more significant is the inability to make global changes to embedded commands in a document.

For example, if you printed out a 15-page report with your subheads centered on the page in bold Times Roman, and then decide that you would rather have the subheads printed flush left in Helvetica, you cannot easily make the change in WordStar (with or without Print-Merge). On the other hand, if you're using Microsoft Word, you'd only have to make a minor adjustment in your style sheet to change the specifications automatically attached to subheads.

The WordStar and PrintMerge approach is good for serious Word-Star users. Another way to get good results with WordStar files is to use them with print formatting utilities for laser printers, described in the next chapter, or to transfer them to the Macintosh computer as described later in this chapter.

If you don't use WordStar, you may find other word processors easier to use with laser printers and typesetters.

Microsoft Word   No other word processing program for the PC comes closer to imitating a Macintosh-like environment than Microsoft Word (a different version of the program is available for the Macintosh, as described earlier). Word combines features such as screen display of how your file will look when printed, different page formats and typefonts, stored vocabularies, and support for using a mouse — all in a single package.

Microsoft Word lets you define a page layout for an entire section of text, called a *division*. For many documents it is useful to define the entire document as one division with a consistent page layout. For non-standard pages like a table of contents, index, and specially-formatted title page, you would define a new division for each unique page layout.

To define a page layout, start by defining where you want the page numbers to fall on the page, the type of page numbering (Arabic, Roman, alphabetic, all upper case letters, etc.), and any headings or footings, as well as the margins for the text. You can change these parameters by defining a new division.

Paragraphs end with a carriage return/line feed code combination. You can format paragraphs to be flush to the left margin (ragged right), centered between the margins, flush right (ragged left), or justified to both margins. You can also specify the type of indent (first line of paragraph, entire paragraph, or "hanging" indent), and whether or not the paragraph can be broken between two pages.

Characters can be formatted as well: bold, italic, underlined, subscripted, superscripted, overstrike and other styles, and typefonts are available in a range of point sizes. Leading control is also available from the menu.

You can use the minimal set of Word keyboard commands and produce documents, and in doing so you'll have the power of Word-Star plus features like "un-do" (the ability to un-do the last action, usually to save something that was deleted by mistake) and multiple typefonts. But you can go much further with Word if you learn more about division layouts and *style sheets*.

All of the design settings under your control for divisions, paragraphs and characters in a document can be saved in a file called a *style sheet*. You can then use the style sheet with the document you created it for, *and* you can use the style sheet for other documents. You can also use other style sheets for the same document.

You can define several style sheets for one document. For example, it might be useful to have a "draft manuscript" style sheet for printing the text double-spaced, and a "screen" style for displaying the text on the screen single-spaced. The typefonts could be a different size on each style sheet.

There are many possible uses of style sheets. You can collect style sheets in the "Gallery" (Word's term for a collection of style sheets), where there might be a separate style sheet for book chapters, magazine articles, letters, memos, reports, greeting cards, and so on. You can have as many style sheets as you like. For a tutorial on stylesheets, read *Word Processing With Style and Microsoft Word* by Peter Rinearson (see Bibliography).

Compared to WordStar, Microsoft Word is richer in features and faster in editing speed. However, many people are put off by products that use the mouse device. The mouse may slow you down if you use it while typing the first draft of a document, because you have to move your hand away from the keyboard to use it. However, when editing and revising text, using a mouse can be quicker than using the arrow keys on the keyboard.

Microsoft Word comes with laser printer drivers for the Apple LaserWriter, H-P LaserJet and LaserJet Plus, Epson-compatible MX, FX and JX printers, the DEC LNO3, Corona LP 300 and Canon LBP laser printers, and the IBM Proprinter, Colorjet and Quietwriter Model 2. With Word you don't usually need special text formatters because the program has a built-in professional approach to text formatting that is better than most word processing programs, with perhaps the exception of XyWrite. However, Fancy Font (described in Chapter 3) has a special print formatting program for use with Microsoft Word.

XyWrite XyWrite III (XyQuest, $195) gives you text-only page makeup and supports over 60 printers, including the Apple LaserWriter, H-P LaserJet and LaserJet Plus, Canon, and Corona laser printers. It also gives you multi-column page layout, microjustified proportionally-spaced text, and automatic or "soft" (also called "discretionary") hyphenation among other advanced features.

Inspired perhaps by typesetting systems, XyWrite is a "what you see is more or less what you get" word processor (WYSIMOLWYG, as industry researcher Jonathan Seybold calls it). You get on-screen display of boldface, underlining, italics, superscripts, and subscripts, and you get to see the page to be printed, complete with columns. However, due to limitations of most PC monitors, the program is designed to display only one monospaced character set. So if you select a smaller type size, for example, your on-screen line extends beyond the margin, although the printed line will still match the margins perfectly.

With XyWrite you can view another document in a window on a split screen, working with up to nine active documents, and quickly move or copy text between active documents.

To print multiple columns, you can set up a single-column to print up to six columns on a page. Text will automatically word-wrap and "snake" to the top of the next column. You can specify a starting position for the first column, spacing between columns, column breaks (following text goes to top of next column), and column length. You can also add footnotes, which print out at the bottom of the column they are referenced in.

XyWrite lets you redefine the keyboard and store text to a predefined key as well as record keystroke sequences for custom macros (procedures). The program can print mathematical symbols and foreign-language characters.

XyWrite's advanced features include the ability to generate a table of contents and an index, with automatic sorting and page numbering, based on phrases you mark in your document. You can paginate a document automatically, with footnotes placed on the proper pages. XyWrite also has "widow" or "orphan" control — a "widow" is a short line of text by itself at the top of a page, and an "orphan" is one or two lines by themselves at the bottom of a page — letting you designate blocks of text to be unbreakable at page endings. XyWrite can also automatically number blocks of texts — paragraphs and lists — and create a numbered outline.

XyWrite numbers footnotes and endnotes (footnotes grouped at the end of a chapter), and can continue footnotes on the next page if they are too long. XyWrite can print multiple files on different subdirectories, with a single run of page and footnote numbers, a single table of contents, and a single index accumulated from across all named files.

These features make XyWrite an excellent tool for writing and producing books and manuals. XyWrite has printer definition files to work with a variety of printers. You can add PostScript or other printer formatting commands to XyWrite printer definition files to make XyWrite work with your printer or accept new fonts and other new features.

Using XyWrite III's built-in LaserWriter printer support and PC MacBridge on the PC, we created this book's index and table of contents on the PC from WordStar text files, and typeset them first on the LaserWriter for proofing and then on the Allied Linotype Linotronic typesetter described in Chapter 3. You can use XyWrite directly with a LaserWriter — the Boeing Computer Services Tech Pubs department uses the system for producing their *SEPG News* (figure 2-7).

ditorial

Welcome To The SEPG Newsletter

We have the pleasure of introducing to you *SEPGNEWS*, a bi-monthly newsletter about the people and products of the Software and Education Products Group. This is where we can become more familiar with one another as a team and with the various projects SEPG supports.

SEPGNEWS is intended to be casual and heavily people-oriented. We're just as interested in the personalities behind the products as we are the products themselves.

This newsletter is produced solely for your enjoyment — so, we are recruiting your support. If you have suggestions for feature columns that have not been included in this issue, please submit them.

BOEING COMPUTER SERVICES
A Division of The Boeing Company

WAT

The Swat Concept In Documentation

SEPG Tech Pubs is now developing a team of writers to handle accelerated and atypical documentation projects exclusively. Dick Burdick conceived the idea of building an accelerated writing team to re-vamp existing manuals to better represent a product in the market place; and, to write new manuals and marketing material for product offerings.

The team is comprised of experienced writers who can research and write quickly while maintaining high quality standards. This writing group is referred to as SWAT, a title for which nobody is claiming responsibiltiy. SWAT is led by Gale Scialdo, an ancient writer who has been producing manuals since the antediluvian era. Her teammates are Jeff Angus, who consumes vast amounts of caffeine and can maintain a pace close to the speed of sound; and, Jim Walsh, a contractor who likes anything accelerated.

Figure 2-7.   Produced with XyWrite on the LaserWriter by WX author Chad Canty, a Boeing systems analyst in desktop publishing technology.

To convert our WordStar files to XyWrite, we used the $35 WX utility from Tech Knowledge. WX strips out WordStar's ASCII "high bits" that cause display problems and unreadable text when you try to use a WordStar document with another word processor (the high bits are used for WordStar's soft carriage returns and for preserving spaces and indents during justification). WX also converts WordStar's underline, bold, margin, and dot commands into XyWrite commands. It also lets you to change the right margin, page length, and forms length and to "unjustify" the text.

WX is a one-way utility — it converts WordStar to XyWrite, but not XyWrite to WordStar. For the most part you don't need a XyWrite to WordStar converter — you can use a XyWrite-saved ASCII file with WordStar. You don't have to strip out the carriage returns first, to preserve paragraph endings, because XyWrite is so fast that it actually creates what appear to be carriage returns and line feeds on the fly (no actual ASCII carriage returns or line feed codes are used). A XyWrite paragraph is actually one long line extending out beyond the margin. You just open the file in WordStar's document mode, reform the document with Control-**B** commands (Control-**QQB** to repeat it indefinitely).

You can edit a XyWrite file with WordStar, but there is no automatic conversion for XyWrite printing codes to WordStar codes. You can leave the XyWrite page layout codes in the file and edit it with WordStar.

Power Writer's Tools

Computers can't write prose, but they can check for spelling errors and typos faster than humans. The word processing phenomenon spawned a multitude of programs that check your spelling, your grammar, your punctuation, even your *writing style*.

Computers are also useful for copying and sorting words. You can now choose from several different programs to prepare an index and a table of contents from a set of text files. You can compare two text files to find the differences, and search an entire disk of text files quickly for a specific phrase or word.

Some functions are provided with the word processing program. Examples are CorrectStar, an optional spell checker that can be installed with WordStar, and XyWrite, which can produce an index and table of contents. However, for the most part the word processing programs do not have the larger spelling dictionaries, the algorithms for checking grammar and punctuation, or the formulas for judging writing style.

A spelling proofreader can help you prepare documents and become a better writer. You can write without worrying about typos, because the program will catch them. The program will also show you the words you habitually misspell, and the process of correcting them will help you remember how to spell them.

The more words a spell checking program has in its dictionary, the better the program checks your spelling. What also makes a proofreading program useful is the ability to *add* words to a dictionary. All of the programs described here have that ability, so that you increase your productivity as you use the program.

Proofreaders and Thesauruses For PCs
A typical spell checking program that runs on CP/M and PC computers is The Word Plus (Oasis Systems, $150). The program can find and correct spelling mistakes with your help and a dictionary with over 45,000 words. The program can also find anagrams, look up words in the dictionary, find rhyming words and help solve crossword puzzles.

The Word Plus works with text from nearly every word processing program for PCs and CP/M computers. WordStar in particular works very well. First you write your text using a word processing program. Then you leave the word processing program and run The Word Plus.

The program displays a total word count and the number of different words and misspelled (unrecognized) words. Then it displays each misspelled word and offers you a choice. You can use the look-up function to see if the word comes close to any word in the dictionary, and if it does, you can use one keystroke to correct the word. You can use the view function to display the word in context (with the line of text it appears in).

If the word is correct but not recognized, you can ignore it and move on, or you can add the word to a special dictionary (many add-on dictionaries are available, often used for technical, legal or medical words) or to an update dictionary (for regular words not recognized by the main dictionary).

The Word Plus includes a hyphenation program that puts "soft" hyphens (hyphens that are printed only when needed to justify lines) in every lengthy word in your file, using a technique described by

Donald Knuth in his book, *TEX and Metafont, New Directions in Typesetting* (Digital Press, Bedford, MA, 1979). HYPHEN uses an elaborate set of rules that describe how to locate appropriate hyphenation points. In addition (because there are always exceptions), HYPHEN refers to a special dictionary of words that defy these rules named HYEXCEPT.TXT (you can add more words to this file as you find them). The "soft" hyphens are compatible with WordStar.

```
0 compatibility
1 computability




REVIEW+  Version 1.2, Copyright 1981 - Oasis Systems

Add word to:                     Other options:
 U>pdate Dictionary                 P>revious word
 S>pec. Dict. "SPECIALS.CMP"        N>ext word
M>ark word                          R>esume review
D>iscard word                       L>ook up word
C>orrect word                       V>iew context

--> COMPATABILITY -__
```

Figure 2-8. The Word Plus finds misspelled words and lets you either look up and correct the word, ignore it, or add it to one of the dictionaries.

Another popular PC spelling checker is Turbo Lightning (Borland International, $100). You load Lightning into memory before writing, and as you write, Lightning looks up the word in its memory-resident dictionary and tells you if it is misspelled. You can then substitute the correct word for the misspelled word with one keystroke, or ignore the word (and leave it as it is), or add it to the dictionary. Turbo Lightning also places the Random House Thesaurus in memory for you to select synonyms.

Spell Finder from Microlytics uses word compression and other advanced programming techniques developed from years of research at the Xerox Palo Alto Research Center (PARC). Licensed from Xerox and used on some of Xerox's Memorywriter typewriters, Spell Finder is one of the fastest spelling checkers on the PC.

Spell Finder manages to pack its program plus over 110,000 dictionary words into just 64K of RAM. Type as fast as you can — you can't get ahead of it. It has the unique ability to recognize and alert you to thousands of capitalized words: major cities, states, countries, major companies, cars, planets, and days of the week, months (it doesn't accept "february" but it accepts "may," which can also be a verb, or "august," which can also be an adjective).

It also recognizes Bach, Berlin, Berlitz, Buick, Einsteinian, and many other names. You can set the level of the alert tone, or if you hate to be beeped, you can select highlighting only, or turn the program off at any time without rebooting and run it later as a "batch" program. U.K. English, French, German, and other versions are in development.

There are several IBM PC electronic thesaurus programs on the market. One of the best is Word Finder (Microlytics/Writing Consultants, $80), which lets you find synonyms in seconds without leaving your word processor. (Word Finder is available with Microlytics' Spell Finder for $100.)

Word Finder (version 3) has 15,000 main word entries and 220,500 synonyms. This is three times larger than the Random House Thesaurus database, which is used by Turbo Lightning and other thesaurus programs — and larger than the 11,000-word printed Random House Thesaurus College Edition.

An unusual feature of Word Finder is "infinite word exploration," which is the ability to explore synonyms of synonyms of synonyms. If you are in search of the perfect word — or even new ideas — you can explore down through the English language's maze of interconnected words and meanings to unlimited depths. Word Finder keeps track of your last ten choices to let you return to previous synonyms or substitute a word into a document.

Word Finder displays synonyms in an "instant" pop-up window, and lets you substitute a synonym for a word in the text with two keystrokes. Word Finder also eliminates the need to delete and retype the new word and retains the capitalization of the original word.

For words not included in the database, Word Finder displays the 30 closest words alphabetically, allowing you to look up synonyms for a related word (searching for "processing" brings up "process" and 29 other words, for example). Word Finder also functions as a memory-resident dictionary — you can quickly check a word's spelling and meaning.

Word Finder is compatible with 12 popular word processors:

WordStar 3.0 to 3.31, WordStar 2000, Multimate, XyWrite 3.03, Word Perfect, Pfs:Write, Microsoft Word, IBM Writing Assistant, Easy Writer II, Framework, Volkswriter Deluxe, OfficeWriter, and Palantir Word Processor.

Proofreaders and Thesauruses For Macs

Hayden:Speller (Hayden Software, $80) is a spell checking program for the Macintosh. You first create your text file with your favorite word processing program, or any application program that can produce text documents (such as ThinkTank, an outlining program described later). You can then use Hayden:Speller to check the file for misspelled words against its 20,000 word dictionary.

Hayden:Speller displays a count of the total number of: words in the file, different words, valid words (words found in the dictionary), and suspect words (not in the dictionary). Words that are not in the dictionary are not necessarily misspelled.

The program's Correct menu offers you two basic choices: the Check Words option displays an alphabetical listing of suspect words, and you can choose one of four actions for each word. You can accept the suspect word (do this if the word is spelled correctly, but not in the dictionary), accept the word and save it in a personal dictionary, replace the word by typing it correctly, or postpone action.

The other choice is the Scan Document option, for displaying the words in context. You can run the Check Words option, and postpone action on any words you want to view in context. The Scan Document option takes more time to complete the changes, but it lets you see the words in context, and it has a lookup option to compare the misspelled word to similar words in the 20,000 word dictionary.

You can correct the words from either of the Correct menu options, or you can choose to mark suspect words for correcting later with your word processing program. You can create a personal dictionary of words you use often that are not in the main dictionary.

Hayden:Speller can't handle files longer than 30K (5000 words, approximately 10 pages), so you have to break large files into smaller chunks to use Hayden:Speller on them.

Other popular spell checking programs for the Macintosh are Mac-Spell+ (Creighton Development Inc.), Mac Spell Right and The Right Word (both from Assimilation).

MacSpell+ ($99) lets you check spelling while you are working in Microsoft Word or MacWrite (versions 2.2 and 4.5). MacSpell+ has a 75,000 word dictionary and a 20,000 word thesaurus. It does automatic hyphenation and searches phonetically for corrections to misspelled words. You can add 3500 words to the main dictionary and also add your own dictionary.

Mac Spell Right ($89) works only on MacWrite files, while The Right Word ($89) works on Microsoft Word, MacWrite, MacPublisher, and other text files (even Jazz text files). Mac Spell Right works from within MacWrite (like a desk accessory), so that you can check spelling while doing word processing. The Right Word uses a 40,000 word dictionary on a floppy disk system, or a 200,000+ word dictionary on a hard disk system. Both programs provide a 15,000 word thesaurus, which on a floppy disk takes more time to use than a standard paper book thesaurus.

MacLightning (Target Software, $100) lives up to its name as the fastest spelling checker on the Macintosh. It has a 71,000-word dictionary (based on the American Heritage), and it runs in memory, always checking words as you type. MacLightning works with MacWrite, Microsoft Word, and most other Macintosh word processing programs. It allows you to type as fast as you like, with a top speed of 68 words a second.

MacLightning is installed as a desk accessory. It beeps whenever you type a misspelled word or make certain grammatical errors. You can look up the correct spelling by hitting the Command-**1** Hot Key, which gives you a list of the closest words in the dictionary. Click on the Paste Bottle icon or hit Command-**2** to automatically replace the incorrect word with the correct one.

You can add words to the dictionary by using a Dictionary Maker utility. MacLightning also displays average word length and the longest word, and checks for proper capitalization.

An unusual feature of MacLightning is that if you use any word more than five times in a given session, it gets stored in a special auxiliary file that is read into RAM memory automatically in the future, which speeds things up for commonly used words.

Target Software also offers the 45,000-word Roget's II Thesaurus from American Heritage, and a programmer's library that checks for correct syntax of C, Pascal, and BASIC programs.

Punctuation, Style and Reading Level Writing is a means of personal expression, not a contest among grammarians and style experts. But if you find spell checking worthwhile, you might find these writing aids worth the cost because they help prevent careless mistakes from diverting attention from what you have to say.

Punctuation & Style (Oasis Systems, $125) is a set of two programs that run on PCs and CP/M computers. The programs point out possible errors in the use of punctuation marks, check for certain typographical errors, and compare your text against various lists of erroneous or inappropriate phrases.

Both programs include provisions for bypassing the flagging of any type of errors, which is especially nice when you don't agree with the program's view of grammar.

You can use the Punctuation and Style programs with any straight text file, plus there are easy setups for WordStar and Perfect Writer. With a little more effort, the programs can be configured for most other popular word processors. Depending on what you request, the programs will either run interactively, asking you to ratify the marking of each suspected error, or in batch mode with output to a file.

These programs are no substitute for good writing or editing — they won't help with organization, pace, tone, verb agreement, content or the finer points of style. If you're looking for the artificial intelligence text processor that changes rough drafts to immortal prose, you'll have to wait a little longer.

The first of the two programs in the package, CLEANUP, is the proofreader part. It checks for misuse of punctuation marks, doubled words (for example, this one one), unusual capitalization, proper number format and pairing of quotes, brackets and other specified symbols. You'd normally use it in addition to a spelling checker, such as Oasis Systems' The Word Plus, described earlier.

The second program is more like a copy editor than a proofreader. The PHRASE program checks your text against a selection of several hundred phrases that the program author feels you should avoid. If you don't agree with the selection, clear instructions are given on how to make your own phrase lists.

The program only matches your text against a list of possible errors rather than actually reading and comprehending it. A word or phrase included in the list because it is inappropriate in one context may the right thing to say in another. You definitely need to consider whether you agree with each point marked by the program, either interactively or by editing a file marked in batch mode.

If you don't have an ear for the difference between passive and active sentences but do agree that passive ones should be avoided, Punctuation & Style will help you spot them. You may find that its rules in this area a bit rigid, but if you have the time to review each objection, you may find it worthwhile.

For the Macintosh, Doug Clapp's Word Tools (Aegis Development, $100) does almost everything you'd want except an extensive spelling check. Doug Clapp, computer magazine columnist and author of *Macintosh! Complete* (Softalk Books), designed Word Tools to provide writers and editors with tools to help them clean up their writing act and eliminate long, wordy, unreadable sentences (like this one).

Using Word Tools is like having your favorite (or most hated) English teacher grade and revise your document. The program counts just about everything in the text: characters (including invisible "control" characters), words, nouns, proper nouns, articles, prepositions, sentences, and paragraphs.

Next, you might have Word Tools check your text for readability, using three respected formulas. The program scores you on "grade level" — the scores are based on the number of syllables per word, words per sentence, and sentences per paragraph. Word Tools will even tell you how "interesting" your writing is.

Another way to check readability is to look for averages and extremes: Word Tools will spot your longest sentences and paragraphs for later revision. If you've got Switcher running in your 512K Macintosh or Macintosh Plus, you can switch back and forth to MacWrite or Word from Word Tools and modify your text on the fly. If you don't have Switcher, you can mark or ignore the "extremes," as you'd like.

You can also create word lists in lots of ways: unsorted, sorted by length, frequency of use, or alphabetically. If you want, you can exclude "noise" words like "a," "the" and "and".

You can also use the program to check for poor writing style — wordiness, slang, hackneyed or redundant phrases, cliches, imprecise words or phrases, and sexist or otherwise offensive, stilted, awkward, overused, and abused words or phrases.

Clapp distilled the best of the *Chicago Manual of Style* — the bible of style books — and other style guides, such as Strunk and White's definitive *Elements of Style*, into a massive suspect/replacement/comment list that blazes through your writing, searching for offending words and phrases.

For example, the phrases "arrive at a decision" and "did not pay attention to" result in the comment "wordy" and the suggested replacements "decide" and "ignored."

If you agree, just click on the Accept option to make the replacement. Or, you can Ignore the suggestion, Postpone your decision until later, Mark the suspect, Mark All the offenders, or — if you dare — Change All the suspects in one swoop.

If you don't agree with the suspect/replacement list itself (it balks at the words "feedback" and "input," for example) you can easily change the list or add to it.

You can also create customized lists to use Word Tools as a search and replace utility. If you've ever used MacWrite or Word to make one global replacement after another until your document looks (and reads) the way it should, you'll appreciate this feature. Just make a list with each word to be replaced and its corresponding replacement, and Word Tools automates the entire process. The feature is useful for preparing text to be exported to data bases, or removing unwanted characters from files downloaded from electronic mail or videotex services, or for creating boilerplate documents.

The custom list feature excels at automating the laborious process of inserting typesetting codes into text. For example, in preparing a document for typesetting, you might need to insert a typesetting code in your text similar to this: `[pr][mp162]QQ[ql][a6]`. Word Tools can change a single ASCII character (including the carriage return character, or any other ASCII character or group of characters) into the above code, automatically, without your having to type it (and possibly misspell it).

Word Tools also checks punctuation, noting common errors such as commas following quotes, single spaces after periods, and incorrect capitalization. Again, each error is explained and you're not forced to change anything. Typos, such as unbalanced parentheses, doubled words, and improper abbreviations, such as "Ave." (always spell it out, the program advises), are also caught by the program.

All of these measures — readability, word counts, wordiness, typos, punctuation errors, and so on — can be printed out or saved to disk as reports for further analysis.

Indexing Programs

Your writing effort on the computer can be proceeding at a rapid pace, but it might slow to an infinite crawl when you reach the task of producing an index and a table of contents for a book or manual. Most word processing programs do not provide indexing capabilities. After spending thousands of dollars on computer equipment and using it to write a comprehensive guide to using computers, you might feel frustrated at the prospect of having to index the book with conventional index cards.

Index (Digital Marketing, $99, based on Documate/Plus) lets you create a multi-leveled index and a table of contents for one or more WordStar files on a PC or CP/M computer. You don't need WordStar to use it — Index commands can be inserted into any text file, regardless of which word processing program you use, and the commands can be processed with Index without WordStar. The program is designed to not interfere with WordStar printing codes, so the commands may show up in the printout if you use another word processor; however, the index and table of contents can be used with any word processing program.

We used Index to produce a large two-level index for a book whose chapters were each stored in separate files. The index was in a form that could be printed instantly, or edited to include typesetting codes. We also used Index to create the table of contents for the book, and to gather together comments and questions within a manuscript.

To prepare an index and table of contents for a text file, you have to place commands in the text file. You can do this while typing the text, or you can edit the file later and insert the commands where they are needed. A typical Index (and the older Documate/Plus) index entry looks like this in your WordStar file:

```
...X file,text
```

The entry **file** is indexed with the descriptive word **text**. Entries and descriptive words can be several words. The first example below places the entire entry `text file` in the index. The second places the entry `file, tabbing in` in the index:

```
...X text file
```

```
...X file, tabbing in
```

The triple periods ("dots" in WordStar jargon) mark the comment line as a Index command. The periods must start in column 1 of your screen. Index uses three periods because WordStar (and its MailMerge add-on package) ignore them. The commands can remain in the text and not show up in the printing. (The commands are treated as comments, to be ignored by the printer.)

Index produces a WordStar file containing an alphabetical index. Each entry includes the page number of every other marked reference to the word. Here are a few entries for `file`:

```
file, data 12, 22
    source, 23, 34
    system, 13, 22, 33
    tabbing in, 23
    text, 14, 23
    verify copy in, 15
```

Page numbers are determined by WordStar's page settings. If you use ordinary page numbers, they will be used to create the index. If you use **.PN** commands to change the page number, these changes are noted by Index also and are used in the index.

Alternatively, Index picks up the page number from your **.HE** (heading) or **.FO** (footing) command. This is useful if you are numbering chapter pages as **2-4**, **3-6**, etc. in a heading or footing. Index finds the prefix by scanning each **.HE** or **.FO** command for the **#** symbol used to mark the place of the page number in a heading or footing.

Index table of contents commands let you define any number of levels of chapter/section headings, starting with . . . **T1**:

```
...T1 Chapter 2: Using DocuMate

...T2 Introduction

...T3 Introducing Index Commands

...T4 Figure 2-1. Summary of index commands.
```

Use these commands in the text at the location of the headings. Index adds the page number defined by WordStar (just as with an index). It then creates a table of contents as a WordStar text file, with page numbers by default at the left margin, and headings following the numbers on the same line.

You can edit the table of contents file to be in any form, or you can use Index commands to format the table of contents differently before producing it. These commands include a column width command, a margin width command, and a command to control indenting sub-level headings.

Most large documents occupy several separate files. You can use Index commands in these separate files, and assemble one index and table of contents from them. Number your pages as you want them to appear; for example, if you want consecutive page numbers throughout the entire document, you must use a `.PN` command at the beginning of each separate file to control the page numbering.

You can change your text file, add more Index commands to the text file, and change page numbers at any time. Run Index on the file after making changes, and the program produces a new sorted index and table of contents. You can also edit the index, since it is a Word-Star text file.

XyWrite, an advanced word processing program described earlier in this chapter, has a built-in indexing and table of contents creation function. The index and table of contents can be produced as part of the XyWrite text file or as separate files, and can be edited with Xy-Write.

You create index and table of contents entries as you write with XyWrite, or when editing the document using XyWrite. The program lets you mark a word or phrase with the cursor and use the **Xn** command to mark it as an entry. The **n** is a number signifying in which set — subject index, author index, table of contents — to place the word or phrase. You can mark words or phrases in the text, or type new words or phrases to be placed into one of the sets.

MacIndex (Boston Software Publishers, $50) is an indexing program for the Macintosh. MacIndex works with MacWrite, Mac-Publisher and MacPublisher II to produce an index using words selected in your document. The package includes Keywords (a desk accessory to select entries in your text) and File Filter, which removes unnecessary words, such as "and" and "the," from the index it generates. The MacIndex package includes the standard Apple Font/Desk Accessory Mover used to move typefonts and desk accessories onto your startup disks.

Text Organizing Programs

There are numerous outlining, notetaking, text organizing and text search tools for PCs and Macs. SideKick (Borland International, $100 for the not-protected Macintosh version including Phonelink for dialing, and $50 for the copy-protected PC version) is a utility that provides a pop-up note taker, scheduler, calculator and modem-phone dialer. SideKick is resident in memory, so you can run it from within most application and word processing programs (see figure 2-9).

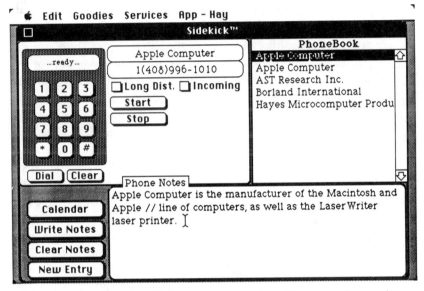

Figure 2-9.   Borland's SideKick is a good companion utility for word processing.

Phonelink, supplied with the not-copy-protected Macintosh version, is a hardware accessory that connects your Mac to a modular phone jack for automatic phone dialing without using a modem.

SideKick's companion product SuperKey (for the PC) lets you record a set of your keystrokes to repeat later by using only one function key. With these tools you can automate many of your routine word processing tasks.

For drawing up outlines, ThinkTank (Living Videotext, $245 for Mac version, $195 for PC version) is the most popular for both the PC and the Mac. ThinkTank provides an outline formatting structure for you to type and organize text. It makes outlining easier because you can easily rearrange the text at any time. The Mac version lets you include MacPaint graphic images or logos in your document.

As you create an outline, the program automatically indents each level of headings and subheads, so that you can visually organize your ideas. You can expand, collapse, or move groupings of heads and sub-heads to reorganize the outline.

Another useful outline program for the PC is Ready! (also from Living Videotext, $100). This program is memory resident — once loaded into memory, you can switch between it and other programs with a single keystroke. You can prepare outlines in Ready! and transfer them to Microsoft Word, for example, with one keystroke.

Imagine the usefulness of having a program that can compare two files and display the differences. There are numerous document comparison programs in the public domain for PC and CP/M computers, including COMPARE.ASM. There is also a file comparison utility in the Norton Utilities for the PC.

For the Macintosh, Document Compare (The Model Office Company, $99) compares two MacWrite files on screen in two windows and highlights the differences in reverse video (white type on black background). It detects changes in typefonts, type sizes, type styles, pictures, words, upper/lower case letters, tabs, page breaks, headers, footers, returns, and rulers. You can tell the program to ignore size, style, and/or case differences. The original files are not changed.

Document Compare also counts words, pictures, and rules, so you know how many times you changed formats (for example, changing from from single to double spacing).

You can print both documents with the differences marked, which is very useful when you want to show an editor or a client, for example, exactly what changes you've made in a document. Document Compare can be a lifesaver when you're on a tight publication deadline.

Document Modeler (The Model Office Company, $299) is an "expert system tool" for automating the creation of documents. It lets you encode your expertise into a "document template" that can be used by any untrained worker to produce documents (see figure 2-10).

To use Document Modeler, the expert writes a "script" in MacWrite or add codes to an existing document to specify standard clauses, variables, conditions, and calculations. For example, if you're creating a sales agreement, you might specify such variables as buyer, price, and item, conditions (when warranties are valid, for example), calculations (such as loan payments or tax calculations), and any standard legal clauses.

Document Modeler converts this script into a document template that prompts your assistant (in this instance, a salesperson) with a series of questions, asking for fill-in-the-blank information or multiple-choice selections. Document Modeler then automatically builds the document on the screen as the salesperson enters responses to each prompt. The document could have appropriate typefonts and styles, a graphic image of the product, automatic paragraph numbering, and even the dealer's letterhead and signature lines. The salesperson can read it over, make changes, print it out, save the responses to disk for later use in a data base, and have the customer sign on the dotted line right on the spot.

Figure 2-10. Document Modeler (The Model Office Company) automates the creation of documents using document templates.

Context-sensitive "Reference Information" automatically appears in a scrollable window at each prompt, providing, for example, advice from a legal authority to a paralegal assistant, medical guidance to a medical clerk, product information for an order clerk, or a standard corporate procedure while filling out a travel requisition.

Document Modeler is compatible with any ASCII text file and can extract data from data bases and update them. It can also import images from MacPaint, MacDraw, Chart, Cricket Graph, and other graphics programs (described in Chapter 4). This allows Document Modeler to create a letterhead or an complete illustrated presentation.

Document Modeler includes sample scripts and a tutorial demonstration template. "Document Maker," the portion of Document Modeler used by "clones" to produce documents, is available separately for $199.

Text Search Software

One serious problem with word processing is that once you've created lots of text files, it's almost impossible to find anything — especially when you have a hard disk with plenty of capacity. This becomes critical in major publishing projects, such as writing a book or editing a magazine, where you may want to see what you've said about a subject before, or group together everything you've collected on a given subject for an article.

This is especially true for users of PCs and CP/M computers, with their limitation of 11-character file names, forcing you to create such cryptic names as ABCCORP1.DAT or WSDOC.123.

True, you could create a data base to keep track of it all. But not only is that a lot of work to create and maintain — it's impossible to predict all of the keywords you'll need for any given search. Wouldn't it be great if you could find any word, instead of just keywords? That's what "full-text search" or "text management" software packages do.

Full-text search software has been used on mainframe computers for searching large databases, such as Lexis and Dialog. Recently, software for micros has also appeared, including 4-1-1, OCRS, and others. One of the best is Professional ZyINDEX (ZyLAB, $295).

Professional ZyINDEX lets you find any word, phrase, number, or combination of these in thousands of text files in seconds. For example, suppose you're looking for a famous quote about art from Oscar Wilde, a 19th Century writer, whose quotes are mixed with many others in several large text files. Just type in **Wilde and art**, and the exact quote ("All art is quite useless") appears on the screen within seconds of starting the search.

ZyINDEX does this by creating a series of index files on disk with "pointers" to every appearance of every word (or number), filtering out "noise words" like "the." The program works with most popular word processors, such as WordStar, Microsoft Word, Multimate,

Volkswriter, XyWrite, and any others that create ASCII text files. Zy-INDEX also has a "map" function to handle special characters in other word processors.

Professional ZyINDEX also allows for more complex Boolean (and/or) searches. For example, say you're looking for everything you've saved on IBM stock performance in connection with the PCjr. You would type **IBM and jr w/20 stock** (**w/20** stands for "within 20 words of"). This would get you all files with both "IBM" and "jr" in them, but only if the word "stock" was within 20 words (to avoid irrelevant mentions of some other stock in the same article).

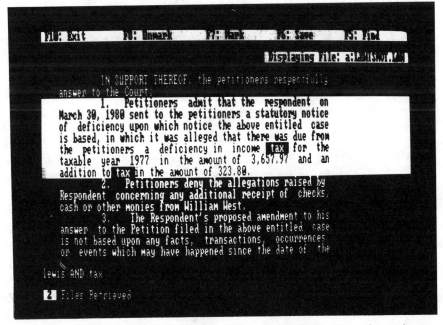

Figure 2-11. Professional ZyINDEX lets you search for a word or phrase throughout a disk filled with text files.

ZyINDEX has an "annotated cut and paste" feature that lets you create a boilerplate file of all paragraphs mentioning a specific topic. If you are an editor supervising a writing effort, or on a writing team, this feature would help you manage the various sections of text. As you go through your text files, you can annotate each paragraph, giving a date, background, or other comments to provide context.

Another useful application of full-text search software is locating specific information in downloaded electronic mail or public database files, which, as many electronic communicators quickly find, becomes worthless in a short time if not carefully catalogued or filed in labelled folders. Full-text search software solves this problem by eliminating the need to catalogue and file hard copy.

On the Macintosh side, Forethought's $150 Factfinder performs some of the same functions. Unlike ZyINDEX, you have to specify the words in the text you want to use as key words, using the mouse to click on each word. You can also access Factfinder files by date or name. The program is equivalent to keeping thousands of 3x5 cards on various subjects, but being able to find one in seconds.

Factfinder for the Mac lets you type up to four pages of notes for each "factsheet" you create. You type your notes into the program as text, without structuring rules. You can type paragraphs, bulleted lists, outlines, or whatever you want, and create keywords for the factsheet. To find all of the factsheets with the same keyword, use the program to do a keyword search of all your factsheets.

Transferring Data

Until now it was very difficult to transfer information from one type of computer to another computer that was not compatible with it. Today you can use a variety of methods to transfer data to and from various computers. The easiest method is by floppy disk, and most computers (except Apple computers) have disk drives that accept PC-formatted 5 1/4-inch disks. You can transfer information by copying files from one disk to another.

To transfer large amounts of data from one PC or compatible to another, or from one Mac to another, you may want the Bernoulli Box (described earlier in the section on hard disks for the Macintosh), which uses removable five-megabyte cartridges to store data, and you can easily carry a Bernoulli cartridge from one PC to another, but not from a PC to a Mac or vice-versa.

To transfer data across the compatibility boundary of PCs and Macs (and PCs to other Apple computers, and from Apple computers to CP/M computers, and so on), you can either use a phone line connection with a modem, as described next, or a direct cable link bypassing the modem but using the modem control software described next. This is accomplished by joining together the serial ports of the two computers with a *null modem* cable (a cable that pretends to be a modem), and using a modem program on both computers to set up communication.

The newest form of data transfer is the *local area network*, popularized first on PCs and then on Macintosh computers. On the PC side there are numerous network arrangements compatible with IBM's SNA network protocol for mainframe computers, and with IBM's personal computer network standard. On the Mac side there is the Apple-Talk network, which connects various Macs and other equipment together. There are "gateways" to and from PC networks and the AppleTalk network that are available from third-party vendors.

Bridging PCs and Macs
Why would you want to bridge the gap between the PC and the Mac? Here are a few reasons:

• You have a file on the Mac that you want to use in your PC page makeup program. Why retype it when you can transfer it to the PC quickly?

• You want to take advantage of the lower-cost, easier-to-use Macintosh page makeup software for what the Macintosh is best at: final layout and integrating text and graphics, while using the PC for what it's best at: quickly creating and storing lots of documents and number files with word processing, database, spreadsheet and other programs.

• You want to share your LaserWriter with several people in your company for better printing economies. Plugging in through a Macintosh, you select the low-cost ($50 per connection) AppleTalk network, instead of the more expensive, hard to use, LaserWriter-incompatible IBM PC networks.

How do you connect a PC to a Mac? There are three typical ways:

1. Direct connection over serial (RS-232C) cable is the least expensive way, using a modem program or transfer program such as Mac-Link (Dataviz, $155). MacLink comes with a cable that plugs into an asynchronous port on the PC and into the modem port on the Macintosh, plus PC and Macintosh communications software to let the machines "talk" to each other.

2. The AppleTalk network is the best bet if you want to share a LaserWriter between Macs and PCs, or if you want to have several Mac users communicating. You can use the PC MacBridge (Tangent Technologies, $650) or equivalent board into your PC. PC MacBridge lets you connect your PC to the AppleTalk network and print Word-Star files on a LaserWriter or other PostScript printer or typesetter. You can connect up to 32 Macs and PC MacBridge units in the Appletalk network. If you're sending messages between Macs, you'll also need some network communications software, such as Videx's $100 Mail Center.

3. Other Networks: You can connect Macs on the AppleTalk network to PCs on other networks, such as 3Com Corporation's 3Com network and Centram's TOPS network. The 3Com network uses a hardware "network server," letting Mac and PC users read or write any file from any other user. Centram's TOPS uses a different approach, using a plug-in AppleTalk board in each IBM PC on a PC-based network of PCs and through software on each machine allowing any PC or Mac user to move data around between IBM or Mac disks.

The 3Com network is suitable for centralized business applications because it relies on a central file server with a large-capacity hard disk and backup device. It is also expensive — the base unit file server (with a 36 megabyte hard disk) is $7,995, each memory expansion board is $995, and the EtherShare software is $695.

Centram's TOPS network is less expensive ($349 for the plug-in card and software package for each PC, $149 for the software package for each Mac). You can use any PC or Mac with a hard disk as a file server with file sharing capabilities.

If network approaches are too expensive, you can transfer data to and from other computers over phone lines using very inexpensive equipment: modems and communication software.

Modems and Communication Software

No communicator should be without the means to communicate data over phone lines. You can send text over a phone line to a typesetting service to get fast turnaround, and you can use electronic mail services to gather text from various sources and combine them into one document, using your word processing program. If everyone used computers and modems, there would be no need to retype information that was already typed once.

Modems are essential for data communications. A modem is a small device that connects to your computer with a wide computer cable (a DB-25 RS232C serial cable connected to your computer's RS232C serial port). You then connect the modem to a telephone line using a standard telephone modular (RJ11 or RJ14 jack) cable.

The typical personal computer modem (Hayes Smartmodem) has an array of lights on the front, telling you what's going on with the modem. The two lights at the far right should be on — they indicate the modem's power is on, and that it senses that a computer is connected to it (both are vital signs that communication can take place). The light at the far left is usually on to indicate that the modem is operating at the "high" data speed setting (usually 1200 baud, approximately 120 characters per second).

The other lights tell you about your connection over the phone line to another computer. If your modem is "talking" to the other computer successfully, the "CD" light (carrier detect) will be on (third light from the left). If you are sending data out through the phone line, the "SD" light will flash with each character sent out; if you are receiving data from another computer over the phone line, the "RD" light will flash with each character received. The "OH" (off-hook) light comes on when you've disconnected from the remote computer.

The "AA" light should only come on if you are using the modem to answer the phone. Why would you want this? Imagine you have a lot of data on your office personal computer, and you want to have access to it from your home computer over the weekend. You would leave your office modem in "answer mode" and set your office computer up for answering the phone and handling your data processing requests. You could then call the office computer at any time from your home computer and request information.

You can use a modem in "answer mode" to control access to a private electronic bulletin board where people can exchange electronic mail and read posted messages. We use a private bulletin board to keep in touch with our contributing editors and writers, to exchange article roughs and rewrites, and to allow callers to post electronic letters to the editor and press releases.

The essential ingredient for using a modem is software to control the modem. You can choose from dozens of communications programs for PCs and Macs. The features to look for include automatic dialing, originate and answer modes, Hayes compatibility (for use with modems that are Hayes-compatible), and the ability to use *protocols* in your text transfers. Protocols let you transfer information with the secure feeling that there will be no errors placed in the data from noisy telephone lines or other electromagnetic interference.

The popular protocols for transferring text files from one computer to another are called "Xmodem," "Kermit," "X.PC" and "MNP." In every case you need to use the same protocol at both ends of the phone transmission.

You can use the Xmodem protocol to transfer files to PCs from Macintosh computers, and to Macs from PCs, and from both types of computers to CP/M and Apple // computers and back again, without loss of data integrity. MacTerminal (Apple Computer, $99) on the Mac has Xmodem, as does VersaTerm (Peripheral Computers and Supplies, $99) and MicroPhone (Software Ventures, $75).

For the PC, we have tried several packages. VMPC's Relay is good for beginners who want simple menu choices or need CRC Xmodem for CompuServe binary file transfers. The program is too slow for more advanced users, who prefer Crosstalk for its quick two-character commands and programming capability. Crosstalk also occupies less disk space (64K), allowing it to fit on a WordStar disk with a spelling checker or thesaurus, for example — important for floppy disk users.

ASCOM IV is for advanced communications applications. It has a communications programming language that lets you control everything down to creating your own protocols. You specify any ASCII or hexadecimal character to be filtered going in or out of the modem. You can set up a list of files to be sent or received and the program keeps a complete log of all transactions. The program has optional menus for beginners, but needs a knowledgeable micro expert to set it up. Unlike Crosstalk, ASCOM IV works with files from any subdirectory — a must for hard disk users.

Translating Between Word Processors

MacLink (DataViz, $155) converts files from WordStar, Multimate, and IBM's DisplayWrite 3 word processors on the PC to MacWrite on the Macintosh, and vice versa. An advanced version of MacLink connects the Macintosh to Wang, DEC and other dedicated word processor systems, also performing translations. The package includes a serial cable with communications, file-transfer, and file-translation software that runs on the PC and Macintosh.

MacLink can translate the WKS, WRK, SYLK, and DIF spreadsheet formats (used on Lotus 1,2,3, Symphony, Multiplan, and VisiCalc) to WKS and SYLK (Jazz and Excel) spreadsheet formats on the Macintosh, and vice versa.

DataViz's TRANSLATE! software (available in versions for the PC and the Mac) performs the same file translations as MacLink, but is designed primarily for connecting with file servers on local area networks, such as AppleTalk and the various PC networks. In such cases you would use the network's built-in file-transfer software instead of MacLink-type communications software.

TRANSLATE! allows people using different machines (PCs and Macs) and different word processors (on the PC or on the Mac) to share a file. A team of writers and editors, for example, can exchange WordStar, Multimate, DisplayWrite 3, and MacWrite documents on the PC or the Mac, as if they were all using the same computer.

For example, suppose you want to use WordStar on a PC to write an article for a newsletter. With the PC connected to an AppleTalk network with PC MacBridge, you can transfer the finished article to a Macintosh, where a copy editor imports it into MacWrite to do some copy editing. The article can be sent back to you for proofing and corrections (which you can make in WordStar). Then it goes to another Mac on the AppleTalk network, where an artist/designer places the article into a newsletter using MacPublisher II, and then prints a proof copy on the LaserWriter.

Here's how it might work: using the TRANSLATE! program on your PC, you translate your WordStar file into an equivalent MacWrite file, complete with rulers (including margins, indents, tabs, paragraphs, etc.), style information (underlining, bold, subscript, superscript, etc.), type sizes (two if you've used WordStar's alternate character size), and proportionally-spaced MacWrite characters.

Then, using Tangent Technologies' Mailbox software (which is bundled with the PC MacBridge card installed in your PC), you send the file as an electronic mail message via the AppleTalk network, where it goes to a file server, which in turn stores the message. The copy editor and artist/designer, who have Macs running Videx's MailCenter software, get a "mail-waiting" alert to tell them to download the file from the file server to their Macs. The file looks like a normal MacWrite file, complete with document icon and name.

TRANSLATE! can also go the other way, translating MacWrite documents to WordStar on the PC. TRANSLATE! looks at MacWrite rulers (margins, indents, tabs, etc.), style (underline, bold, shadow, subscripts, superscripts, etc.), and type size and translates it all to WordStar, Multimate, DisplayWrite 3, ASCII text, or other formats.

When the program translates the document from MacWrite back to WordStar (which only supports two typefonts), two different typefonts are translated. It can translate more than two if you're converting it to a Multimate format or other word processor that has more than two typefonts.

If you want to be immediately notified of incoming mail to your PC, you can use Tangent Technologies' BX Mail software (a $50 upgrade to PC MacBridge/Mailbox users), which is an 8K memory-resident background utility. The program alerts you instantly to any incoming mail, even when you are working in an application program.

You can also use TRANSLATE! to convert your MCI Mail and other electronic mail files, stripping out carriage returns so you don't have to do this chore manually.

What We Use   To publish *Desktop Publishing* magazine, we receive most outside articles over the phone — through use of a modem and personal computer. Writers with personal computers and modems can send articles directly to our electronic bulletin board system, which runs on a CP/M computer. If the long distance rates are too costly, writers can alternatively drop the articles off on MCI Mail, CompuServe or The Source, where we have electronic "mailboxes."

To facilitate communications, we use a variety of modem communications programs and a variety of Hayes-compatible modems, along with our Hayes Smartmodem 1200. The bulletin board system uses a Prometheus 1200 (Hayes-compatible) and has been running for several months without major problems. The software for the bulletin board is called Heavy Metal and is available from Delphi Data Systems.

The Hayes Smartmodem 1200 has served us well for three years, pausing only once with a burnt-out power supply (which was promptly replaced by Hayes at no charge). We use it to call networks such as MCI Mail, CompuServe and The Source. Our version of the public domain Modem7 program has automatic dialing functions, a built-in phone list, and function keys for sending complicated log-on messages and passwords.

We started using the public domain Modem7 program on different CP/M computers. We wanted a modem program that had the Xmodem protocol because it was a method of transferring computer files with guaranteed accuracy. This is important to us — if even one byte of the file is changed during transmission, it could affect a word and cause a typo, or it might affect a typesetting code and cause a block of text to be typeset incorrectly.

From PC to Mac and Back

After much trial and error, in which articles were transferred to the Mac, only to be dumped because there were too many strange characters in the file, or because each line was treated as a separate paragraph, we settled upon a standard method of transferring text files that works every time.

The articles came from various sources, including PC disks, although much of the text came to us via MCI Mail. The articles were edited with WordStar and other word processing programs, then converted into simple text files in the standard ASCII format. Some word processing programs have ASCII text files as a save option; others, like WordStar, do not convert files to simple text files — you need a utility program such as UNWS, available in the public domain. On CP/M systems, you can use the PIP command with the Z option (the most reliable method of turning a WordStar or similar text file into a straight ASCII text file).

With straight ASCII text files on a PC or CP/M system, we were then able to transfer them to the Macintosh by cabling the computers together via their modem ports, and running communications software on both computers that could create a telecommunications link. We also used our bulletin board system to deposit articles ready for typesetting, and then called the bulletin board with the Mac to retrieve the articles.

On the PC we used MITE (Mycroft Labs, $195 for the PC version, $150 for the CP/M version) and, at other times, a public domain program called MODEM (a PC version of Modem7, the popular CP/M program). On the CP/M systems we used MITE, Modem7 (public domain) and, at other times, Mastercom (The Software Store, $150). All of these programs are excellent, and all of them offer the Xmodem protocol which is necessary for error-free file transfer.

On the Macintosh there are many communications programs offering the Xmodem protocol. Apple's MacTerminal has the Xmodem and Text options, but for some reason they were not adequate — boxes (indicating a parity error) would appear at the beginning of each line, and we couldn't search globally to get rid of the boxes using MacWrite or Microsoft Word.

We switched to VersaTerm (Peripheral Computers, $99), which has three versions of Xmodem as well as the Kermit protocol. We used the

"Text Xmodem" protocol and the boxes disappeared.

But that wasn't the only problem. The carriage returns caused by typing the Return key are used to mark *ends of paragraphs* in both Microsoft Word and MacWrite, and also in WordStar and other PC word processing programs. However, converting the file to the ASCII format meant that each line break contained a carriage return/line feed at the end. This caused every line of the text file to be treated as a separate paragraph by the Macintosh word processing programs.

The only solution was to modify the text file *before* converting it into straight ASCII format for transferring to the Mac. We performed the following steps using the find/substitute function of our PC-based word processing program:

1. We made sure that every "hard" line (i.e., single line considered as a separate paragraph) was consistently followed by a blank line; consequently, to get a blank line in the output, we used two blank lines.

2. We then substituted a marker for every end of paragraph (easy to find in our text files — just search for every end of line that is followed by a five-space indent).

3. Then we substituted another marker for every instance of two blank lines. By that point we had substituted markers for all the places where we actually wanted to have carriage returns.

4. We could then do a substitution to get rid of all remaining carriage returns.

5. Finally we reverse the above substitutions: a carriage return and a tab for every end-of-paragraph marker, and a carriage return for every blank line marker.

The file is then ready for conversion to straight ASCII text. On CP/M computers use PIP with the Z option; on PCs use a conversion utility such as UNWS.

We use a PC or CP/M communications program with the Xmodem protocol to send the text file directly to the Macintosh via cable or modem, or to a bulletin board where it can be retrieved by the Macintosh via modem. On the Macintosh we use a communications program such as VersaTerm with the Xmodem Text protocol to receive the file.

The end result is a text file with carriage returns only in those places where Microsoft Word or MacWrite (or JustText, described in Chapter 7) can use them as paragraph markers. This text file, transferred to the Macintosh, is now ready for typefont changes and formatting for pouring into PageMaker pages (as described in Chapter 5).

CHAPTER THREE

Using Printers
and Typesetters

The "paperless office" today makes about as much sense as a paperless toilet.

— Amy Wohl

Overview　The name of the publishing game is *output*. Word processing is where you start your publishing effort, but the quality of your results is directly related to what you can produce with a printer or typesetter. The paramount indication of whether a printer or typesetter is right for your application is the *print quality*. There is no way to tell without seeing actual samples from the equipment vendor.

Most personal computer users don't buy typesetters because the machines are too expensive, too slow for the usual printing chores related to computing, and of such high-quality that you'd only want to use one for final typesetting. The paper from the typesetter has to be developed by a processor, which uses chemicals, so you need a ventilated room for the processor. We include generic information about typesetters in this chapter to compare them to laser printers.

The most popular printer for personal computer users is the *dot matrix* printer, named after the dot pattern used to form characters. Examples are the Epson FX and MX series, the Apple ImageWriter series, and printers made by Okidata and Gemini.

Also in use, but outdated, are *daisy wheel* printers. These printers resemble large typewriters (in fact, some of them are typewriters outfitted to run with computers). The print head is a circular "daisy" wheel of characters, or a ball-shaped typing element as in IBM

Selectric typewriters. The most popular daisy wheel printers are the Diablo (now owned by Xerox) series and the NEC Spinwriter.

The daisy wheel printers produced type that looked like it came from a typewriter. This threshold print quality came to be known as "letter quality" printing and was used as a measure to compare the newer dot matrix printers.

Daisy wheel and dot matrix printers are noisy compared to the recently developed laser, ink-jet and thermal printers. The dot matrix printers have improved to be "near-letter-quality" and acceptable for correspondence and report printing. Many are capable of using different typefonts. Laser printers have recently taken the market by storm. They are generally bought for desktop publishing applications and to replace daisy wheel printers in offices.

Typesetters are available as output devices in copy centers and typesetting services. You can prepare text for them directly or use a laser printer to proof your pages inexpensively before using the typesetter.

With all of these choices available, your first step should be to decide what print quality suits your application. You may want to consider using dot matrix printers for most of the output, and a laser printer shared by several computers in a network for high-quality printing.

Laser Printers   Laser printers are credited with ushering in the new age of desktop publishing. The Apple LaserWriter, awarded Product of the Year in 1985 by *InfoWorld*, is a feature-packed machine that can deliver the promise of desktop publishing, and the H-P LaserJet and other laser printers are price/performance breakthroughs for office printing.

Although laser printers are not fast for producing each page of a document, they can quickly turn out copies (duplicate originals) of each page. They work quietly and provide the best resolution — 300 x 300 dots per square inch. Most laser printers have multiple typefonts and the ability to print a page of graphics at high resolution.

Laser printers were derived from the technology used in photocopiers. Most of the laser printers for personal computers are based on the Canon LPB-CX "engine" (the cartridge that contains the toner, belt and printing mechanism), which was derived from the Canon Personal Copier Cartridge line of photocopiers. Examples of Canon-based laser printers are the Apple LaserWriter, the H-P LaserJet and LaserJet Plus, and the Cordata (formerly Corona) LP300.

Others, such as Quadram's Quadlaser and the Ricoh LP4120, use the Ricoh engine, which has a toner that is independent of the optical belt. The difference is that with the Canon, if you run out of toner, the optical device could still be good but you still have to change the entire cartridge. The Ricoh, on the other hand, lets you change the toner without changing the optical device. The manufacturers of Ricoh-based laser printers claim that the Ricoh engine is less expensive to maintain in the long run.

Figure 3-1. The Apple LaserWriter, based on the Canon engine, is the first Post-Script laser printer for use with personal computers.

Laser printers are similar to photocopiers in that both machines harness light to transfer an image onto a photoconductive print drum. However, laser printers use a beam to scan the image, leaving a positive electrical image on the drum, whereas copy machines use reflected light to create a negative image. The toner in a laser printer attracts to the positively-charged organic-photo-conductor belt, whereas in copy machines the toner attracts to the negative areas. As the drum in a laser printer rotates, the mechanism pulls the paper between the drum and a special string called a *corona*. The corona never touches the drum, but transfers the image from the drum to the paper. The machine then fixates the characters to the paper with a fusing process that uses heat or pressure rollers.

Both the Canon and Ricoh engines provide near-typeset-quality output at 300 dots per inch. To get the best possible quality, the laser printer manufacturers add memory, a processor and some type of page description language or set of printing commands. The quality of the output depends on the way the printer's controller electronics and software handle the arrangement of dot patterns to represent letters and images.

Figure 3-2. The Ricoh LP4120 laser printer uses the Ricoh engine.

With enough memory a laser printer can print an entire 8½ x 11 inch page of graphics and text at 300 dots per inch. Some printers have enough memory to do this; others, like the H-P LaserJet, have only enough memory to fill one-quarter of a page with graphics at 300 dots per inch, or the entire page with only 72 dots per inch.

Another difference that affects the quality of output is the way the printer handles typefonts. Printers like the H-P LaserJet accept font cartridges that you plug into the machine; the LaserJet Plus also lets you store typefonts on disk and download them to the machine's memory when you want to use them. These typefonts are defined as dot patterns, and you can only purchase one size of a typefont in a cartridge or disk font, because the machine cannot change the size of the dot patterns to get larger letters. For example, you can mix in a maximum of a quarter page of Fancy Font fonts (treated as graphics by the LaserJet) mixed in with the H-P regular cartridge font text on the LaserJet, or up to a full page of Fancy Font fonts (or graphics, or H-P cartridge fonts, or a mixture) per page with the H-P LaserJet Plus.

The other basic way of defining a typefont is by its *outline* or *shape* expressed as an algorithm rather than as a fixed dot pattern. Because they can be scaled to any size and manipulated as graphic images, the *outline* fonts, as they are called, are vastly superior to the dot pattern fonts. You can buy one outline typefont that can be used at any size. The letters of outline fonts can also be twisted, rotated, printed sideways, or otherwise distorted on purpose, using a special language that manipulates the typefonts.

To get outline fonts, you must get a laser printer that is driven by a *page description language* such as Adobe's PostScript (Apple Laser-Writer and other machines use PostScript) or Xerox's Interpress. The PostScript language is fast becoming a standard among the "high end" laser printers that are to be used in place of typesetting machines, because it inexpensively combines an excellent graphics description language with outline fonts.

A printer driven by PostScript usually has enough memory and processor power to produce a full page of graphics and text at 300 dots per inch or greater resolution. This is why the PostScript printers are more expensive than some other laser printers. However, the advantage of PostScript is better graphics, built-in typefonts (no need to buy typefont cartridges), and more flexibility with typefonts.

Laser printers are capable of producing near-typeset-quality output. Some printing processes, such as newspaper printing, reduce the image resolution so much that laser printing and typesetting are nearly indistinguishable. In such cases you can save money by laser printing rather than typesetting.

Most professional publishers require the resolution of real typesetting, but can use laser printers as "proof" printers for the typesetting, so that they can save on expensive typesetting paper or the typesetting service charges. PostScript-driven laser printers are especially useful as "proof" printers because they are 100% compatible with PostScript-driven typesetters such as the Allied Linotronic 100 (1270 dots per inch) and Linotronic 300 (2540 dots per inch).

With a laser printer you can get excellent results that could be used in place of typesetting. For example, with most printers you can print your text at a 200% enlargement of its original size, and then reduce the printed pages by 50% with a stat camera. An image printed at 300 x 300 dots per square inch and reduced by 50% will reproduce at 600 x 600 dots per square inch, which is a step closer to real typesetting (usually 1000 x 1000 dots per square inch). However, the Apple LaserWriter and most other laser printers do not print pages that are larger than 8½ x 11 inches, so you have to paste printed pages together or print your text in columns.

The Dataproducts LZR 2660/65 laser printer ($22,900, figure 3-3) can produce 11 x 17 inch pages, and operates at a much higher speed (up to 26 pages per minute) than most laser printers designed for desktop and office use.

Figure 3-3. The Dataproducts LZR-2660/65 PostScript laser printer can use 11 x 17 inch paper and print at speeds up to 26 pages per minute.

Laser printers vary from high-volume high-priced very fast printers, such as the IBM 3800 ($365,000) to low-volume eight-page-per-minute laser printers, such as the H-P LaserJet ($3495). However, the price per page is better with the higher-volume printers, because their duty cycles are high and their maintenance costs are relatively low per page. The duty cycle is the number of hours per month of actual printing divided by the total number of hours per month in which the printing power is on.

THIS IS NOT

Photo-typesetting

or *LASER* printing!

All the type in this sample was actually set on an Epson dot-matrix printer by the program Type-Set-It using an IBM-PC with a Hercules graphics card.

BIG OR SMALL TYPE *FAT* OR SKINNY TYPESTYLES AS WELL

A trial disk that contains the entire Type-Set-It program (but prints the letters S and E backwards) is offered for $10 by Good Ideas. It allows potential users to see copy produced on their own equipment and to experience the simplicity of operation.

Figure 3-4. Reduced output from an Epson dot matrix printer using the Type-Set-It system from Good Ideas.

The IBM 3800 can print between 2.2 million and 4.5 million pages per month, whereas Canon-based printers such as the LaserJet have a practical limit of about 12,000 pages a month, and Canon recommends a duty cycle of 3000 pages a month. The LaserJet is theoretically capable of printing 83,000 pages in a month, but you will spend more in maintenance costs if you have many months of such printing volume — it pays then to get a higher-volume printer like the Dataproducts LZR-2660.

Dot Matrix Printers

Dot matrix printers are impact printers that are less expensive, faster and more compact than daisy wheel printers. Full-featured dot matrix printers cost between $250-$800 and can print at speeds ranging from 80-400 characters per second.

In a dot matrix printer, the print head strikes an inked ribbon to print characters on regular paper. Rather than having pre-formed characters on a daisy wheel or typing element, the dot matrix print head consists of a column of tiny round or square-faced impact rods. For example, the Epson FX printer's print head has nine impact rods in each vertical column. Each rod is individually controlled so that any combination of rods can be forced forward to strike the ribbon against the paper. The printer can print any combination of dots to produce a character of text or a graphic image.

The dot matrix printers range in price and features, but generally they can print characters in several sizes (usually 5, 10 and 17 characters per inch), print them in bold and double-strike densities, and in several styles (italic, expanded, condensed, etc.). Dot matrix printers can print high-resolution bit mapped graphic images. The output quality of dot matrix printers varies considerably over the price range. With the right software, you can print typefonts that rival laser printer typefonts, especially when printed at a large size and then reduced with a stat camera. Figure 3-4 shows a sample of reduced dot matrix printing from an Epson MX (with Graftrax) and the Type-Set-It program (Good Ideas, $395).

The most popular dot matrix printers are made by Epson (MX, FX and other series), Okidata, Gemini, NEC (Prowriter), IBM, and Apple (ImageWriter series). The command set for driving an Epson dot matrix printer is becoming a standard on the PC side of the industry, and the ImageWriter is the standard on the Apple side.

Color dot matrix printers (using color ribbons or ribbon cartridges) are becoming available, such as the Apple ImageWriter II and the NEC Color Pinwriter, which includes software (Colormate) to let you specify colors for the printout, even if your file was created on a black and white Macintosh computer.

Ink Jet Printers   Ink jet printers work by firing drops of ink at paper, using high pressure nozzles. The impact area of the ink drops is controlled so that the drops expelled from the nozzles hit the paper in the right places to form the dots that make up characters.

The technologies used in low cost ink jet printers include the *bubble-jet* (named after the Canon Bubblejet ink jet printer) and *drop-on-demand* (also called *piezoelectric*) printing.

The bubble-jet mechanism uses resistance heaters to boil the ink, which changes to vapor as pressure dramatically increases. The ink is forced through a nozzle with enough velocity to strike the paper. This method is used by both the H-P ThinkJet and the Canon Bubblejet. The advantage of the ThinkJet is simplicity: the ink supply and print nozzles are in one cartridge that must be replaced when the ink runs dry. However, in the Bubblejet, the ink is enclosed in a separate cartridge.

In drop-on-demand printing, a piezoelectric crystal, which is an electrical-to-pressure transducer, is subjected to an increase in pressure, which causes an electromotive force to deform the crystal. The crystal is mounted in such a way that the deformation increases pressure in a small amount of ink around the crystal, which forces ink through the nozzle. This technology is better for working with colored inks and is used successfully in four-color ink-jet printers. An example of this technology is the Canon PJ1088 color ink-jet printer. So far the bubble-jet technique works best with black ink printers.

The major advantage of ink-jet printers is that they are quiet as well as inexpensive (in the range of $400-$800). The H-P ThinkJet ($495) is relatively slower at 150 characters per second, but less expensive than the others. The Canon Bubblejet printer is faster (220 characters per second in draft mode, 110 in letter-quality mode), but is more expensive ($599).

Color ink-jet printers ($1000 and up) are for graphics printing; they are not designed for letter-quality printing or word processing. Color ink-jet printers can print on transparencies for presentations, and are used in business and educational applications where four-color graphics on the screen need to be printed.

Thermal Printers   Thermal printers are useful in many computer applications, especially printing video images (what appears on the screen). The main applications for video image printing are medical imaging and industrial and commercial security, but there are inexpensive printers in the $400-$800 range (black and white) for video printing at home or in a small business. At the other end of the spectrum, Sony is releasing a full-color thermal printer for $13,000.

Direct thermal printing, the oldest of the thermal printing techniques, is attractive for its simplicity. A heated printing element causes a chemical change in special thermal paper. There are no ribbon or ink cartridges and very few moving parts. One example is the Mitsubishi P-70, which can print 640 dots per line and reproduce exactly a graphic or text image as displayed on a monochrome PC monitor with a color or monochrome graphics display adaptor.

The main disadvantage to the direct approach is the requirement for special thermal paper, and the low print density. The special paper is not normally available as stationery or business forms, and it feels strange, not like regular paper. The printed dots are not sharp enough for characters to appear as crisp as they do with other types of printers. The direct thermal printers are not attractive for word processing applications, but the print density and fuzzier dots are attractive for printing video images.

The maintenance and operation costs of direct thermal are moderate compared to other printers. The special paper is a few cents per page, but you don't need ribbons or cartridges, and the print heads last a long time and yet are replaceable.

Thermal transfer is the most popular technique of thermal printing for PC printers. These printers melt ink on a separate ribbon or transfer sheet; when hot, the ink sticks to the paper to produce the image. This technique helps manufacturers produce small and lightweight portable printers, and you can use common office paper.

The thermal transfer method requires a ribbon or transfer sheet containing the ink, but the method is still very simple. The type of ink used can be dark enough to produce very dark images. It is also possible to have ribbons or sheets that carry several colors, in order to print color images. The ink can be deposited in several layers, which makes it possible to mix colors.

The Canon F-60 is a thermal transfer printer that offers cartridge selection of print styles with four colors. It prints 360 x 180 dots per square inch at 20 characters per second.

Thermal printers form characters and graphics with dots in the same manner as dot-matrix impact printers. However, there's no impact with thermal printing, so the printers are less noisy. Thermal printers are much better at producing video images, but characters of text are not as sharp as with conventional dot matrix printers. However, the lightweight and portable thermal printers are often the least expensive alternative for printing in color or printing video images.

Typesetters   The typesetting machines available today are in the $18,000-$200,000 range. Programs are available to drive them from personal computers acting as "front ends." One example is the $18,000 Digitek 4000 system and PC workstation from Itek. The system comes with a graphics-equipped PC XT or AT and Itek's WYSIWYG page makeup software.

Another such system is the Allied Linotype Linotronic 100 (at about $30,000), which can be shared by several Macintosh computers in an AppleTalk network or driven by one Mac.

The typesetters controlled by computer are called *phototypesetters* or laser typesetters. These totally electronic typesetters form a character using very small dots (usually more than 900 x 900 dots per square inch). The resulting image is transferred to photographic material, usually by a burst of light from a xenon flash lamp or laser. The photographic material can be photopaper, film, or in some cases offset plate. Large phototypesetters are capable of very high speeds, such as 1000 lines a minute (30-character 8-point lines). Less expensive typesetters average 50-150 lines per minute.

The traditional method of getting text into the typesetter's "front end" computer was to retype it, using the special keyboard. However, you can prepare a disk for a typesetting service (if they can read your disk format) to avoid re-keying the text. The most popular typesetting machines are made by Compugraphic, Allied Linotype, Alphatype, Autologic, AM Varityper and Itek. All are driven by a computer that can read PC disks, and some can read Macintosh disks. If the typesetter can use a modem as an input device to receive your text, disk compatibility isn't needed.

The number one manufacturer of typesetters is Compugraphic, and most of the programs for typesetting and page makeup on PCs can produce output for the Compugraphic 8400 and 8600. Programs that drive the 8400 and 8600 include MagnaType, DO-IT, PagePlanner and SuperPage (these programs are described in Chapter 7).

Autologic typesetting systems (APS-55/200 plain paper typesetter, APS-5 and APS Micro-5) do not offer the same wide selection of typefonts but are also driven by the PC software mentioned above, as are AM Varityper typesetters.

Allied Linotype Linotronic typesetters can be driven directly, just as LaserWriters can be driven, by PCs as well as by Macintosh computers over the AppleTalk network (as described in the previous chapter).

PostScript Printers and Typesetters

Not all laser printers are alike in functionality, even if they all print at 300 dots per inch. For example, the H-P LaserJet can print only one-quarter of a page of graphics at 300 dots per inch, whereas the Apple LaserWriter can print a full page.

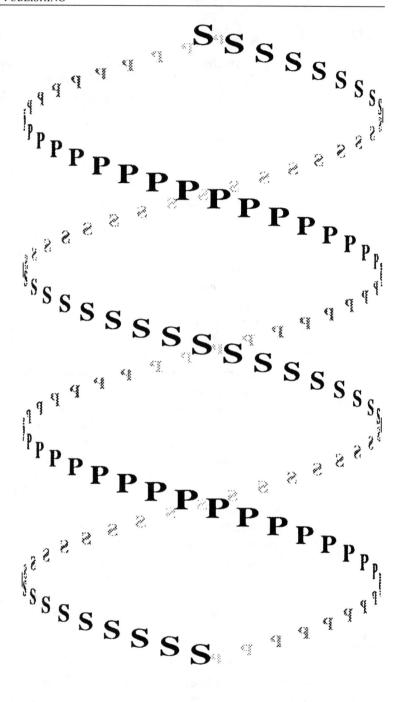

Figure 3-5.   Special effects printed on the LaserWriter using PostScript.

Both printers use the same Canon engine as laser printers from other manufacturers, with the 68000 processor and memory as the others also use, but with one major difference: the LaserWriter uses software and enough internal memory to process entire pages at a time. You can therefore mix text and graphics on a page and print it at 300 dots per inch.

This difference is largely due to the software that runs inside the LaserWriter — a graphics and page description language called Post-Script (created by Adobe Systems of Palo Alto, CA). PostScript is also responsible for making it easy for typesetting manufacturers like Allied Linotype to make a typesetter that is compatible with the Laser-Writer and the Macintosh.

PostScript printers have the advantage of a page description language that defines typefonts as *outline fonts* rather than dot matrix fonts. With some printers, you load a typefont at a specific point size. If you use a lot of different sizes you have to load separate cartridges or disk fonts. This is not the case with PostScript printers. You can scale each PostScript typefont to any size, make the characters italic or bold, and do underlining, outlining or shadowing. You can rotate text around objects, twist and swirl characters through objects, print sideways or at any angle, and do other special effects with PostScript commands.

PostScript laser printers are compatible with PostScript typesetters. This compatibility means you can prepare text and graphics on a personal computer and print pages on the PostScript laser printer for proofing, then typeset the pages on the PostScript typesetter *without any recoding*, and get the same result, because PostScript knows about the difference in resolution of these devices (computer screen, laser printer and typesetter), and produces the correct output resolution. This is a tremendous improvement in productivity over the traditional methods of reproducing line art and graphics.

Apple LaserWriter

Awarded *InfoWorld*'s Product of the Year in 1985, the Apple Laser-Writer is the breakthrough product that most industry-watchers credit as the catalyst for the desktop publishing market.

The LaserWriter is the most functional laser printer on the market, outclassing the others by virtue of its PostScript software and relatively low price. The LaserWriter can produce near-typeset-quality output with a full range of typefonts and full-page graphics at 300 dots per inch; the only laser printers that can do all of these things are other

PostScript printers.

Like other laser printers, the LaserWriter has a Canon engine, but it also has a 68000 processor, 1.5 megabytes of RAM for image processing, a half-megabyte of ROM for storing typefonts and PostScript, and thirteen different typefonts (four faces, thirteen fonts, counting bold, italic, etc. versions as separate fonts) that can be sized as small as 4 points and as large as 720 points. The LaserWriter Plus has 1.5 megabytes of RAM plus a full megabyte of ROM to hold more typefonts.

The LaserWriter (PostScript included, with Times Roman, Helvetica, Courier and Symbol typefonts) is $6000. More typefonts, available for the LaserWriter (an $800 upgrade kit includes fonts and replacement ROM chips), and included with the LaserWriter Plus ($6800), include Avant Garde, Bookman, New Century Schoolbook, Palatino, Zapf Chancery and Zapf Dingbats. These typefonts are actual ITC fonts created with PostScript as outline fonts that can be scaled to any point size from 4 point to 192 point. In addition you can manipulate all of these fonts, using PostScript commands to stretch or reduce words, print letters black on gray or white on black background, rotate letters at any angle, or even wrap letters around graphics.

When the LaserWriter (or LaserWriter Plus) is first powered on and warmed up, and finished with its self-test, it prints a test page. The page has a number that is incremented for each page you print, so that whenever you print a test page, you can read the actual number of copies made so far with the machine. This is useful information — after 2000 to 3000 copies you should change the toner cartridge (the cartridge color bar changes from green to red when the cartridge needs replacing, and new cartridges cost about $99). Changing the cartridge takes about five minutes (you need only a scissors to cut open the protective lining around the cartridge). For over a year we have been printing proof pages for two bi-monthly magazines and one book on the LaserWriter, and we have found it to be reliable.

The LaserWriter takes about ten seconds more time to print a single page than the H-P LaserJet (with graphics the printing time is slower). The speed difference is due in part to the different ways the computers communicate with the laser printers — the Macintosh communicates to the LaserWriter via the slower AppleTalk network rather than directly, and the PC can communicate with a LaserJet directly through a parallel port. The difference in speed is also due to PostScript —

recreating the size and shape of each letter by algorithm takes time. Three typefont styles — 10-point Courier, 12-point Helvetica and 12-point Times Roman — are stored in ROM for fast printing, but other styles and point sizes must be calculated and stored in the printer's RAM before printing.

The differences in speed are not that great, and you would probably not care if you want real scaleable typefonts and full-page 300 dot-per-inch graphics.

Allied Linotype Linotronic

The LaserWriter can perform many typesetting jobs, but not all. However, the LaserWriter is 100% compatible with typesetting machines that can do professional-quality typesetting — the Allied Linotype Linotronic 100 and 300. You can create pages on a Macintosh screen, save them to a Macintosh disk, and print them on the LaserWriter for proofing, *then* typeset them on the Linotronic without having to change anything.

The Linotronic 100 and 300 are PostScript typesetting machines that can be connected via the AppleTalk network to one or more Macintosh computers. The Macintosh programs that can send output to the LaserWriter need no modification — the Allied Linotype typesetters act like LaserWriters, but at much higher resolution (the Linotronic 100 typesets at 1270 dots per inch, and the 300 typesets at 2540 dots per inch).

Allied Linotype, which bought Merganthaler (the largest typesetting equipment manufacturer in Europe, second largest in the U.S.), owns the Merganthaler and ITC catalogs of typefonts, which they intend to make available in PostScript form for their typesetting machines. As they become available in PostScript, the fonts will also be available for the Apple LaserWriter.

The Linotronic 100 and 300 are probably not items you would want to purchase unless you have the need for real typesetting on a regular basis. However, these typesetters are becoming popular among progressive typesetting services, copy centers and print shops, because all they need is a Macintosh (and AppleTalk cable) to offer full-page typesetting to their customers, or a PC with software or an add-on card that translates text and graphics to PostScript.

So if you own a Macintosh, or a PC with PostScript capability, you can now use a service much like a copy center to do laser printing *and* typesetting. If you don't own a Macintosh, you can rent time on one and do desktop publishing at the copy center.

Macs With PostScript Printers

The Apple LaserWriter is the PostScript printer of choice for Macintosh users. It comes with a simple installation program that loads the PostScript typefonts into your system for use with the LaserWriter. Now that large-capacity hard disks are readily available for the Macintosh, you can load as many typefonts as your system disk can hold. As Adobe Systems or Apple announce new PostScript typefonts, the companies make them available on Macintosh disk. You can also buy fonts from third party vendors.

As for printing text, most application programs have a Print selection in their File menu. Before clicking this option, you can use the Choose Printer desktop accessory (called the Chooser in newer versions of the software) to select the LaserWriter. The LaserWriter connects via the AppleTalk network to your printer or modem port.

When you click on the Print selection in the pull-down File menu, also select the Font Substitution in the subsequent LaserWriter menu. This selection tells the LaserWriter to substitute real PostScript fonts for the Macintosh screen fonts. If you don't select font substitution, your fonts will be printed exactly as they appear on the Macintosh screen (which has 72 dots-per-inch resolution). They may have the "jaggies" in their bit mapped (lower resolution) full size, but you could reduce the whole page to smooth the edges of your characters, or substitute PostScript (outline) fonts.

PCs With PostScript Printers

There are two ways to connect a PC to a PostScript printer such as the Apple LaserWriter: direct through a serial port, or through an interface to the AppleTalk network. If you use the direct approach, your software must already be capable of translating your text and graphics into PostScript.

For example, Microsoft Word for the PC comes with PostScript support built-in, so no cards or programs are required. Windows (Microsoft, $99) and other Microsoft products also support PostScript. The GEM Desktop and system software (Digital Research) for the PC support PostScript. Programs like DO-IT (Studio Software) and SuperPage (BestInfo) also support PostScript and run on a PC (these are described in Chapter 7).

If your software doesn't come with PostScript support, you can use Tangent Technologies' $250 LaserScript/S software. LaserScript/S supports WordStar, Multimate, any software that generates ASCII text files, and software with Diablo 630 printer emulation. It also allows Lotus 1-2-3 and other software to generate graphics on PostScript printers, and provides full control of type fonts, sizes, and styles.

But while you can use Microsoft Word or other application programs with a standard RS-232 cable to connect your computer to the LaserWriter, an advantage of using a network interface board (such as the PC MacBridge from Tangent Technologies, described next) is that it lets several users of PCs and Macs share one Laser-Writer over the low-cost ($50 per connection) AppleTalk network.

You can connect an IBM PC, XT, or AT or compatible to an AppleTalk network cable with Tangent Technologies' PC MacBridge ($650). PC MacBridge is a card that plugs into a PC slot and provides a "gateway" to the AppleTalk world. You can have one or more LaserWriters, Linotronic typesetters, and Macs connected to the AppleTalk at the same time, sharing data with the PC MacBridge in your PC.

```
^A^B^DThanks For Reading On!!^B^D^N

^RThis letter was prepared to show you more features of the ^B^DLaserScript^D^B  WordStar-To-
PostScript conversion program.  It was prepared using WordStar 3.3,  an IBM PC AT,
and Apple LaserWriter Plus, and ^B^DPC MacBridge^B^D.

This page is prepared using the ^BTimes-Roman^B and ^Y^BHelvetica^Y font families. These fonts are
distinctive, proportional-spaced fonts.

In the Times-Roman and ^YHelvetica^Y font families, you prepare WordStar documents ^Dalmost^D
exactly as you would using a standard printer, such as a Diablo 630. You can freely change
between different font families and you have a wide variety of desirable print features at
your fingertips.

For example,  you can change between the normal Times-Roman typeface, ^Ba bolded Times-Roman
typeface^B,  ^Dan italic Times-Roman typeface (which replaces shadow print)^D, and a ^B^Dbold-italic
Times-Roman typeface^D^B.

^YYou can also use the Helvetica typeface,  used for this paragraph.  In Helvetica you  have
the  normal  typeface^B,   ^Ba bolded Helvetica typeface^B,   ^Dan italic Helvetica typeface  (which
replaces shadow print)^D, and a ^B^Dbold-italic Helvetica typeface.^Y

You ^Scan always use the underscore feature^S,  as well as ^Xstrikeout^X.  Ordinary features  like
^Tsuperscript^T  and ^Vsubscript^V are avaliable as they  should be.^R

Your text can be left justified,
flush against the left margin...

^Q^Y^DOr it can be perfectly centered
between margins...^Y^Q

^Q^ROr flush against
the right margin.^R^Q

^AYou Can Even Insert A Digitized Image!!!^N
./wips >< \tom\convert\datacopy\camera .5




^A^Q^BThe Datacopy Camera^B^N^Q
.pa
```

Figure 3-6. WordStar text with Control codes embedded for printing via PC Mac-Bridge on the LaserWriter or other PostScript device.

PC MacBridge converts your text from WordStar 3.3, MultiMate 3.3, Microsoft Word, or any straight ASCII text file (such as Lotus 1-2-3 ".PRN" files), and your graphics (from 1-2-3 and ".PIC" files) into PostScript instructions for printing on PostScript printers connected via the AppleTalk network. MacBridge works with any other program that generates "Diablo 630-compatible" or ASCII files (check with your dealer or your software manual to see if this applies to your software).

You'll need to add special commands to your WordStar text files to change typefonts. For example, you can get the LaserWriter to print in the Helvetica Bold font by adding Control-`PB` (for bold) and Control-`PY` (for Helvetica) before the text you want printed (see figure 3-6 and 3-7).

Thanks For Reading On!!

This letter was prepared to show you more features of the *LaserScript* WordStar-To-PostScript conversion program. It was was prepared using WordStar 3.3, an IBM PC AT, and Apple LaserWriter Plus, and *PC MacBridge*.

This page is prepared using the **Times-Roman** and **Helvetica** font families. These fonts are distinctive, proportional-spaced fonts.

In the Times-Roman and Helvetica font families, you prepare WordStar documents *almost* exactly as you would using a standard printer, such as a Diablo 630. You can freely change between different font families and you have a wide variety of desirable print features at your fingertips.

For example, you can change between the normal Times-Roman typeface, **a bolded Times-Roman** typeface, *an italic Times-Roman typeface (which replaces shadow print)*, and a ***bold-italic Times-Roman typeface.***

You can also use the Helvetica typeface, used for this paragraph. In Helvetica you have the normal typeface, **a bolded Helvetica typeface**, *an italic Helvetica typeface (which replaces shadow print)*, and a ***bold-italic Helvetica typeface.***

You <u>can always use the underscore feature</u>, as well as ~~strikeout~~. Ordinary features like superscript and subscript are avaliable as they should be.

Your text can be left justified,

Figure 3-7. The text in figure 3-6 converted to PostScript by PC MacBridge and output on the LaserWriter.

You can select other LaserWriter and LaserWriter Plus typefonts, in any size, and several type styles (italic, oblique, and normal), with underlining, superscript or subscript characters, special characters, centering, justification, page format (margins, height, width, and offset), and line spacing.

PC MacBridge lets you print Lotus 1-2-3 spreadsheets and graphs on the LaserWriter. The supplied LaserGraph program also lets you create bar, pie, and line charts and put them in a WordStar document or print them directly via the PC MacBridge on a LaserWriter or other PostScript device connected via the AppleTalk network.

You can connect the AppleTalk network, or connect a Macintosh directly into a PC-based local area network such as 3Com Corporation's 3Com EtherSeries or Centram's TOPS network. The 3Com network uses a hardware "network server," letting Mac and PC users read or write any file from any other user. Centram's TOPS uses a different approach, with a plug-in AppleTalk card in each PC on a PC-based network, and software that lets you move data from PCs to Macs and back to PCs. The software uses Macintosh-style icons to access both Macintosh and PC files.

Sharing the $6000 LaserWriter with several PC and Mac users helps you get the maximum use of your investment. On pure cost-effectiveness it is a better solution than having cheaper printers for each computer.

Hewlett-Packard LaserJet

One of the most popular printers for PCs is the H-P LaserJet ($2995), a fast, quiet, economical page printer. However, the LaserJet does not use PostScript, nor does it have as much memory as the LaserWriter and other PostScript printers; it is therefore limited in its ability to create smoothed fonts and graphics at high resolution.

The LaserJet is based on the Canon engine, with a 68000 processor, 59K of internal memory, and typefonts in cartridges ($225-$400 each). The LaserJet has two built-in typefonts (Courier 12 point and Compressed Line Printer 8.5 point) and a limitation of eight different typefonts on a single page (the most one cartridge can hold). Style variations of typefonts include bold, italic, vertical and horizontal orientation, and different point sizes. The typefonts are dot matrix fonts — composed of dot patterns, not by algorithm (as PostScript fonts are composed).

You can control the printer directly using a series of Escape codes that form the Printer Control Language (PCL). The printer is capable of printing at a resolution of 300 dots per inch, but graphics are printed at 75 dots per inch unless the graphics program uses the Printer Control Language. The printer is also limited to printing a 5.4-square-inch graphic image at 300 dots per inch resolution, due to the limited amount of RAM. The LaserJet can print a 21.5-square-inch image at 150 dots per inch, and a full page at 75 dots per inch. Text is typeset at 300 dots per inch.

Figure 3-8.   The H-P LaserJet Plus laser printer, based on the Canon engine, has expanded memory and downloadable typefonts.

The LaserJet Plus ($3995) is an enhanced version with 512K of internal memory (117K of ROM for more built-in typefonts, and 395K of RAM for printing larger graphic images and downloading more typefonts), and a parallel port for faster data transfer (the LaserJet has only a serial port). With the LaserJet Plus you can access as many as

32 downloadable typefonts at one time plus a set of cartridge fonts. However, you are still limited to 16 typefonts on a single page. New commands in the Printer Control Language (PCL) include solid line rules, shading and fill patterns for graphics. You can print a full page of graphics at 150 dots per inch, or a half page at 300 dots per inch.

The LaserJet Plus model includes *macros*, which are for storing a long string of commands in the printer. Macros let you define an overlay form or letterhead by name so that you can load it into the printer and then use it repeatedly. You can store up to 32 different macros to be used as automatic office forms (invoices, statements), signatures, letterhead, etc. Another application of macros is to simulate another printer control language.

Many application programs support the LaserJet and LaserJet Plus, including Microsoft Word, WordStar 2000, Lotus 1-2-3, Multimate, and all of the page makeup programs for PCs that are described in Chapter 5. Many of these programs are cost-effective for doing desktop publishing with the inexpensive LaserJet.

PCs With the LaserJet
The LaserJet and LaserJet Plus printers are easy to connect to any PC or compatible. The LaserJet has an RS-232C serial port into which you can plug the supplied RS-232C cable as if it were any daisy wheel printer. The LaserJet Plus has both the RS-232C serial and IBM-style (Centronics) parallel port options, but you must specify which one you want when you order. You can reconfigure the RS-232C to be an RS-422 port.

The power and flexibility of using the LaserJet or LaserJet Plus is directly related to the software that controls it. Word processing and graphics programs with their own LaserJet drivers produce output that varies in quality. For example, figure 3-9 shows a Lotus 1-2-3 graph printed with the LaserJet driver in the Lotus package, and figure 3-10 shows the same graph printed with LaserControl 100 ($150, Insight Development Corp.).

LaserControl puts the LaserJet in a special mode that emulates the Diablo 630, the NEC 5510 or 7710, the Qume Sprint V, and the Epson MX-80 printers. If you have a program that already works with one of these printers, you can use the program with the LaserJet.

For Lotus users, the Epson emulation is especially useful as a substitute for the 1-2-3 LaserJet driver, which prints at a resolution of only 75 dots per inch. Under Epson emulation (density 3), LaserControl prints at 150 dots per inch.

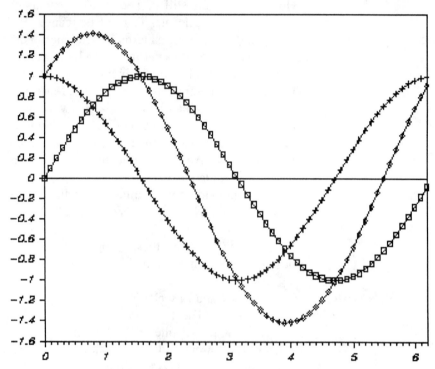

Figure 3-9. A Lotus 1-2-3 graph printed with the Lotus-supplied H-P LaserJet driver at 75 dots per inch resolution.

Hewlett-Packard supplies a free utility program called PrintScreen that is loaded into the RAM of your PC, where it remains until you turn off or reboot your computer. PrintScreen sends a picture of the screen to the printer whenever you press the Shift-PrtSc (print screen) key combination. You can use PrintScreen with a standard monochrome monitor, plus an IBM color/graphics board, or a Hercules graphics board.

PCLPak is another utility available from Hewlett-Packard for $79, or free with a package of soft fonts. PCLPak lets you select Printer Control Language functions from a menu. For example, to print a wide spreadsheet using Lotus 1-2-3, you can use PCLPak to select the LaserJet's landscape (sideways) option with legal-sized paper and the 8.5-point Line Printer landscape font on the 92286B cartridge. You can then return to Lotus 1-2-3 and print the spreadsheet.

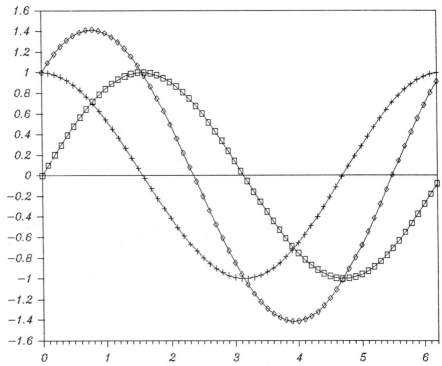

Example LaserControl/1-2-3 Graph

Figure 3-10. The graph in Figure 3-9 printed with LaserControl 100 on a LaserJet Plus at 150 dots per inch resolution.

PCLPak also provides a simple method for downloading the "soft fonts" of the LaserJet Plus. You can load any soft font from a floppy disk into the Plus's memory, delete a soft font from the printer's memory, and keep track of the fonts you currently have available. In addition, it lets you create simple rectangular bars and fill them with any of eight shades of gray and six patterns.

PCLPak is well-designed but it is limited to working as a stand-alone program — you can't use it from within an application. There are other utilities available that reside in RAM and can be used from within another application program, such as CtlLaser (Rabar Systems, $65), described next, and some of the utilities control the H-P and other laser printers, described later in this chapter.

The purpose of CtlLaser is to send commands to the printer without leaving a program. When you load CtlLaser into memory, it occupies

14K of RAM. You can then use other programs. However, at any time you can type Alt-**H**, and the CtlLaser menu appears, with 21 types of LaserJet control commands. If you select command 3 (Orientation), a second menu appears showing your options (Portrait or Landscape). The CtlLaser program has room for 23 printer commands in its menu, so you can add your own commands.

CtlLaser is useful for sending a control string to the printer without having to understand the H-P Escape codes. You can set up the page format with margins and orientation. It is not useful for switching typefonts within text, because it sends codes to the printer at the time you select them.

We describe more powerful print formatting programs for the LaserJet later in this chapter.

Macs With the LaserJet (and Canon Printers) Although the Apple Macintosh works best with Apple's LaserWriter, the price of the LaserWriter is much higher than the Hewlett-Packard LaserJet and Canon laser printers and you also have to buy the Apple-Talk network cables (another $100-$200). There are several utilities for the Mac that make it work properly with the LaserJet and LaserJet Plus and the Canon Laser Beam Printers.

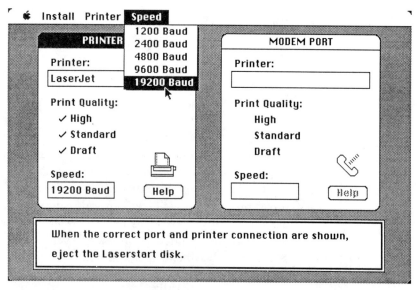

Figure 3-11. The Laserstart Plus utility lets you use the LaserJet from a Mac. This menu presents LaserJet typefonts.

Laserstart Plus ($145, SoftStyle) lets you connect the LaserJet to a Mac with a standard ImageWriter cable (AppleTalk is not needed) and print text and graphics produced by virtually every Macintosh program. Laserstart Plus is easy to install — the installation adds a new driver to the system folder. You can then use a Choose Printer desk accessory to choose the LaserJet, LaserJet Plus, Canon Laser Beam Printer, or Xerox 4045 laser printer/copier.

You also use Laserstart Plus to modify your MacWrite or other application disk. The modified programs are then able to print on these laser printers.

Laserstart Plus supports all normal Macintosh printing modes: standard, high, and draft. The standard mode prints the image you see on the screen, but reduced to 96% of its original size to avoid text being chopped off on the edges by the printer. Since the resolution of the Macintosh screen is 72 pixels per inch and the possible resolution of the LaserJet is 300 pixels per inch, Laserstart Plus combines the dots into four by four boxes of dots and produces output at 75 pixels per inch. Surprisingly, a LaserJet can paint an entire page of graphics at 75 dots per inch, using Laserstart Plus, even though the LaserJet only has 64K of memory.

The high mode prints what you see on the screen, but at 150 pixels per inch — twice the resolution of standard mode (the resolution the LaserWriter uses when you're not using one of its built-in fonts). In high mode, MacDraw graphics look outstanding, but MacPaint graphics, created at 72 pixels per inch, look better in standard mode. In high mode, you'll get better results with text if you choose a font with a point size that is twice the size of the original.

The draft mode uses the built-in LaserJet or LaserJet Plus typefonts rather than Macintosh fonts. Normally, you'll have problems with random extra spaces in this mode unless your Macintosh font is close to the LaserJet font in size and style. Laserstart Plus solves that problem by including several fonts that exactly match the spacing of many LaserJet font cartridges and by seeking out the LaserJet font that matches as closely as possible the font you're using on the Macintosh.

In addition to the three conventional Macintosh printing modes, Laserstart Plus lets you combine 300-dot-per-inch fonts with MacPaint or other images pasted into MacWrite or Word, so you get the best of both worlds.

Laserstart Plus lets you print an entire screen, and it can print Mac-Paint's bit-mapped graphics faster on the LaserJet than the Mac can print them on the LaserWriter. Also, if a LaserWriter font is not built in, the LaserWriter has to do a two-minute download of the font from the Mac before it can be used. LaserStart Plus "rasterizes" (converts the font to a dot pattern) as it prints, saving you printing time when you're using special fonts.

Another utility for using a LaserJet with a Macintosh is ProPrint ($74-$225, Creighton Development). ProPrint can print MacWrite text only — no graphics output, no other word processors (to print Mac-Paint files and other graphics, consider using LaserStart).

The program is easy to use: you select from a list the file you want to print and ProPrint takes care of the rest. The main drawback of ProPrint is the lack of typefont selection — it uses the default typefont on whatever cartridge you are using.

Another excellent utility for the Macintosh is Magic ($399 without camera, New Image Technology). Magic is a complete digitizing system (described in the next chapter) that includes a camera and supporting software for converting photographs and other images into Mac-Paint files. Part of the software lets you print any MacPaint file on a LaserJet (not just files created by Magic).

Magic gives you a choice of four sizes that correspond to 300, 150, 100 and 75 dots per inch. At 300 dpi each pixel on the screen is converted to one LaserJet dot, resulting in a screen image printed at the size of a matchbook. At 150 dpi the image doubles in size; at 75 dots you get an image that is 96% of the original size.

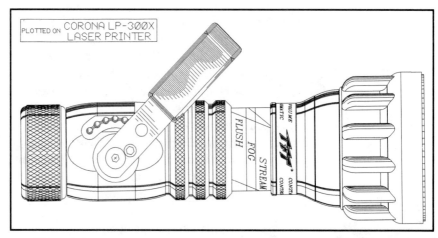

Figure 3-12.   An AutoCAD image plotted on the Cordata LP300 laser printer.

**Other Laser
Printers**

New laser printers are appearing in the market with expanded memory, faster and more durable print engines, sophisticated font capabilities and emulation modes. The emulation modes make it possible to run popular "off the shelf" software with the printers.

The first low-cost laser printer to appear in the market was the Cordata LP300 (formerly Corona). Although the H-P LaserJet stole the media show, the Cordata LP300 was available first at the low price of $3395. Since that time there have been many low-end laser printers introduced, as well as some on the high end of the price spectrum.

**Low-end Office
Printers**

The Cordata LP300 ($3395) leads the pack in performance and features of the low-priced laser printers. Cordata supplies the printer with a plug-in PC card for interfacing the printer to any PC or compatible computer (including their own Cordata compatible computers).

The LP300 includes 38 disk-downloadable fonts. This method for downloading fonts is more flexible and less expensive than the cartridge font loading method used by the LaserJet and other printers.

The LP300 is driven by a page and typesetting language with about 100 commands to take advantage of the built-in features. The language is similar to the LaserJet escape code sequences, but it includes a macro capability for emulating other laser printers. You can take any word processing program command and translate it to any command on the printer. Any word processing software can be used to generate the macros. You have to embed the graphics codes in your text file to mix graphics with text .

You can print graphics anywhere you tell the software to position them, and you can expand images horizontally by factors of 2, 4, 8, and vertically by any integer factor. You can compensate for the fact that most display screens do not have a square aspect ratio (such as the PC monochrome monitors).

The Cordata printer is faster than most printers because it stores the graphic image on the interface card, and does not have to transfer the image to the laser printer's memory. Other printers have to receive bit-mapped images through a serial port; some, like the H-P LaserJet, take up to 20 minutes to completely produce an image. The Cordata interface card, on the other hand, uses direct input/output of blocks of memory to the laser printer, so printing of graphic images takes only eight seconds.

A variety of application programs support the Cordata LP300. For example, Microsoft Word has an LP300 driver, and the printer is also compatible with every word processor that runs on the PC and works with an Epson printer, because it has an Epson compatibility mode (including Epson graphics).

One of the lowest priced laser printers is the QMS Kiss ($1995), which is limited in functions and fonts but is designed to replace daisy wheel and dot matrix printers. The Kiss emulates an Epson FX printer with 300 dots per inch resolution (a maximum of 240 x 72 dots per square inch of graphics). The QMS SmartWriter ($3850) is based on the Canon LBP-CX engine and prints 8 pages a minute, with better graphics (QMS also makes high-end printers, such as the PS-800, which uses PostScript).

Figure 3-13. The QMS SmartWriter has 128K of RAM for downloaded fonts and Qume, Diablo and Epson printer emulation.

Qume also has two low-priced printers — the LaserTEN ($2795) and LaserTEN Plus ($3395), designed to compete directly against the LaserJet and LaserJet Plus. The LaserTEN has 128K of memory and the LaserTEN Plus has 512K. Both printers feature downloadable fonts, a 250-page input paper tray, face-down collated output and a 5000-page maintenance cycle. The printers have several emulation modes, including H-P LaserJet, IBM ProPrinter, and the Qume Sprint 11 daisy wheel printer.

Genicom also has a low-cost laser printer with several emulation modes. The Genicom 5010 ($2995) uses the 10-page per minute Hitachi engine and "personality modules" that contain emulation codes, including those for the IBM Graphics Printer, the Diablo 630 daisy wheel printer, and the H-P LaserJet.

High-end CAD/CAM and Graphics Printers

Xerox was one of the first manufacturers to use laser technology in printers designed for CAD/CAM (computer aided design and manufacturing) and sophisticated graphic arts.

The Xerox laser printers ($20,000 to $40,000) are high-speed graphics and typesetting printers using Xerox's Interpress language.

Figure 3-14. The Genicom 5010 uses "personality cartridges" to emulate various printers, including IBM Graphics Printer, Diablo 630 and LaserJet.

The Xerox printers produce output faster than the Canon engine. The Xerox 4045 Laser CP printer ($4995) has Xerox 2700 and Diablo 630 emulation modes and can print 10 pages a minute. Xerox also offers complete "desktop publishing" systems starting at around $12,000.

QMS manufacturers the Lasergrafix series of laser printers that use a control-code language called QUIC. The desktop model (800) uses the Canon engine and the larger, faster models use the Xerox engines. QMS also sells PostScript-compatible printers (LaserGrafix 1200/A and QMS PS 800 are both PostScript laser printers).

IMAGEN makes several laser printers, based on the Canon, Ricoh and Xerox engines, that use the imPRESS language. IMAGEN was founded to market a patented rasterization process developed at Stanford University for placing dots on a page, using only 1 to 2 percent of the memory required by the more common full-page processes.

The Dataproducts laser printers use the 26-page-per-minute Toshiba engine. Dataproducts has the LZR-1230 for $15,000 that offers Diablo 630 emulation, and the $23,000 LZR-6600/65 that uses PostScript. The printers are designed for high volume applications.

Typefont and Printer Utilities

To meet the need for control over inexpensive laser printers such as the H-P LaserJet, companies have introduced *utility programs* that let you download typefonts to the printers, change from one typefont to another, and control margins and orientation. Some of these are designed to be run before you start your application or word processing program, and others are designed to be run while momentarily suspending operation of your application or word processing program.

Most word processing programs have margin and line spacing controls that are designed to work with daisy wheel or dot matrix printers, not laser printers. You can put printing codes in the word processing program to control typefont changes, and other codes to control other special effects, but you may still need a utility to *start the laser printer* or set margins and other settings.

Printworks For Lasers

Printworks for Lasers (SoftStyle, $125) is a memory-resident printing utility that you can instantly call up while in any application program, giving you an easy, low-cost way to get total control over all of the printing functions on the LaserJet, LaserJet Plus, Canon LBP-8A1 and

LBP-8A2 Laser Beam Printers, NCR 6416 and Xerox 4045.

For example, with Printworks loaded into your PC or compatible computer's memory, if you are using WordStar and you want to print on the LaserJet, you can press the Shift and Print Screen keys, and Printworks for Lasers pops up a menu that lets you select type fonts, image size, lines per inch, page size, character width and spacing (including proportional spacing), margins, manual or internal tray sheet feed, page orientation (allowing for sideways printing for spreadsheets), normal or reverse characters and graphics printing, number of copies to print, and other printer features — all with one or two keystrokes.

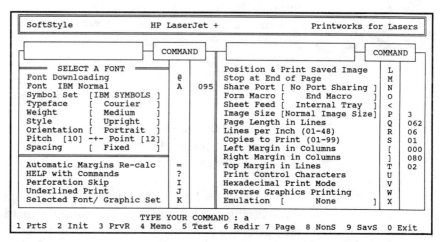

Figure 3-15.   Printworks for Lasers is a memory-resident utility for controlling printing functions on the LaserJet and other Canon-based printers.

Also included in Printworks for Lasers is a memory-resident, single-page "Memo Writer" — a word processor allowing you to quickly create and print short memos or letters, address envelopes, or add a caption to a graph.

You can cut and paste bit-mapped images to any position on the page. For example, while you're in Lotus 1-2-3 or in ExecuVision creating presentation graphics, you can pop up Printworks for Lasers, save the screen to a file, reduce or enlarge the image to fit, paste it into a document in WordStar (Macintosh-style), and print out the resulting page on a laser or dot matrix printer.

You can also print the complete IBM PC character set without having to purchase special H-P font cartridges (costing around $300). The IBM character set includes the standard keys on your keyboard plus foreign characters, mathematical and scientific symbols, and special characters used in certain word processors (such as character number 21 in DisplayWrite 3, the document section symbol).

Printworks for Lasers includes line-drawing symbols (character numbers 176 to 223) that you can embed in your document to create forms, simple logos, borders, boxes, and other simple graphics and merge them with text.

The ability to use line-drawing symbols will also come in handy if you're using Lotus 1-2-3 with a monochrome monitor, since Lotus uses line-drawing characters instead of bit-mapped graphics to create its monochrome charts.

Some word processors, such as WordStar, won't let you use the upper 128 (number 128 to 255) characters, because they're reserved for use by WordStar. However, you can use this feature of Printworks for Lasers with WordPerfect, Volkswriter Deluxe, Microsoft Word, Multimate, XyWrite, and some other word processors.

If you want to experiment on your PC using Printworks for Lasers and you don't have a word processor that lets you use these characters, exit from your program into DOS, hold down the Alt key, type any number from 128 to 255, and release the Alt key to see the upper 128 characters.

Printworks for Lasers also has a Power Printing feature that lets you do typesetting on laser printers as well as dot matrix printers. You use it by placing any of the 40 Power Printing commands in your text files created by any word processor. The commands then perform basic typesetting functions on the LaserJet and LaserJet Plus, Canon, NCR, and other laser printers as well as most dot matrix printers when you print the file.

Using a backslash (\), you can insert simple typesetting codes throughout a document (place a code at any column position and on any line), to select from the printer's built-in typefaces (six downloaded fonts are optional), plus up to five font cartridge slots (such as those available on the Xerox 4045 laser printer/copier. Other codes give you up to 25 foreign-language and mathematical symbol sets, 26 point sizes (in one-point increments), six pitches, three line spacings, eight special shadings, a variety of styles (italic, compressed, wide, double-high, proportional, landscape, underlined, etc.), and other print formatting commands.

One subtlety you should know about laser printers and PCs: they are normally connected to the IBM PC serial port. However, most PC-DOS software prints to the parallel port, so you have to type the MODE command on the PC-DOS command line in order to redirect output to the serial port. With the MODE command you must specify the baud rate, parity, data bits, and stop bits for the serial port.

Printworks for Lasers' install program avoids this by prompting you to assign printers to ports, and has defaults for screen colors and the print font. You can later select, via menu, a dot matrix printer for lower-cost draft copies, for example, and then switch to a laser printer for final copies. You can also unthrottle your laser printer to receive data at its full 19,200-baud rate, instead of being restricted to the slower 9600-baud DOS limit.

Printworks for Lasers makes the Hewlett-Packard LaserJet or Canon laser printers look like an IBM Graphics Printer or Epson MX-80 dot matrix printer (including graphics mode) to application programs (DisplayWrite 3 and others). You can therefore use programs that are configured to work with the industry-standard Epson or IBM Graphics Printer. Since most business software on the market supports Epson and IBM Graphics Printers, you can make your business software work with Hewlett-Packard LaserJet and Canon laser printers — in both text and graphics modes, without changing your software.

With the Canon Laser Beam printers, Printworks for Lasers can also emulate the Diablo 630 — one of the most widely supported daisy wheel printers, as well as the Epson MX-80.

If you're using the LaserJet Plus printer, you can create "form macros" that will automatically overlay text and graphics — a masthead, for example — on every page. You can also download up to six typefonts at a time from disk and select them via menu.

Printworks for Dot Matrix ($75, SoftStyle) gives you all of these Printworks for Lasers features on dot matrix printers, such as the IBM Quietwriter, or higher-end Epson, NEC, TI, Toshiba, and other printers — which typically have 24 or more wires and can print text and graphics at near-letter-quality, but at lower prices than laser printers.. Printworks for Dot Matrix takes full advantage of the higher resolution matrix of these printers.

You'll need a typesetting-style word processor like Microsoft Word or XyWrite to take full advantage of all these features (such as printing IBM graphics characters).

Fancy Font   The Fancy Font system (SoftCraft, $180) is a complete print formatting program for PCs, PC-compatibles and CP/M computers that is fully compatible with Epson dot matrix printers and Canon-based laser printers. The Fancy Font system offers a library of typefonts and styles, a complete printing control language, a program for editing existing fonts, and a utility to create new fonts.

Fancy Font can produce excellent results on an Epson dot matrix printer. The program has several draft printing modes for dot matrix printers that print at 240 dots per inch with one or more passes of the print head. Fancy Font prints at 300 dots per inch on the H-P LaserJet and the Canon LBP-8A1 laser printers (there are no other draft printing modes in the laser printer version).

Fancy Font formatting commands are designed to be embedded in any text file produced by any word processing program. You can even put Fancy Font commands in data bases and spreadsheet data saved in ASCII format.

The Fancy Font language includes dozens of print control commands that can change typefonts and sizes, control pagination with running heads and footers, justified or ragged margins, nested and hanging indents, and control relative horizontal and vertical motion of the print head.

Fancy Font uses the graphics mode of the LaserJet and Canon printers to draw its typefont characters. The LaserJet is limited to one-fourth of a page of high-resolution 300-dot-per-inch graphics. Therefore, you can use Fancy Font typefonts for headlines and such (up to one-fourth of a page), and use the cartridge fonts for most of your text. The LaserJet Plus, however, can print a full page of Fancy Font typefonts. Fancy Font can mix its own typefonts and the printer's cartridge fonts (or "native" disk fonts) on the same line of text, so you can do special effects.

Fancy Font works with any straight ASCII text file produced by any word processing program, but SoftCraft provides a special program for use with Microsoft Word on the PC. Fancy Word ($140, includes 25 fonts, additional fonts are $15 per disk) prints Microsoft Word documents using Fancy Font typefonts and printing features. You can use Microsoft Word as you normally would, with all of Word's formatting features, plus Fancy Font features if you want to add them. Versions of Fancy Word are configured for specific printers including the Epson FX and MX series, the Epson LQ-1500, the Toshiba and the LaserJet.

Logo Creation

The font editing program allows you to edit characters in existing fonts or create new characters or logos from scratch. Logos, such as ![hp] can be created and then printed just as any other character. An optional font editing program provides an enlarged display, powerful editing commands and is compatible with the Microsoft Mouse. The following screen depicts a character editing session.

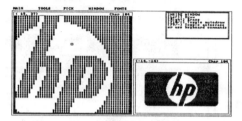

Logos or pictures can also be digitized with a camera or other digitizer and then printed in the middle of a document with *Fancy Font*.

Font Variety

Fonts Are

Available

In Many 𝕯𝖎𝖋𝖋𝖊𝖗𝖊𝖓𝖙 𝕾𝖙𝖞𝖑𝖊𝖘

And

Sizes

$$\pi(n) = \sum_{k=2}^{n} \left\lfloor \frac{\phi(k)}{k-1} \right\rfloor$$

Figure 3-16. Sample Fancy Font output from an H-P LaserJet.

Figure 3-17. FONTASY for the PC has a catalog of over 250 typefonts. This sample (shown actual size) was printed at 300 dots per inch on the LaserJet Plus.

Fontasy

Fontasy ($50, PROSOFT) gives you one-page layout and typesetting with a catalog of typefonts for the LaserJet Plus as well as Epson dot matrix printers and the IBM Proprinter. The program runs on PCs and works with the Hercules Monochrome card or the IBM Color Graphics Adaptor. If provides proportionally-spaced printing with up to 28 typefonts at a time and over 250 typefonts available from the vendor.

The program can do kerning of type as well as right justification and centering. You can draw images with or without a mouse. FONTASY helps you draw rectangles, straight lines and ovals, and you can fill in areas using a palette 95 different fill patterns. You can move images, turn them sideways or upside down, and print both text and graphics in reversed white on black background.

You can supply text by typing it directly into FONTASY or "pouring" it into your multi-column template from a straight ASCII text file.

FONTASY has many highly-decorative fonts ($25 each) for use in invitations, menus, maps, flyers and other documents where flamboyant type is called for. Logos and letterhead are easy to design, as are banners to be printed sideways.

WordStar Print Formatting Programs

If you want more typefonts and special effects from your WordStar text, one low-cost approach is to buy an inexpensive *text formatting* program (sometimes called a *text processor* or "pretty-printing" program). These typically work in conjunction with WordStar or another word processing program to print the text on laser printers with multiple-font capabilities.

To control the LaserJet or any laser printer with LaserJet emulation from within a WordStar text file, you can use PrintMerge (Polaris Software, $99) or StarJet (Control-C Software, $150). StarBeam (Control-C) is for printing on Canon Laser Beam printers; the company also offers MultiJet (for printing Multimate files on the LaserJet) and MultiBeam (for Multimate files on the Canon printers).

PrintMerge works as a substitute print function for WordStar text files and translates WordStar "dot" commands and Control-**P** commands into LaserJet functions. The program provides a number of formatting commands that let you switch from one font to another within a document, and specify margins, page length, headings and footings, underlining, and superscripts.

One of the important features of PrintMerge is its ability to produce double-justified text even when you use several different fonts on one line. Another feature lets you incorporate charts created by Microsoft Chart into WordStar documents. PrintMerge also gives you a set of merge commands that allow for conditional comparisons in printing multiple versions of form letters.

With version 2.00 of PrintMerge, you can download soft fonts to the LaserJet Plus and assign them a Font Selection Letter. Then you can switch to a soft font within the text file with a simple Control-**P** command using the Font Selection Letter.

Version 2.00 of PrintMerge has commands for graphics and tables. For example, to create a box, use the command `.BX` followed by the coordinates of the box, the width of lines, the patterns or shades to fill the box with, and the pattern or shade to use to print the borders of the box. Even if you are using a variable-spaced font like Times Roman-,you can align tables verticallywith the **.FX** command.

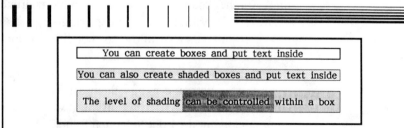

StarBeam prints WordStar files on the Canon LBP-8A1 Laser Beam printer *as is* without wasting time and money on retyping and relearning.

No new steps for **StarBeam!** It is the <u>easiest</u> and <u>most complete</u> path from WordStar to the Laser Beam! Other programs redefine Wordstar commands and force you to take extra steps; learn new commands, create intermediate ASCII files, and re-edit existing documents before you can print them out with laser-sharpness.

With **StarBeam**, line breaks print as you see them on the screen so <u>what you see is what you get!</u>

The advanced features of the Laser Beam are easily utilized by adding special **StarBeam** commands to WordStar documents.

STARBEAM FEATURES

* Print WordStar documents *as is*
* Use many different fonts
* Horizontal and vertical lines
* Shaded and unshaded boxes
* Text in boxes
* Multiple columns per page
* Proportional spacing with justification
* Underline spaces

ACCESS TO MANY FONT STYLES

StarBeam gives WordStar the ability to use many styles and sizes of print by using different fonts. For example:

You can print normal characters, or small characters, or Bold face type.

You can expand characters vertically, horizontally or

vertically and horizontally at the same time.

StarBeam allows printing in three different fonts per line.

GRAPHIC EFFECTS

StarBeam lets you incorporate graphics into your documents. For example, you can draw horizontal and vertical lines of different thicknesses:

You can create boxes and put text inside

You can also create shaded boxes and put text inside

The level of shading can be controlled within a box

Figure 3-18.   StarBeam for the Canon Laser Beam printers has the same features as StarJet for the LaserJet. Both programs print WordStar files.

PrintMerge 2.00 also supports macros. It works like this: if you create a special letterhead or logo, and store it as **macro #3** in the printer, you can add the command **.RM 3** to a text file, and then when you print the file, this letterhead or logo is included.

StarJet and StarBeam are similar to PrintMerge — StarJet translates WordStar's Control-**P** and "dot" commands into LaserJet codes, and StarBeam translates them into Canon Laser Beam codes. StarJet/StarBeam recognize most of the "dot" commands and add a few more (called "dotstar" commands) for setting the default typefont for bold and italic styles, drawing lines and boxes, printing multiple columns, controlling paper and envelope loading, and performing other printing functions not available in WordStar "dot" commands.

StarJet lets you set a different typefont to be used for headings and footings. The user-defined Control-**P** codes are set to emphasized mode (**^PE**), extended symbol sets (**^PR**), and proportional column justification (**^PQ**). The proportional column justification makes it possible to justify columns of a table using a proportional font.

StarJet calculates the interword and inter-character spacing needed to justify the text with proportional fonts. What you see on the WordStar screen will not be exactly what you get in print, but the result with StarJet is better proportional spacing than if you used WordStar with embedded LaserJet codes.

You cannot print with the MailMerge option of WordStar and get form letters with the PrintMerge or StarJet features, but you can use MailMerge to "print" to a disk file and then put the PrintMerge or StarJet codes in the resulting "print" file.

Both PrintMerge and StarJet are powerful printing programs, but they rely on WordStar's dot command style of formatting and the Control-**P** style of switching typefonts. This style is not necessarily the style you want to use, and you have less choices for typesetting control than with real typesetting programs. To publish a book or large manual, you may want to use a real typesetting program (described in Chapter 7), and if you want to merge graphics with the text, you might prefer to use a page makeup program (Chapter 5).

Sharing Laser Printers

Show us an office with a new laser printer and we'll show you a battlefield. If that describes your office, you may be ready for a printer sharing device. With the LaserWriter, the AppleTalk network performs printer sharing via cables, so you don't have to worry about a printer connection if you have AppleTalk connected to your computer.

With the LaserJet and other laser printers, you have a choice: buy additional laser printers (the expensive alternative), or buy a printer sharing device, typically priced at $300 on up, depending on features. These devices are switches with built-in buffer memory that allows you to connect several computers to a laser printer, and "spool" files (send files to it for printing, then use your computer for some other purpose).

Here's a brief checklist of options you might want to shop for, depending on your specific needs:

- How many PCs can be plugged in?

- Does it handle both PCs and Macs?

- Which laser printers will it support?

- Does it allow for connecting to both laser and other dot matrix printers (this feature allows you to print drafts on a dot matrix printer and final copies on the laser printer)? Make sure it can support your specific printers.

- What's the buffer capacity (what is the maximum size document you can spool to the printer)?

- How fast can it print a specific length document on your laser printer? (Compare with normal printing speed on your laser printer for the same document.)

Printer sharing device vendors include Hayes, ACT, Extended Systems, and INTEK. The cost per user may be a lot less than it would otherwise cost to have a dot matrix graphics printer for each user. And the next chapter provides many graphic reasons for having access to a laser printer.

CHAPTER FOUR

Working With Graphics and Images

What sort of profession is it for a grown man to sit around drawing pictures?
— cartoonist B. Kliban

Overview of Graphics

Graphic images are just as important as text in conveying information; sometimes they are more important. A chart depicting a growth or slump in sales will have more of an effect on the reader than a spreadsheet with numbers. A diagram of how to open and service a gum wrapping machine will communicate far more readily-understandable information than paragraphs describing the machine.

If you don't feel artistic, or even talented enough to draw a straight line, you may not think to mix graphics with your text. Using a personal computer with a graphics program solves this problem. The computer software is talented enough to draw all the straight lines you'll need. In fact, the computer can draw straight lines with more accuracy than any artist can draw by hand. Once you have an image on the screen in a "painting" or "drawing" program, it is easy to quickly duplicate the image several times and place copies in several places.

Painting and drawing programs make it possible for artists to use the screen as an erasable canvas, letting them play "what if" with images without wasting ink, paper and materials.

Graphic images can be created and printed on black and white output devices, such as laser printers (for high resolution) and dot matrix printers (for lower resolution and a "softer" feeling). Images can also be printed on the newest color printers that are becoming available (described later in this chapter). For preparing documents, images can be brought into page makeup programs and integrated with the text for one-pass printing/typesetting of pages.

Not all graphic images have to be created from scratch. *Digitizers* (also called *scanners*) are available to transform an image printed on paper or captured with a video camera into digital form to be edited with "paint" or "draw" programs. The scanned image can be incorporated into painted or drawn graphics (figure 4-1). There are several digitizers that work with Macs and PCs for digitizing black and white images, and one scanner that can scan color images.

Figure 4-1.   A MacPaint graphic (by Mick Wiggins) incorporating a digitized image.

Color images can be handled in a new way, thanks to advances in typesetting technology. It is now possible to take a color screen image, save it on disk, and produce digitally the color-separated film needed for mass-printing the image, all without using an expensive photographic separation process.

The only problem with "digital four-color separations," as they are now called, is that the image resolution available on personal computers is very low compared to photographic images. Unless you want the "pixelated" effect, the graphic images derived from personal computers will be too rough for magazines, advertisements and books, but not for newspapers and newsletters.

The two personal computers that have all the tools available for using graphics in desktop publishing applications are IBM PCs and compatibles, and the Apple Macintosh. Of these two types of computers, the Macintosh is the strongest in graphic applications, even though it does not use color; the PC can use color if you have a color graphics card and monitor, otherwise it can do high-resolution black and white (but not as high as the Macintosh screen resolution). The graphics resolution is determined by the screen display in both cases.

There is one more reason for the Macintosh's superiority: today's standard features of "painting" and drawing programs appeared first on the Macintosh. It helps to see how they are implemented on the Mac even if you are going to use PCs, because the PC programs emulate the Mac approach to graphics.

Macintosh Graphics

The Apple Macintosh computer was not the first computer to offer graphics, nor was it the first to be easy to use. It was the first mass-market computer to use icons and a mouse in its operation, and it triggered an icon-and-mouse phenomenon in the personal computer industry. It was also the first computer to be designed for and extensively marketed to artists, writers and craftspeople.

The Mac is the easiest computer to use for drawing and manipulating black and white images. MacPaint lets you draw and manipulate images with ease; practically every "paint" program for every personal computer was designed to look similar to MacPaint.

The MacPaint program provides "paintbrushes" that draw lines of varying sizes, or draw patterns. Using the "fat bits" feature, you can also change the image dot-by-dot. Make a mistake? Use the "eraser."

MacDraw is a more sophisticated program that gives you tools for producing blueprints and designs. MacDraw lets you draw straight lines, boxes and polygons quickly, and enlarge, reduce or stretch boxes and other polygons by clicking and pulling with the mouse (or drawing tablet).

You can create any type of graphic with the combination of Mac-Paint and MacDraw, and print the graphic with the best results using MacDraw. You can also get enhancement utilities or replacements for MacPaint/MacDraw from third party vendors who specialize in graphics (we describe some of these programs later).

There are a variety of drawing and painting accessories for working with MacPaint and MacDraw. For example, the MacTablet (Summagraphics, $495) comes with a light pen for drawing freestyle, with a 6 x 9 inch drawing area. The tablet connects to either the printer or modem port, and you activate the tablet by choosing the desk accessory software. The light pen can be used in place of the mouse as the pointing device.

The professional MM1812 Digitizing Tablet (Summagraphics, $995) is excellent for tracing images that are larger than the Mac screen (figure 4-2). You can place an image on the tablet (a 12 x 18 tracing area) and trace it with the mouse using the cross-hairs.

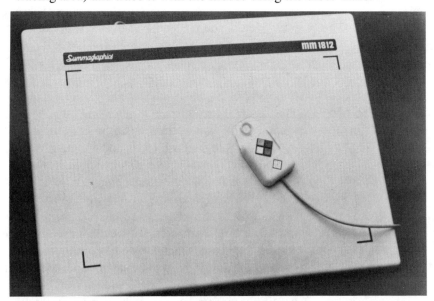

Figure 4-2.   The Summagraphics MM1812 Digitizing Tablet has a 12 x 18 inch tracing area and two scales of reduction.

MacPaint   MacPaint is the program that invented "painting" on personal computers. You can "paint" with a "brush" controlled by either the mouse or a drawing tablet, such as the Summagraphics MacTablet.

The brush strokes can be extremely thin to extremely thick. You can define a shape of any size and fill it with any of the patterns available. You can use a "spray can" to spray-paint black on a white canvas, or white on a black canvas. You can copy a graphic or portion of a graphic many times, using the Clipboard, position the copies anywhere on the MacPaint page, and even invert them (see figure 4-3). Portions of the graphic image can be copied into the Clipboard, and then pasted into another drawing, or saved in the Mac Scrapbook for use in many drawings (figure 4-4).

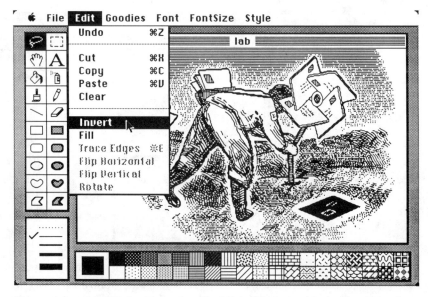

Figure 4-3. A MacPaint illustration (by Mick Wiggins) with small graphic pieces copied to the Clipboard, rotated and moved into position on the page. One piece is defined by the lasso and inverted to black.

MacPaint also lets you type letters and numbers to mix in with your graphics or to use as captions. However, there are no word processing functions. You can bring word processed text from MacWrite or Microsoft Word into MacPaint through use of the Scrapbook and Clipboard (or just the Clipboard).

MacPaint has several limitations — it does not substitute laser printer typefonts for text in its images, and it cannot change the size of an image or print with a reduction or enlargement percentage. The typefonts you see are "smoothed" along with the graphic images when you use the Print Final selection in the File menu. Neither the graphics nor the typefonts are "smoothed" (modified for the higher resolution laser printer) if you use the Print Draft selection.

Another limitation is that you can only save to the Clipboard an image the size of your screen, and you can't reduce or enlarge your image. There are a number of MacPaint enhancement products, such as Art Grabber and Paint Cutter, that let you copy larger images to the Clipboard and Scrapbook. These are described later in utilities.

Figure 4-4.   The MacPaint illustration from figure 4-3, with a portion copied to the Scrapbook for use in another illustration.

MacDraw   Apple Computer's MacDraw ($125) makes up for many of Mac-Paint's limitations. MacDraw's LaserWriter print menu lets you choose the reduction or enlargement percentage to change the size of the printed graphic, and it gives you the option to employ a "smoothing" algorithm to redraw as it prints images at the higher resolution of the laser printer. It also provides typefont substitution so that text is printed using the PostScript typefonts.

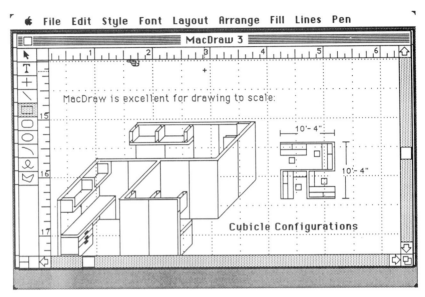

Figure 4-5. MacDraw has more tools for drawing straight lines, angles, boxes and polygons, and lets you reduce, enlarge, stretch or compress images.

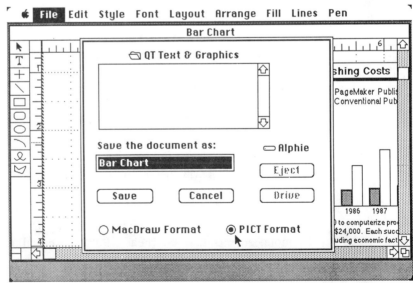

Figure 4-6. To use MacDraw images with page makeup programs such as Mac-Publisher, ReadySetGo and PageMaker, save the images in the "PICT" format.

MacDraw is an excellent tool for drawing straight lines, 45-degree and 90-degree angles, boxes and polygons. Each separately-drawn item can be moved, duplicated many times on-screen, enlarged, reduced, stretched, compressed, rotated or have its characteristics (line width and pattern) changed.

MacDraw lets you type text within a box and control the leading, but you can't bring large amounts of text into a MacDraw screen from a MacWrite file or other type of text file. Once you press Return, MacDraw treats the line of text as a single graphic object — you cannot change the typefont of individual words unless you first make them separate graphic objects, which is a very cumbersome procedure.

MacPaint and MacDraw are best used for creating graphic images, and MacDraw is the best for printing them. You can then save the graphic images in the "PICT" (picture) format, as shown in figure 4-6, to prepare them for use with page makeup programs.

There are many things MacPaint and MacDraw can't do, and the programs, desktop accessories and clip art libraries (described next) try to overcome these limitations.

Electronic Clip Art

Clip art is art that is in the public domain (permission has been given to copy it) and available for use in your publications. Examples of clip art images are fancy borders and letters, everyday household items, amusing or out-of-the-ordinary images, and so on.

Electronic clip art images are usually saved in MacPaint files, and you can edit the images with MacPaint or manipulate them with Mac-Draw (including improving their printed appearance with MacDraw's "smoothing" algorithm). There is a lot of clip art on CompuServe, the leading videotex service, which you can call with your computer and modem and download files. You can download CompuServe's collection of Macintosh graphics into a Macintosh, using almost any Mac communications program (such as MacTerminal), or into a PC, using T/Maker's Personal Publisher program.

ClickArt (T/Maker Graphics, $50 each disk) are collections of images on disks saved in MacPaint files. You can select from Personal Graphics (Einstein, cartoons, animals, Michelangelo's David, city skyline, cars, wine bottle — mostly used in invitations, announcements, and letterhead); Publications (illustrated headlines, map of USA and Europe, illuminated alphabets — mostly used in newsletters, flyers and invitations); Letters (24, 36 and 48 point sizes are included in MacPaint files, and you can set 72 point type, in 15 installable fonts from 24 available typestyles and typefaces, and Holiday Images (a disk of seasonal holiday images for Christmas and birthday cards, invitations, and more). A catalog of other disks in the ClickArt series is available from T/Maker Graphics.

Figure 4-7. Examples of electronic clip art (for use with MacPaint and MacDraw) from T/Maker Graphics and ImageWorld.

In addition to ClickArt clip art images, you can select from many other collections of art, including The Mac Art Dept. (Simon & Schuster, $40) and McPic! and McPic! Volume 2 (Magnum Software, $50 each).

Mac the Knife Volume 1 ($40) and Volume 3:Mac the Ripper ($60, both from Miles Computing Inc.) contain drawings and illustrations, fonts and clip art. Borders and clip art for special occasions and holidays can be used to design invitations, stationery, greeting cards or bulletins.

Maccessories Graphic Accents (Kensington Microware, $50) are professional illustrations. You can get a large library of clip art from the Mac-Art Library (CompuCRAFT, $200), or by volume ($30 per disk).

Choose from Famous People (High Flyers Volume 1, $30 from Macadam Publishing Inc.), airplane templates (The Great International Paper Airplane Construction Kit, $40 from Simon and Schuster), or Q-Art ($35 from Queue Inc.), which contains over 200 personal and business clip art images.

The MacMemories Catalog (ImageWorld, $40) is a representative sampler of the other twelve themed disks from ImageWorld (the entire set is $400) which include "Art Nouveau," "Wild Wild West" and "Tools, Machines and Merchandise" images. The Pattern Collection Volume One ($13 from RoZet) contains patterns and shapes. Finally, grids, scales, rulers and charts for MacPaint are found in GRIDS ($38 from Soft Wares).

Desk Accessories and Utilities

T/Maker Graphics makes a utility disk called ClickArt Effects ($50). ClickArt Effects let you do four special effects not available in Mac-Paint: rotate, slant, distort, or give perspective to text and images while in MacPaint. You load ClickArt Effects into your system disk as a desk accessory (a desk accessory loader is provided). Then, when you are in MacPaint, you can use it to do things MacPaint can't do, like rotate an object in one degree increments, slant the object left or right, distort (stretch) the image, or give it one-point perspective, as in a highway stretching ahead into the distance. Select any of the four effects by selecting its icon.

One of the problems of using ClickArt Effects is that while Effects are being used, you can't use any of the usual MacPaint commands. Effects leaves your images with a case of the jaggies that you will want to clean up using MacPaint's FatBits feature, which zooms into the individual pixels and lets you edit them. The manual offers tips on which order is best to use the different Effects, otherwise you could end up with an unrecognizable mess.

ClickArt Effects works only with the current MacPaint Window. To work on larger images, you have to work on pieces of your page at a time, moving the window around the page.

MacPaint and MacDraw can print images that are up to 8 by 10 inches, but you cannot copy a MacPaint image larger than the screen window into the Clipboard to get it into MacDraw for "smooth" printing or merging with MacDraw images. You can only copy the MacPaint image window by window into the Scrapbook, and then copy and paste the windows from the Scrapbook into a MacDraw document. You can use the following desk accessories that make it easier to copy large MacPaint images.

One MacPaint "add-on" utility is Paint Cutter (Silicon Beach Software, $39). Paint Cutter lets you select a portion of a MacPaint image as large as 8 by 10 inches. You can then flip, rotate, invert, or copy the image to the Clipboard or Scrapbook. Paint Cutter can open four document files at one time, if you have a 512K Mac, and you can select images to copy between them. If you have a 128K Mac, you can have only one document open.

Paint Cutter automatically scrolls your screen in the direction you move your mouse, even if you try to move your mouse past the edge of the window. You scroll in the direction of the mouse, all around the page, until you have drawn a selection box that contains your image.

Once selected, images can be rotated in 90 degree increments, flipped horizontally and vertically, and inverted (switch from black to white and white to black). You can select portions of images with the MacPaint selection rectangle tool, and the effects take place only for the part of the image selected (inside the rectangle).

The Paint Cutter disk includes MacPaint Rulers (measure in inches, centimeters, or pixels); Coordinates, an accessory for displaying the location of your pointer (arrow) relative to any point on the screen; and these other accessories: Screen Saver, Quickeject, and Silicon Beach Font, plus Apple's Desk Accessory/Font Mover. With Paint Cutter you can print the entire document (or selected portions) in final or draft mode, either at full size, or reduced 50%.

You have to leave whatever application you are in to use Paint Cutter, because it is not a desk accessory. QuickPaint (Enterset, $50) and Art Grabber+ (Hayden Software, $50) are desk accessories you can install on your startup disk and use without quitting MacDraw, MacPaint or whatever application program you're using. Art Grabber+ is supplied on the MacroMind Utility Disk (Hayden) that includes CheapPaint, which makes some of the features of MacPaint available as a desk accessory to use while using another application program. Art Grabber+ can copy an entire MacPaint document (if you are using a 512K Mac or Mac Plus) for pasting into MacDraw, MacPaint or text files.

To print a MacDraw image that is two pages wide, select No Breaks Between Pages from the MacDraw Page Setup menu (pull down the File menu), then choose a paper size and a reduction factor (50% or 100%). If you get the message `The Print Command was not completed`, it usually is because you don't have enough disk space to hold the MacDraw temporary print file. To avoid the message, print long documents by selecting just a few pages at a time, or copy your MacDraw program to a disk that does not contain the System Folder.

You can buy additional disks of fonts, and move them onto the desired disks with the Font Mover utility. Fonts range from PostScript fonts ($450 from Altsys Corp.; $185 for a single printer package or $375 for a multi-printer license from Adobe Systems), which are installed by downloading to your LaserWriter, to MacWrite/MacPaint fonts available from numerous sources. Altsys also sells FONTastic, a $50 font editing program you use to create new fonts from scratch or edit existing ones.

LaserFonts Microfonts (Century Software, $30) lets you print the LaserWriter's built-in fonts in sizes below 9 points when using programs (like MacWrite) where the font size menu does not let you select point sizes below 9 point. Microfonts also prints condensed and expanded versions of the built-in LaserWriter fonts.

LaserFonts Willamette (Century Software, $30), also designed for the LaserWriter, comes in several weights and widths, with enough professional typesetter's features to make your documents look typeset. You get a set of bullets, em, en, and thin spaces, accent and diacritical marks.

There are many foreign language fonts available, with the widest selection offered by Linguists Software for $100 to $180 per set; each set includes several languages.

Finally, Font Explorer ($25 from Heizer Software) is a font utility that includes The Font Well, which can be pasted into any document to reveal and allow the use of all 256 characters in a font, including hidden characters that cannot be reached from the keyboard.

Microsoft Chart   You can create charts and graphs with spreadsheet programs, but they tend to look like dot matrix printouts, even when printed on laser printers. However, Microsoft Chart for the Macintosh (Microsoft Corp., $125) has its own LaserWriter driver and produces excellent charts and graphs from data you supply to the program. Microsoft Chart requires only 128K, but runs much faster on a 512K Mac.

Select up to 40 different chart types, and supply data by typing it or importing it from spreadsheet programs, such as Multiplan.

You can have up to 64 sets of values corresponding to categories in a data series. You can have a series based on the sequence of categories; or a time line as the category, with dates incremented by days, weeks, months, or years; or a series of text labels; or a series of numeric labels. You specify the first category and the amount to increment for each additional category.

New series based on existing ones can be created with the Analyze command. The data values for the new series can be the average of the old values, or the cumulative sum, or the difference between two successive values, or the percentage of the total value for each category, or values derived from an exponential growth curve using the old values as the base.

You place markers by each series to plot in a chart, and you can change the order of the list of series to be plotted. You can plot one series at a time or multiple series with the same format and chart. You can also create a combination chart with one or more series in the background and an overlay of additional series.

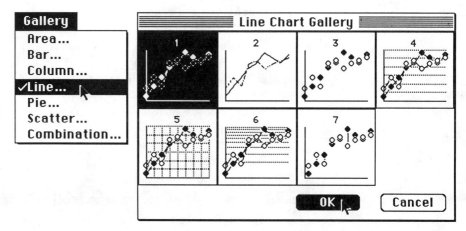

Figure 4-8. Microsoft Chart for the Mac produces seven types of charts and graphs: area, bar, column, line, pie, scatter and combination. Shown are various line charts.

There are seven basic charts included in the program: area, bar, column, line, pie, scatter and combination. Unless you specify one, you get a column chart with categories plotted on the horizontal (x) axis and corresponding values on the vertical (y) axis. The axes are labeled with the names you choose when you create the data series.

If you want a different type of chart, you can select from among the basic types in the Gallery menu and choose a variation of one of these for a special effect. Variations include changing individual values to a percentage of the total, stacking values of multiple series, or adding a background grid.

Charts can be customized: you can change the intersection of the two axes to establish a new reference point, and add legends, arrows, and tick marks on the axes. You can change the pattern used to fill columns or pie chart areas, select from several types of frames to put around your chart, and use different typefonts for labels and titles.

Other Chart and Graph Programs

Cricket Graph ($195 from Cricket Software) provides color presentation graphics and page layout for science and business applications. With Cricket Graph, you can create color charts and graphs for your Excel, Jazz, and other spreadsheets, for example, and print them in color on the ImageWriter II or on plotters, several color printers, and color slide film recorders — all at higher quality than you can get from Microsoft Chart and other Macintosh graphics software (which is also limited to black and white).

You can also import Cricket Graph's color graphs and charts directly into MacPublisher II (described in Chapter 5) and merge them with color text and images to create eight-color newsletters, newspapers, and other documents, using the ImageWriter II printer.

Cricket Graph has a multiple-graph page layout feature — up to ten graphs can be moved, resized, overlayed, and otherwise positioned on a page. Cricket Graph stores its graphics internally in "PICT" files (as in MacDraw) rather than bit-mapped files, so it is not limited to the resolution of the Macintosh screen or LaserWriter — it redraws all graphics at the full resolution of the output device, allowing for very high-resolution plotting. Color information is retained even when the graphs are passed to MacWrite, Word, and PageMaker, allowing these black-and-white applications to print graphics in color.

Cricket Graph lets you graph the twelve most popular science and business graph and chart types: scatter, line, area, bar, column, pie, stacked bar, stacked column, polar, quality control, double Y, and text.

Cricket Graph also lets you do high-quality plotting of over 2000 data points per series — compared to 64 in Microsoft Chart and 100 in Excel. The program allows for regression curve fits, 3-D "depth," and "error bars" to indicate confidence regions.

You enter data in rows and columns in a spreadsheet-like form, or directly import data from SYLK (Multiplan, Chart, Excel, Omnis 3, or OverVUE) files, text-only (MacWrite or Microsoft Word) files, Cricket Software's StatWorks statistical software, or from Jazz and other applications via the Clipboard. You can import data from mainframes or Macintosh data bases in tab-delimited format. You can also save graphs in "PICT" form, allowing for exporting directly to MacDraw, MacDraft, and PageMaker. Switcher is included with Cricket Graph for fast data transfers to and from other applications.

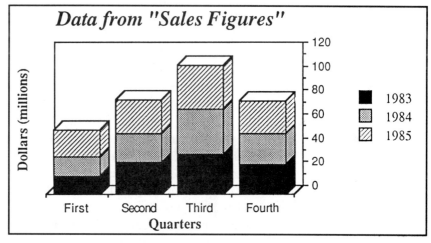

Figure 4-9. Cricket Graph can create high-resolution color transparencies on the Hewlett-Packard 7474A plotter and other color printers, up to 10 graphs on a page.

Cricket Graph offers data manipulation and editing capabilities: data can be sorted, grouped by ranges of values, smoothed, and transformed by logarithmic, trigonometric, exponential, and statistical functions. You can edit the graph or chart by simply clicking on any portion. A dialog box allows for changing axis tick marks and labels, plot symbols, and bar patterns. And you can resize the plot frame and explode pie chart segments.

You can enter text for labels and legends in all available styles, sizes and fonts, with lines, arrows, rectangles and rounded rectangles. "Graphic macros" let you save standard formats in icon-identified files for future use and distribution throughout an organization.

Cricket Graph offers color graph printing on a Macintosh with a color printer. You can assign any of eight printer ribbon or pen hues and 16 fill patterns, allowing for 128 different colors. Cricket Graph supports color printing on the Apple ImageWriter II, Apple Color Plotter, and Hewlett-Packard 7470A and 7475A color plotters, and black and white printing on the ImageWriter and LaserWriter (including transparencies).

Special versions of Cricket Graph ($495 each) are available for 13 other color printers, including the Xerox 6500 color laser, Hewlett-Packard ColorPro and 7550 plotters, Tektronix 4691 and 4695 color ink jets, Benson Colorscan ink jet, Seiko D-Scan CH-5201B, Applicon AP5500, Diablo Series C, Printacolor GP-1040, ACT-2, Versatec ECP-42 color electrostatic, Trilog C100 Colorplot, Lasergraphics CPS-200, and Gulton CP-80C.

These special versions of Cricket Graph let you create color transparencies (35 mm to 8 x 10 inches, including instant Polaroid photographs) on the Dunn Instruments "Color Macintosh" slide-making system (which bundles Cricket Graph software and the Mac-Paint-like Dunn Color software with the Dunn MicroColor film recorder), as well as the Matrix QCR, Hewlett-Packard 7510, and Lasergraphics MPS-2000 film recorders.

Another Macintosh graphing program is ClickOn Worksheet (T/Maker Graphics, $80), a 50-row by 20-column spreadsheet with eleven other functions that you can use from within MacWrite. This type of program is generically called a "desk accessory," and lets you bring up multiple windows on screen to perform calculations, graph data, etc. without leaving the application you are currently working in. ClickOn Worksheet does not have a print function — you either paste the graph into a program that does have a print function, or print the contents of the screen by pressing the Command-Shift-4 keys simultaneously (the Command key is one that has a cloverleaf icon).

PC Graphics

The IBM PC and PC XT are not supplied with sufficient hardware to do medium-resolution or high-resolution graphics, but you can add graphics cards and monitors to the PC or PC XT. Some compatible computers have graphics cards and medium- or high-resolution monitors built into the system. You can also add a mouse or a drawing pad to a PC — popular ones are the Microsoft Mouse ($140 bundled with PC Paint), the Mouse Systems mouse ($140 with PC Paint bundled in the package), and the Summagraphics SummaSketch tablet (with PC Paintbrush bundled in the package).

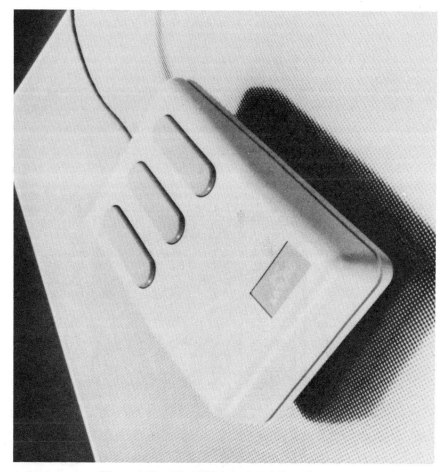

Figure 4-10. The PC Mouse from Mouse Systems.

The most popular add-on cards for the PC to get black and white or color graphics are the IBM Color/Graphics Adapter, the IBM EGA (Enhanced Graphics Adapter), the Hercules Color Graphics Card or the Hercules High-resolution Monochrome Card. Monitors that can display 640 x 350 pixels are adequate for displaying high-resolution PC graphics.

When the PC or PC XT displays high-resolution graphics, the pixels are 640 x 350 (your screen is divided into 640 columns by 350 rows), which means the aspect ratio of pixels is closer to 2 to 1 rather than 1 to 1 (not square like Macintosh pixels). This means that typical Macintosh graphics, where the aspect ratio is 1 to 1, are distorted on the PC screen to be long and thin.

PC Paint   PC Paint (Mouse Systems, $99 or $220 with Mouse Systems mouse) is a medium-resolution "painting" program modeled after MacPaint. PC Paint requires a PC with 256K of RAM, an IBM Color/Graphics Adapter or Hercules Color Card (or equivalent), and an RS-232C serial port for the mouse. PC Paint also works with the Logitech Logimouse.

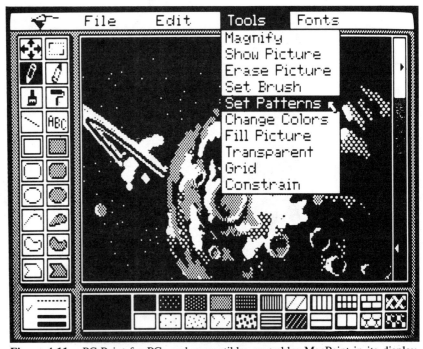

Figure 4-11. PC Paint for PCs and compatibles resembles MacPaint in its display and features.

The graphics resolution in PC Paint is 320 by 200 pixels (medium resolution for standard IBM graphics), with four colors. If you add an STB Graphix Plus II board to your PC you can increase the display to 16 colors.

PC Paint resembles MacPaint in the display it shows, with 44 fill patterns along the bottom edge of your screen. The top row of your screen shows File, Edit, Tools, and Fonts, which are four menus that you pull down with your mouse as you would on a Macintosh. The left margin of the screen displays icons for the various tools, and the bottom left corner contains a menu of line types (ranging from dashed to heavy). You can choose colors from a color bar running along the right margin of your screen (use the mouse to select colors as from a palette). The center area of the screen is the window in which you can "paint" images.

Painting tools include an electronic pencil, spraypaint, paintbrush, paint roller, text, lines, boxes, circles, ovals, polygons, and curved lines. You can choose patterns to fill objects, change your paintbrush width and paint, or change the pattern of the spraypaint in your spraycan. Use the eraser tool to cover up mistakes, but beware of double clicking your mouse when you have the eraser icon selected, unless you really do want to erase your entire image. Luckily, the Undo command, found in the Edit menu, can bring back the drawing, unless you erased it with the Erase Picture Command.

Other tools can be found in the pull down menus, such as a Grid that attracts elements to fixed points on a grid, useful for aligning objects or text. If you print the drawing with the grid displayed, the grid will be printed with the drawing, just as it appears on your screen.

PC Paint gives you a choice of five fonts for text, in three sizes: small, medium and large. Newer versions (after 2.5) of PC Paint, such as PC Paint Plus, let you import any of the over 110 fonts supplied with Fontrix (Data Transforms, $155). PC Paint Plus ($99) lets you adapt graphics from such other programs as Lotus 1-2-3.

When typing text into your PC Paint window, press Return to start a new line as you get close the the right margin of your window, or the text will continue out of sight past the right margin (MacPaint has this same characteristic, while MacDraw automatically wraps words to the next line if you type within a box). Select the icon that shows arrows pointing in four directions to move the edges of your drawing/text out from behind the window.

PC Paint prints your entire screen in an area that is 5½ by 8 inches.

PC Paint can't print part of your screen (selected items only), and if you want to print more than the screen area, after shifting the screen position several times and printing several versions of the image, you have to cut and paste them together by hand. PC Paint Plus lets you print a full page of graphics, and includes ready to use clip art images.

Use the Capture program to capture the medium-resolution graphics screens from other programs, such as Lotus 1-2-3, Symphony, Framework, SuperCalc3 and others. You can then bring the screens into PC Paint (they are converted to PC Paint's file format) for painting/fine tuning, and save the enhanced screens to disk and print them when you are ready. You can't convert the PC Paint screen into a form that the other programs can read; the conversion is one way.

PC Paint supports various dot matrix printers, including the IBM Graphics Printer, Epson dot matrix printers, and the Quadram QuadJet Ink Jet Printer. Color printers supported include the IBM Color Graphics Printer, the Epson JX-80, and the Tandy CGP-220 Color Ink Jet Printer.

PC Paintbrush

PC Paintbrush is a high-resolution "paint" program from IMSI (International Microcomputer Software Inc.) and costs $139, or $189 with the Logitech Mouse. The software is also bundled with the Summa-Sketch graphics tablet (Summagraphics) and the Summapad MM961 (6 by 9 inches) for $495.

The program requires a PC with at least 192K of RAM, a color or high-resolution monochrome monitor, and either the IBM Color/Graphics Adapter, the IBM EGA (Enhanced Graphics Adapter), or the Hercules Color Graphics Card or high-resolution monochrome card (or equivalent).

The main difference between PC Paint and PC Paintbrush is that PC Paintbrush offers more but is harder to learn how to use. PC Paintbrush offers more colors, higher-resolution graphics (but requires a more expensive high-resolution monitor), and works with digitizing pads, mice, joysticks and a touch screen.

PC Paintbrush tools are similar to those in PC Paint (paintbrush, spraycan, pencil, text, and line). However, PC Paintbrush does not have a polygon, curved line or rectangle with rounded corners (all found in PC Paint). PC Paintbrush has both an eraser (same as PC Paint), and a color eraser to selectively erase areas in the selected color.

When you start the program, you see a menu across the top of your screen with the Undo command and six other choices. Undo will undo any choice except Clear Screen. The other six menus are Page, Edit, Style, Size, Pick and Misc. To select choices from the Edit menu, you must have the scissors icon selected, and to select choices from the Pick menu, you select the icon of two rectangles (next to the scissors).

The icons of tools, including scissors, two rectangles, text, line, erasers, paintbrush, and others are displayed along the left margin of your screen. Ten line weights can be chosen from the line box in the bottom left corner, while the bottom row displays 32 patterns. You can edit the supplied patterns, and save your customized patterns to use in other drawings.

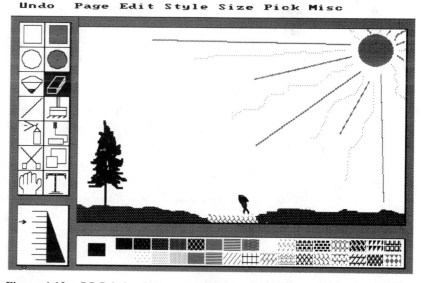

Figure 4-12. PC Paintbrush has more features and higher resolution, but requires more hardware.

PC Paintbrush offers effects similar to PC Paint: the ability to rotate selected areas of a drawing in 90 degree increments, flip selected images vertically and horizontally, and reverse colors. In addition, PC Paintbrush can tilt, shrink and grow images. Select an area of the screen to Shrink or Grow; use Tilt to attach a parallelogram to an area of a drawing (for a simple one-point perspective), then tilt it to a specified angle and fill it with a mirror image of the original.

You can Save images to disk, and use Edit to copy or move pictures or selected portions of pictures into files (give them names first with the Name Is option, or they overwrite the last file saved). You can then paste them into another image file. Move deletes the original image, while Copy makes a duplicate of the image.

PC Paintbrush has two levels of "fat bits:" you can zoom into a point on the screen and magnify the pixels so you can edit them, then zoom into that point and further magnify the pixels.

PC Paintbrush typefonts are created with vectors and fills, and eight styles are provided. Five bit-mapped fonts are also included. Vector (Stroke) fonts are best used in high-resolution mode, because they show jagged edges in lower resolutions, while bit-mapped fonts show jagged edges in both lower and higher resolutions. Bit-mapped fonts are best for medium resolution.

Font attributes include light, medium or boldface, and italic, underline, shadow and kerning. To size vector (Stroke) fonts, you can select from nine point sizes. You have four bit-mapped font scaling choices for adjusting height and width.

The program also has a "freeze" utility (called FRIEZE) that can capture text and graphics from other programs, such as Lotus 1-2-3, Microsoft Word, WordPerfect, SuperCalc3, DR Draw and even PC Paint, and convert the files for use with PC Paintbrush. The FRIEZE utility gives a choice of image sizes before you bring them into PC Paintbrush. Select an entire screen or part of the screen, and you can choose a height and width (up to 24 feet wide), plus you have a choice of printing sideways.

PC Paintbrush can print selected items, your screen, or the full image. The program supports various dot matrix and laser printers, including the IBM Graphics Printer, Epson dot matrix printers, and the H-P LaserJet laser printer. Color printers supported include the IBM Color Graphics Printer, the Epson JX-80, and the Tandy CGP-220 Color Ink Jet Printer.

Microsoft Windows Paint

Microsoft Windows Paint is included free with Microsoft Windows (Microsoft, $99), and lets you create, zoom in and improve, save and print artwork. Also included free with Windows is Microsoft Windows Write.

The top left of the Windows Paint screen is a display of the tool in use, selected line weight, brush shape, and paint pattern. Seven menus are labeled across the top lines of the display screen, and a Palette of tools stretches across the top lines of the screen. This type of display leaves your screen free from edge to edge, allowing a wider drawing window (although also vertically smaller) than other paint programs. The window you see on screen is just part of the complete "canvas," an area equal to the maximum printable dimensions of your printer.

Pull down the Palette menu to select brush shapes, patterns, and line weights. Select Tools from the palette menu to choose Paint's tools when they are concealed by another drawing window.

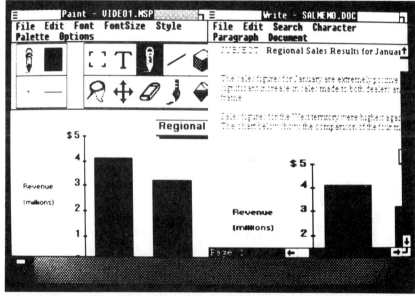

Figure 4-13. Microsoft Windows is a graphic environment for the PC XT and PC AT that includes a paint and draw program.

The menus are labeled (from left to right) File, Edit, Font, FontSize, Palette and Style. The Options menu is last. Tools include Zoom in and out, grid controls, and Edit Pattern (edit the current pattern).

When you save the image, the program saves the entire canvas to disk. Since the display is not a full page display, use the Scroll tool (icon of arrows in four directions) to move your window on the canvas to let you move your workspace (drawing window) around on the page (canvas).

An icon showing four right angles forming the corners of a box is the selection rectangle, used to enclose a portion of an image for editing. Once you select the area, the Edit commands let you cut, copy, invert, trace edges (of patterns, text and shapes), or flip the selected image horizontally or vertically. Other commands under the Edit menu include paste, erase, undo, and clear.

Tools include those already described (selection rectangle, text and scroll), plus pencil, brush, line, eraser, fill curve, airbrush, 3-D, and selection net (selects closer to dimensions of a non-square object than selection rectangle). Shapes let you draw boxes, rounded boxes, circles, ovals, polygons and freehand polygons.

Text can be typed when the text tool is selected, but once you click away from the text, or select another tool, you can't change the typefont, size or style again. You are limited in typefonts and sizes to those that have been installed on your system disk.

The Windows Utilities disk contains fonts you can download to your system disk. Helv, Courier and Tms Roman are bit-mapped (raster) fonts, and Roman, Modern and Script are "stroke" (vector) fonts. Add fonts using the control panel installation menu.

Raster fonts are used for the screen and dot matrix printers, and are in fixed sizes. Set 1 contains the stroke font, while Sets 2, 3, 4 and 5 are raster fonts. Set 2 was designed for a screen resolution of 640 by 200, which is the resolution of the IBM Color Graphics Adapter or compatible. Set 3 was designed for the higher-resolution (640 by 350) Hercules Graphics Card, and IBM Enhanced Graphics Adapter, also popular with near letter quality dot matrix printers. Set 4 was designed for printers with only 60 dots-per-inch resolution, and Set 5 was designed for printers with 120 dots-per-inch resolution.

You can select from styles that include plain, bold, italic, underline, outline and strikeout, and your text can be styled to align left, right or center. Opaque offers the standard solid white background for text, while Transparent lets the background pattern show through the text.

Paint graphics can be used by Cardfile, a standard Microsoft Windows desktop aid. Other Windows desktop aids are Notepad (text oriented), Terminal (software to connect your computer to a modem, for calling CompuServe, Dow/Jones or other computers), Calendar (with an alarm to remind you of appointments), Calculator, Clock and Reversi (a logic game that pits you against the computer).

GEM Paint and GEM Draw   GEM (Graphics Environment Manager) from Digital Research is a complete graphics-oriented operating system for PCs and compatibles (a version also runs in the Atari 520ST).

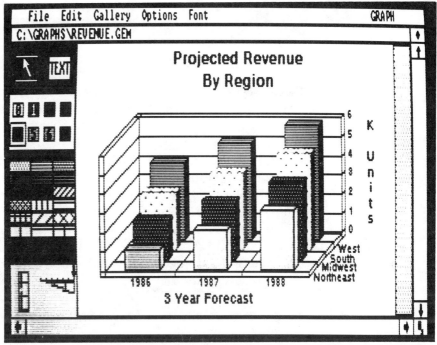

Figure 4-14. GEM Graph produces charts and graphs and runs in the GEM Desktop, which provides a Mac-like graphics environment on the PC XT and PC AT.

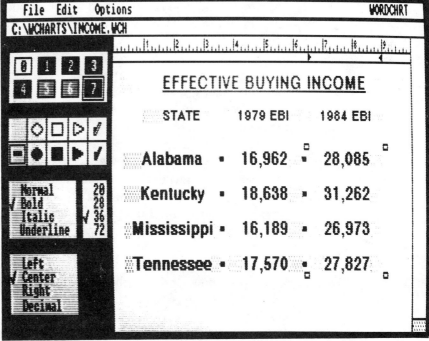

Figure 4-15. GEM Wordchart lets you mix typefonts, borders and tables.

The GEM Desktop ($50) provides a Macintosh-like desktop with mouse support, pull-down menus and icons for organizing files and directories. GEM Draw ($249) is a sophisticated drawing tool for CAD/CAM applications that runs on the GEM Desktop, and the GEM Collection ($199) includes GEM Paint (similar to PC Paint) and GEM Write (similar to Volkswriter, with the ability to merge text and graphics).

GEM Graph ($249) is also available for producing charts and graphs from spreadsheet data, and GEM Wordchart ($149) creates up to eight color "slides," single page documents with mixed typestyles and sizes, with border and table templates included for use.

Charts and Graphs

There are numerous chart and graph-making programs for PCs. The super-spreadsheet programs (Lotus 1-2-3, Symphony, and SuperCalc 3) all produce charts and graphs from spreadsheet data. You can use various utilities with the H-P LaserJet (such as Lasercontrol 100, described in Chapter 3) to get better output on a LaserJet than the spreadsheet can produce by itself.

Graphwriter (Graphics Communications, Inc., $595) is a professional chart and graph maker for PCs that requires only 192K of RAM. Charts and graphs can be sent to your monitor, plotter, LaserJet printer or Polaroid Palette Computer Image Recorder to produce 35mm slides.

The program comes in two versions: the "basic set" has general chart types, such as horizontal bar and vertical column charts, pie charts, line graphs, scatter plots and text-chart formats. The "extension set" includes Gantt charts, organizational charts, bubble charts and nine specialized charts.

The program offers a variety of typefonts in several sizes, and you can change both the color and the location of words on a chart. You can rotate pie segments and change labels accordingly, expand or compress bars in a bar or column chart, and fill bars or columns with color or a crosshatching pattern. You can also set up a combination of chart types, such as a bar chart with a line graph, or a bar chart with a pie chart.

Graphwriter can import spreadsheet data from DIF and SYLK data files (used by popular spreadsheet programs). The program provides more graphic features that make it useful to spreadsheet programs like Lotus 1-2-3.

Page formats can be either horizontal or vertical, and a page can contain more than one chart. You can print charts on plain or glossy paper or on projection transparencies.

Graphwriter supports various plotters and dot matrix printers including Epson, IBM Graphics Printer and Okidata 82 with Okigraph. The program also supports the H-P LaserJet.

Microsoft has a version of Chart for the PC ($250) that has nearly all of the features of Chart for the Macintosh (described with Macintosh graphics in this chapter). Microsoft Chart for the PC requires 128K of RAM and a graphics card with monitor. The PC version includes high-low charts similar to the ones used to show stock market activity. All of the features of the Macintosh version are present in the PC version.

Digitizers

Digitizers (also called scanners) let you record a video image from a camera in digital form for use in a computer. They are based on image processing technology, which dates back to the early 1960s, when NASA converted video images, beamed down from Ranger 7 on the lunar surface, into digital form in order to remove distortions with a computer program. Image processing basically involves converting a video signal into digital form (a process known as "digitizing"), then processing it through various circuits and computer programs to clear up the image.

Image processing systems have been traditionally priced at tens or hundreds of thousands of dollars and have been designed for applications such as medical CAT scanners and analysis of spy satellite imagery. But in late 1984, several companies introduced low-cost digitizers for the Macintosh and PC, making this technology accessible to the rest of us.

Basically, digitizers are peripherals that connect to the serial port of a Macintosh or PC (there are specific digitizers for Macintosh computers and PCs). They either read a video "frame" (one complete television screen image) from a video camera, or they can read documents or materials placed on a flatbed scanner that looks like a copy machine, or fed through a slot and scanned line by line as the page scrolls past a platen (such as ThunderScan for the Macintosh, which uses the ImageWriter printer as a scan device). The digitizer converts the image to data that can be fed into the computer for display and for saving on disk. This data is in the form of numbers representing the brightness of each pixel (picture element, or dot on the screen, representing a point on the image). They are typically two- or three-bit numbers representing four or eight levels of gray, respectively.

This data is then converted to an screen image that simulates shades of gray, corresponding to the brightness of small areas of the image. The most common type of program for this purpose is "dithering," which creates geometric patterns based on the average brightness level of a group of pixels.

Digitizers are fun to play with, and the applications for today's models range from image data bases (for example, a realtor's data base of homes for sale, with images of the homes that can be displayed on the screen and printed) to security checks (digitizing signatures or faces for use on badges) to newsletter, book and magazine graphics.

Are digitized images as good as photographic images reproduced through conventional methods? A halftone (photograph screened for printing, described in Chapter 6) has a resolution of 85 dots per inch. However, halftone dots come in infinitely varying sizes (10% of a dot, 20% of a dot, etc.). Laser printers can print at 300 dots per inch, but these dots are fixed in size. If your eye can distinguish forty different shades of gray in a screened-print halftone (40 different sizes of dots packed in, 85 to the inch), then you are actually able to see 3400 dots per linear inch, compared to the laser printer's 300. Even if you use the best typesetter and the highest-resolution computer graphic software available to date, your digitized image will not match the quality of a photographic screened print. However, digitizer technology is rapidly advancing into this area.

The true value of digitizing is in preserving with accuracy drawings, blueprints and sensitive documents. The Smithsonian's Air and Space Museum is using a Datacopy digitizer with PCs to archive many thousands of sensitive documents that will eventually decay and be lost. The digitized images, however, last much longer than paper,and they are more accurate than hand-drawn images and less expensive than halftones or photostats. The Smithsonian started digitizing in 1984, and they had scanned close to 60,000 documents as of the end of 1985, but they are not even half done.

Engineers and architects can use digitizers to store drawings and 3D models, use graphic editing software to modify them without expensive redrawing, and send them to clients or other offices via modem and telephone as an alternative to postal carrier services.

Graphic artists and designers can build an "electronic portfolio" of illustrations for magazine and advertising layouts, newsletters, story boards, presentations, technical publications and so on, combining images from renditions, real-world objects, "clip art" and video tape. Illustrations can be quickly sent to clients via modem for fast review and for changes to meet tight advertising and boardroom deadlines, for example.

Real estate developers can store existing maps and modify only small sections, instead of redrawing the entire map. Maps can include digitized photographs of houses, office buildings, parks, and other features that would have been prohibitively costly to include previously. They can then include these images in promotional mailings, newsletters, ads, and other materials.

You'll want to use a hard disk for any serious work with the scanner, since one image can generate a lot of data (one image can use up 512K of disk space after it's compressed, depending on the resolution and data storage method of your scanner and its software).

For the Macintosh MacPaint (Apple Computer, $125) is well suited for editing the pixels of black-and-white images, and the LaserWriter (and any other PostScript-driven laser printer) can provide the best resolution of all the laser printers for black-and-white images. Manufacturers realizing this potential have introduced low-cost image digitizers for the Mac.

It seems only natural to be able to scan a photograph or illustration and bring it into MacPaint. The two most popular digitizers are Mac-Vision and ThunderScan.

Koala's $399 MacVision includes a box that connects between a video camera or videocassette recorder and the Macintosh serial port and software that operates as a desk accessory. Select "Camera" on the menu, adjust the brightness and contrast, and copy the image (using "copy" from the Edit menu). Then you can paste the image into any Macintosh document or touch it up with MacPaint.

MacVision is easy to use, but limited in resolution (320 x 240 dots, compared to the Mac's full 512 x 342 capacity). Another problem with MacVision (and most other video digitizers) is that the video image must be stationary, which means asking people to stand still for up to 18 seconds. This puts video digitizers in the category of primitive cameras of the early 1900s. For the same reason, videocassette recorders must be freeze-framed, complicating things and reducing image quality.

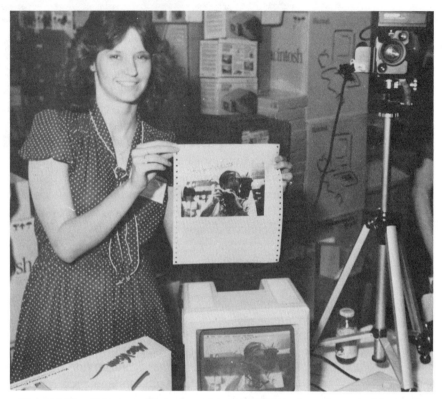

Figure 4-16.   Using any video camera (shown at right) or recorder, and a Macintosh, you can digitize images with MacVision.

Figure 4-17.   This image was digitized with MacVision, printed on an Apple ImageWriter, and reduced to 50% of actual size.

Another problem with video digitizers is that the geometric patterns created by dithering are annoyingly visible, turning a perfectly fine nose into a jungle of vines, for example. Other digitizers use a variable-density dot system to display brightness, creating areas with obvious jumps in gray tones.

If you want a high-quality image, you should look at Thunderware's $229 ThunderScan. Created by Macintosh guru Andy Hertzfeld, ThunderScan is an optical scanning cartridge that replaces your ImageWriter printer ribbon cartridge.

Plug the ThunderScan cartridge into a standard or wide-carriage ImageWriter, feed the picture to be scanned into the printer, and ThunderScan creates an amazingly high-quality image on the Macintosh screen. You can get even higher quality when you print out the image on the LaserWriter if you pass it through the Laser Tools program from Knowledge Engineering, which can reduce the image before printing for higher resolution (Laser Tools is available with JustText, described in Chapter 7).

While the ThunderScan is very simple to use and produces high-quality images, it has some limitations: it only accepts whatever can

Figure 4-18. ThunderScan attaches to an ImageWriter printer and produces high-quality digitized images on the Mac. This image was saved as a MacPaint document, placed into a PageMaker document, reduced and printed on an Apple LaserWriter.

fit into the ImageWriter printer and it takes a long time to digitize each picture: up to 15 minutes or more.

MacViz (Microvision Company, $299) overcomes some of these problems. MacViz lets you display, archive, manipulate, and telecommunicate images from any standard video source to a Macintosh computer, without requiring stationary images.

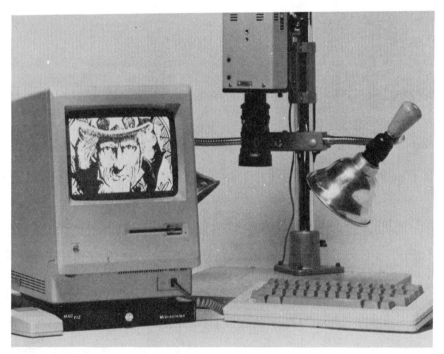

Figure 4-19. The MacViz digitizer accepts images from several video sources without requiring stationary images.

MacViz includes a small box that fits under a Macintosh computer and connects to any standard video source — TV camera, TV monitor, or videocassette recorder, or any TV set with a video output. You point the camera at the object, focus it, set the contrast on MacViz for the best picture, and click the mouse to take the picture.

MacViz creates high-resolution pictures with 512 x 512 dots, which is larger than the Macintosh screen (you scroll down to see it all). The digitizer uses a "spray paint" technique to create a wide range of shades of gray using dots instead of obvious geometric patterns and visible gray-scale steps.

Data sent to the computer consists of only one black or white bit. MacViz creates an image on the Macintosh screen in which darker areas are represented with denser random dots and lighter areas by less-dense random dots or no dots. You can fine-tune the contrast of each image with a knob on MacViz and by selecting one of three contrast modes from a screen menu.

Seen at a distance or reduced, images created by the MacViz on the Macintosh screen, ImageWriter printer or LaserWriter printer are slightly closer to photographic quality, and can be photocopied with virtually no loss of image quality.

MacViz also simplifies the process of taking a picture. Unlike other video digitizers that require complex adjustments and an external TV monitor, MacViz has one simple knob for adjusting brightness and contrast. MacViz uses the full Macintosh screen itself, rather than an external TV monitor, to provide an equivalent WYSIWYG ("what you see is what you get") display of the image.

The MacViz creates images in MacPaint file format so that you can touch up the image, cut and paste it into other images or into Mac-Write or Word documents, or transmit it via modem to other Macintosh computers. Approximately 16-20 images (depending on image complexity) can be stored on a standard 400K Macintosh disk (assuming no other files are on it), or you can store 400 to 450 images on a 10 megabyte hard disk.

Another way to get images into a Mac is a flat document scanner. This device uses a laser beam and a photosensitive device to scan images, outputting a signal. SpectraFAX Corporation (formerly Laser-FAX Inc.) offers the SpectraFAX 200 Digital Photocopier ($3995), which scans photographs and art work into a 512K Macintosh or a Mac Plus (there is also a PC version available, described next in the PC digitizer section). Using software developed by SoftStyle and included with the scanner, you can input color images to Colormate files or black-and-white images to MacPaint files (Colormate is described later in this chapter).

SpectraFAX's scanner is essentially a "digital photocopier" that looks and works like a regular photocopier. You put the art work or photo on top (you can scan books and other solid objects) of the glass plate, lay the cover on top of the object, and control the scanner with a pull-down menu on a special version of Colormate, which is bundled with the scanner, or Colormate II.

You can edit the scanned images with Colormate or Colormate II and print them on the ImageWriter II or NEC color Pinwriter printers, in full color. You can also print in black-and-white on any other printer the Macintosh can connect to. Using the Clipboard, you can "clip" and move the images (in black-and-white form) to other applications.

Also included with the SpectraFAX scanner is PaintScan, which lets you scan black-and-white images directly into MacPaint at 72 dots per inch (the full MacPaint resolution), without smoothing.

Several image management programs are available for the Macintosh that let you manage images as records in a data base, along with text and numbers. Filevision (Telos Software Products, $195) lets you store and manage images in records with a short text description of each image. Microsoft File ($195) is another data base manager that stores pictures, text and numbers on the Macintosh.

For PCs and Compatibles
Two relatively low cost digitizers are now available for PCs and compatible computers: the Datacopy Model 730 (which includes the ability to scan text as well as graphic images) and the PC Scan from Dest Corp.

The Datacopy Model 730 desktop scanner (300 dots-per-inch resolution) comes with an interface "half" card for your PC and the WIPS text and image processing software ($4950). The Model 720 (200 dots per inch) also comes with a card and WIPS ($3950). With both models you can add the CIR character recognition software described in Chapter 2.

Either scanner requires 640K of RAM in your PC and a Hercules monochrome graphics card (for high-resolution displays). The Model 720 and 730 support 64 shades of gray, which is adequate for most applications. The more expensive Model 920 supports 256 shades of gray (the Smithsonian is using the Model 920 and Fastore system, described below, to scan archives of airplane designs, among other things).

WIPS is a "shell" over PC-DOS that lets you control the scanner, and save and load images to disk. You can overlay several images, then save the composite as one image.

Two utility programs are included which run independently of WIPS. Imprint merges word processed text with images to print to an Epson printer, H-P LaserJet or QMS laser printer. You can embed graphics commands in your text file using your favorite word processing program.

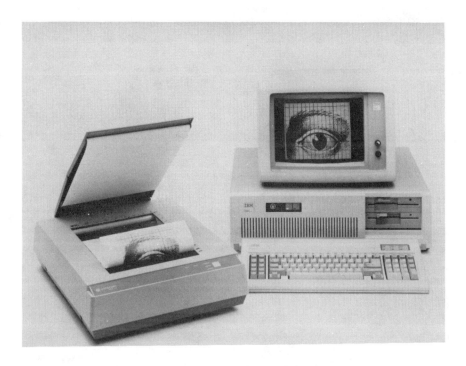

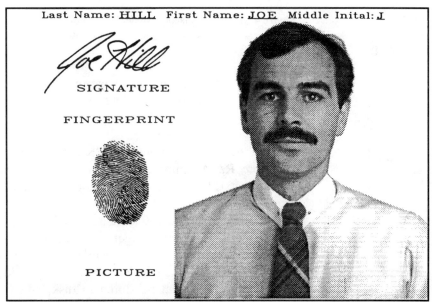

Figure 4-20. The Datacopy Model 730 document scanner for PCs and compatibles can digitize and edit graphic images and photos, and scan text into text files.

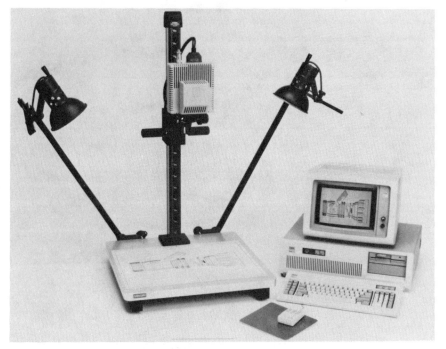

Figure 4-21.   The Datacopy Model 920 can digitize an image of a three-dimensional object and reproduce 256 shades of gray.

Preview lets you view an image on the high-resolution monitor to check if it fits in your document text (while in your word processing program). You can then "Release" the image from the document, and rescale the graphics to fit.

WIPS needs a minimum of 512K RAM on an IBM PC XT or AT, but more RAM improves performance by speeding up operations. With only 512K available, the computer quickly fills up and runs out of memory.

The Model 720 and 730 store a single bit per pixel. The Model 900 stores eight bits per pixel to get 256 gray levels. The Model 730 scans at 300 dots-per-inch resolution, while the Model 900 varies in resolution — the dots per inch depend on the camera and focal length.

Gray scale data can be stored to disk, where a programmer can manipulate the data. The model 730 has 4 bits of gray scale, and the Model 720 has 2 bits. Both models can scan a document in 30 seconds. Images are scanned in either a "threshold" mode (where each picture element is converted to black or white — good for line art and text) or a "halftone" mode (dot patterns simulate shades of gray).

WIPS (Word Image Processing System) provides image manipulation functions such as scaling and rotation. You can zoom into an image, selectively erase portions by filling with white or black, and invert portions from black to white or white to black. You can also choose to employ a data compression technique to store images, using less disk space. The desktop scanners are designed to be shared in an office environment. The WIPS software can save your scan settings so that you can retrieve them easily.

Datacopy is in the business of providing high-end digitizing equipment as well as scanners for PCs. Datacopy's Fastore system includes a camera mounted above an image table for recording three-dimensional objects, a 200 dots-per-inch full page display system (screen and controller box), and software to connect to your PC, all for $44,500. Other interfaces available include those required to use the Intel Multibus, Sun Microsystems, Apollo Computers, and Digital Equipment Corp. MicroVAX systems.

The PC Scan (Dest Corp., $1995) is a compact page scanner that digitizes images, and with the optional Text Pac software ($595) scans text on pages into text files.

The PC Scan digitizes images with 300 dots-per-inch resolution and scans a page of text in 25 seconds. The software can save the text in various word processing formats, including WordStar and MultiMate. Text Pac inserts tabs, centered text, underscored text and end of page codes in the text file as if they were typed at the keyboard.

The scanner scans one sheet at a time. Pages placed right side up emerge face down to be in the right sequence for multiple-page documents. An automatic video threshold feature adjusts the scanning contrast to accommodate variance in paper color.

The PC Scan can be connected to any PC, PC XT, PC AT or compatible through a SCSI interface, and requires no extra hardware.

SpectraFAX Corporation (formerly LaserFAX Inc.) offers the SpectraFAX 200 digital photocopier ($3995) for the IBM PC and compatibles. The SpectraFAX digital photocopier scans photographs, art work, and text. Documents up to 8½ x 14 inches can be scanned in black-and-white or color and can then be manipulated using the graphics editing software that comes bundled with the machine.

You can print out images on dot matrix or laser printers and other devices. You can also print in color, using ink-jet, dot matrix, or thermal-transfer devices.

The SpectraFAX scanner features an open-architecture design, so third-party companies can add new functions to the scanner by adding boards. SpectraFAX offers two boards: one for optical character recognition (OCR), and one for facsimile.

The TEXreader OCR board ($995) does optical character recognition on scanned documents, converting them into ASCII text files. It is capable of recognizing eight fonts and learning additional ones.

The SpectraFAXimile board ($1995) converts the scanner into a Group II or III facsimile machine, allowing offices to transmit and receive images via voice-grade telephone lines to the large installed base of Group II and III facsimile machines. A 9600-baud asynchronous modem is built in, allowing the scanner to function as a standalone modem for phone line communication or for direct connection to micros, minis, and mainframes.

Working with Color

PCs and compatibles can display colors, depending on the type of color graphics card you use. All of the PC "paint" programs described in this chapter can produce color images you can print on color ink jet printers, but the quality is not good enough for magazines and books.

To produce color images conventionally, you have a *color separation* performed, where four pieces of film are produced to use with the four basic printing press inks: cyan, magenta, yellow, and black. The conventional way to get a color-separated image from the computer screen is to photograph the screen with color film and have it color-separated by a graphics house; it usually costs from $200 to $500 or more for each image.

Now there are several inexpensive ways to get separated color images. Even artists using the Macintosh (which can only draw in black-and-white) can produce reproduction-quality prints directly from the LaserWriter or Linotronic typesetter. You can start with a black-and-white image, and make several copies of the image quickly — both "positive" (as the image was created) and "negative" (reversed — white becomes black, black becomes white). Then you can eliminate certain graphic elements from each copy so that each copy can be used to make a registered, color-separated plate, and specify a process color percentage for each copy. The result would be a series of Macintosh screen drawings, each an exact duplicate of the original with only certain elements missing (the ones that are not in the process color specified for that copy). Make final corrections from a color proof.

Another way to add color to a black-and-white Macintosh image is by producing a reproduction-quality print from the Linotronic (or LaserWriter), then using dyes to color the output.

There are services starting to offer "digital color separations" from a graphic image stored in a PC or Macintosh disk file. ImageSet (San Francisco, CA) can take images from a variety of computers, including PCs, Macs, Apple // models, Atari 520ST and the Commodore Amiga. Their clients (computer magazines, book companies, software houses and hardware houses) want to show computer images in print.

ImageSet wrote an image-capturing program for the PC called IM-CAP and put it in public domain libraries (distributed free by user groups). The program captures the screen image and writes it to a disk file. Another program called IMSHOW displays the image again.

The Macintosh has a built-in function (Command-Shift-3) to capture a screen to a disk file. For Commodore Amiga images, ImageSet can take GraphicCraft files (the paint program for the Amiga).

ImageSet sends the black-and-white disk images to a typesetter and the color images through a digital separation process that breaks the image into the component four-colors for four-color printing.

The digital separation process does not enhance the resolution of the image — it matches the resolution of the original image. The Allied Linotype Linotronic 100 and 300 typesetters enhance the PostScript images generated by Macintosh computers and PCs (through PC MacBridge or PostScript driver for an application program).

For MacPaint images, ImageSet has a special procedure for black-and-white images that are to be converted into color. You supply ImageSet with a disk containing a MacPaint image broken out into the component colors, each color in a separate MacPaint file with a descriptive title telling ImageSet which process color to use for that part of the image. ImageSet merges the separate files into color tints. Each color can be proofed on the LaserWriter in black-and-white and printed on a transparency to compare it to the other images. ImageSet adds/subtracts appropriate color tints to produce four pieces of film corresponding to the four printing colors (cyan, magenta, yellow and black).

Color printers are getting better at producing quality color images. For example Fuji has an ink jet printer that produces two by three foot color posters that are not as good as four-color printing, but good enough for a short-run poster or one-time use as a poster.

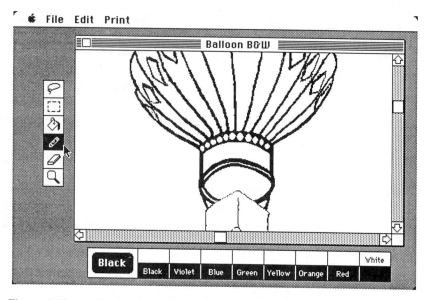

Figure 4-22. A Macintosh graphic before coloring it with Colormate. The icons represent tools for adding color to images.

Colormate and Colormate II

One low-cost way to print in color with the Macintosh is with Apple's ImageWriter II printer, using SoftStyle's Colormate program ($125). Colormate lets you color and print pictures or text created by Mac-Paint, MacWrite, MacDraw, and other Macintosh software. You can then print on the ImageWriter II printer or on the NEC color Pinwriter printer, using eight colors — violet, blue, green, yellow, orange, red, black, and white.

Colormate provides on-screen tools to "colorize" images and text. Working like similar tools in MacPaint, the Lasso and Selection Rectangle let you color an irregular object or one contained in a selected rectangle, and the Paint Bucket lets you fill a foreground or background area in any color. You can use the Eraser to erase any part of the image, or the Crayon to sketch freehand or do precise touchup work in any color.

Colormate also has tools completely new to MacPaint users. The ColorBits command lets you designate colors of specific pixels, similar to what MacPaint's FatBits option does with black-and-white pixels.

The Magnifying Glass lets you examine an area or even a dot to see which color it will be printed in (the color is indicated by a letter or a black or white square). The eight Display Selection Blocks emulate color filters on a camera, identifying all appearances of one or more selected colors on the screen.

Colormate also lets you create additional colors by mixing ("dithering") the original eight colors on MacPaint patterns. Colormate users can directly open full-size MacPaint documents, color them, and print full-color in a single pass.

You can copy to the Clipboard black-and-white images from another application's document (created by Microsoft Chart or Mac-Write, for example) into Colormate for coloring. You might find Colormate handy for color-coding a document or highlighting words for emphasis.

You can also use Colormate to create four-color separations — one for each color of ink used in the printing process: cyan, magenta, yellow, and black. Normally this is very expensive, costing hundreds of dollars when done using digital color separation services.

Colormate can help you prepare "digital" color separations. First, put registration marks in the four corners of your image. Then use the Colormate Display Selection Blocks as color filters. To create the "cyan" separation, turn off all colors in the image except blue, violet, and green and print out the screen in black. For magenta, keep red, orange, and violet. For yellow, keep green, yellow, and orange. And for black, just keep black. These four images — all printed in black — go to the printer for printing.

You can use any dot matrix printer that works with the Macintosh, including the NEC color Pinwriter or Apple ImageWriter II. But for better results with alignment between the four colors and a crisper image, a LaserWriter is better.

SoftStyle's Colormate II takes color images a step further. The program is like a full-color MacPaint, with all of the standard Mac-Paint tools plus the Colormate tools. Colormate II is the ultimate tool for creating color separations on the Macintosh. The program automatically separates out the four process colors and prints out four images, complete with automatic registration marks and identification of the four separations.

Colormate II is also designed to work with the SpectraFAX 200scanner (Mac) to produce color separations in one fast operation, using Colormate II to preview the colors and touch them up before going into the expensive printing process. Essentially Colormate II functions as a set of "color filters," similar to how the cameras that create expensive color separations work.

Colormate II also stores its images at the full 200 dots-per-inch scanner density (in addition to a 72 dots-per-inch version for presentation on the Macintosh screen). Images created with Colormate II will print at full 200 dots per inch on black-and-white laser or dot matrix printers, and on color ink jet and color laser printers, as they become available for the Macintosh.

Other applications of Colormate II are to create color comps (used by ad agencies to preview color ads for clients), color illustrations, and presentation graphics. You can import a scanned image into Colormate II, or you can import black-and-white images from MacPaint and then add color. Then you can print out the results on an ImageWriter II and feed the resulting color print into a color Xerox machine for instant conversion to a color overhead transparency.

You can use Printworks for the Mac ($75 from SoftStyle) to supplement Colormate for color printing with"object-oriented" drawing, drafting, and charting applications. These are applications, like Mac-Draw, that store graphics mathematically instead of as pixels (bit-mapped dots), allowing you to enlarge or reduce the image without losing resolution and to print at higher resolution. Printworks for the Mac creates color documents by converting patterns (such as crosshatches) you've used in MacDraw, Chart, Excel, Jazz, MacDraft, MacPublisher, MacPublisher II, MacAuthor — and any other application that creates patterns — into eight colors on the ImageWriter II.

Printworks for the Mac installs as a desk accessory in your application and lets you assign a specific pattern to each color. After that, color printing is automatic. While you'd normally use Colormate for converting MacPaint images to color, you can also use Printworks for the Mac to print an image entirely in one color.

Printworks for the Mac also lets you do something previously impossible on the ImageWriter II: combine near-letter-quality (NLQ) printing and graphics (in black or white or color) on the same page. The problem in doing this previously was that NLQ printing — which uses the ImageWriter II's built-in fonts — requires draft mode, while graphics can only be printed in standard or high printing modes. Printworks for the Mac manages to get around that.

Printworks for the Mac comes with five fonts in standard sizes that exactly match the ImageWriter II's NLQ text printing fonts. If you use these fonts, you'll avoid the frustrating irregular spacing you get when you use draft mode.

Printworks for the Mac also lets you do simultaneous background printing of a file in standard or high modes from most applications, except MacPaint.

You can create art with some of these painting and drawing programs, but most users will want to create graphics for use with text in documents. You can print graphics separately and hand-paste them into documents, but the new page makeup programs available for Macs and PCs (described in the next chapter) make hand-pasteup obsolete — you can mix already-created and saved graphic images with text on electronic pages, and in some cases change the sizes of the graphic images to fit the page specifications. You can then use the page makeup program to print the entire page, including graphics.

CHAPTER FIVE

Page Makeup

You shall see them on a beautiful quarto page, where a neat rivulet of text shall meander through a meadow of margin.

— Richard Brinsley Sheridan

Overview   Page makeup on the screen is a vast improvement over manual paste-up. It may take you the same amount of time to create a page layout electronically as it does manually, but it takes far less time to *change* an electronic layout. With manual paste-up, changes are harder to make, and you have to separate layout and paste-up into two steps, using copies of the real typesetting galleys for layout, and the galleys for final paste-up.

On-screen page makeup means no more galleys, no more missing scraps of text, no more use of noxious chemical sprays, and no more cutting with knives and pasting with glue or wax. Final pages roll off the printer or typesetting machine ready to be sent to the print shop.

Although the programs are easy to use, page makeup on personal computers does not automatically turn users into designers or artists. It takes training and experience to build design skills, and good design is as necessary for effective communication as good illustrations and art. The role of the artist and designer is to use the personal computer tools to produce roughs and layouts, and let their clients experiment with them to get what they want. The final camera-ready can be prepared by the client or the artist or designer without having to spend a lot of money on typesetting and manual paste-up.

Programs that do page makeup on the Macintosh have been available since early 1985. They have been extensively revised and purged of bugs, and are perhaps the most reliable programs for personal computer page makeup.

PageMaker from Aldus Corp. ($495) is regarded as the first true page makeup program for the Macintosh that could handle more than two pages at a time. A less expensive package for the Macintosh is ReadySetGo (2.0) from Manhattan Graphics ($195). MacPublisher ($99) from Boston Software Publishers was the first page makeup program, and its low price compensates for its limitations — it can be useful for many applications, but does not provide as much flexibility or control as PageMaker, which costs more than three times as much. MacPublisher II ($145) provides more flexibility and control.

Unlike the programs for the Macintosh, page makeup programs for PCs and compatibles range from the super-sophisticated and expensive (SuperPage from BestInfo for $7000, described in Chapter 7) to the simple, effective and inexpensive (Personal Publisher from T/Maker for $185 for the ImageWriter version, $335 for Laser-Writer/LaserJet version). Aldus is developing a version of PageMaker for the PC AT and PC XT that works with Microsoft Windows and provides almost exactly the same type of system as a Macintosh, with icons and pull-down menus. Ventura Publisher (Ventura Software, $695), which runs on the PC XT and PC AT, is the mid-range program that provides sophisticated features but is less expensive than Superpage and other professional packages.

There is more of a shakeout in the PC area of the market — inexpensive page makeup programs are being introduced that challenge the professional page makeup systems. We describe the new inexpensive packages in this chapter, and reserve discussion of the professional packages to Chapter 7; this way you can get a little background in typography and design (Chapter 6) before reading about super-sophisticated typographic and design features.

Merging Text and Graphics   Most of the page makeup programs accept text characteristics (typefonts and tabs) from word processing programs, and all of them accept unformatted ASCII text as saved from programs like Microsoft Word, or as converted by programs (like UNWS for WordStar files) for filtering control characters. Some programs, like PageMaker, accept text characteristics from Microsoft Word files; for example, PageMaker accepts and uses any tabs, typefont settings and soft hyphens already in Word files.

All of the page makeup programs let you type text directly onto the page as displayed. However, with the exception of JustText, the page makeup programs do not have typical word processing functions, such as the ability to find text and substitute new text, or save the text to a file that can be used with other word processing programs.

Of the page makeup programs that allow text editing, only Ventura Publisher transfers the text changes you make to the original text file. In almost every other program you can make text changes on pages, but the changes are not transferable to the original text files. The preferred method in these cases is to make the text change in the original file and restart your page makeup operation with the newly-changed text file.

You can put graphics on the page with Macintosh page makeup programs by using the Mac's Clipboard and Scrapbook, or directly from MacPaint or MacDraw "PICT" files. Most sources for Macintosh clip art supply the art as Macintosh MacPaint files. For example, T/Maker Graphics publishes ClickArt (a collection of clip art images you can use in your documents) — each ClickArt image is a separate piece stored in a MacPaint file. You can copy the file and make alterations as you please. CompuServe also publishes clip art in the public domain — all you need is a modem and communications software (described in Chapter 2), and you can download free graphics to your Macintosh.

You can use graphics with some PC page makeup programs that can read PC Paint files. Other programs cannot place graphics on the page with text, but you can draw rules to define empty areas, or draw empty boxes for areas where you can place graphic images by hand. T/Maker's Personal Publisher, which runs on a PC, has a special function for reading Macintosh "PICT" files into a PC for use with Personal Publisher. You can dial CompuServe with a modem and a PC and receive Macintosh clip art for use with Personal Publisher, or connect a Macintosh directly to your PC and transfer the graphic files.

Most page makeup programs let you enlarge or reduce graphic images and keep the aspect ratio intact so that images look the same. Some let you crop images — keep only the portion within an imaginary rectangular frame. Some let you compress and expand images as well as enlarge and reduce them, so that as the aspect ratio changes, the image is distorted into a new image. All of the page makeup programs let you use a mouse to position text and graphic images.

All of the page makeup programs have ways to "wrap" text around graphic images. The page makeup programs are designed to be easy to use for laying out pages with graphics and text, because this merging of text and graphics is a function that doesn't work too well in word processing programs or in paint/draw programs. It is easier to develop text and graphics separately, store them in separate files, and merge the finished text and graphic images on a page, using a page makeup program.

Typesetting Features   The page makeup programs are mostly WYSIWYG (What You See on the screen Is What You Get on paper). A WYSIWYG program makes it an easy task to do page makeup for newsletters, advertising and marketing literature, and even some books. However, for professional magazine, newspaper or book production, two essential ingredients are mostly missing from WYSIWYG programs: automatic pagination, automatic hyphenation, kerning, and other advanced typesetting features.

JustText (described in Chapter 7), with its non-WYSIWYG approach, provides automatic hyphenation and pagination, kerning, and most of the advanced typesetting features. Ventura Publisher also provides automatic hyphenation and pagination, and kerning, but in a WYSIWYG format that is easier to use. *Kerning* is the process of moving letters closer together to improve their appearance. We explain kerning and other typographical concepts in Chapter 6.

The page makeup programs described in this chapter have limited typesetting features but are easy to use. The typesetting parameters — typefont point size, leading, automatic kerning, interword spacing and others — are preset to default settings in page makeup programs so that you don't have to learn about typography to get your newsletter published. For many desktop publishing applications, these features are enough, but for those applications requiring more control over the typesetting, one of the more expensive programs in Chapter 7 may be the right choice.

Page Makeup on the Macintosh   There is more desktop publishing software available at this time for Macintosh computers than for any other. This is largely due to the design of the Macintosh and its system software. The Macintosh has a high-resolution screen, icons and pull-down menus, built-in screen and laser printer typefonts, and support for a mouse, a digitizer, and a graphics tablet.

The built-in support makes it easier and faster for software publishers to provide such features in their application programs. This is why PageMaker — which produces typeset pages after showing you the pages on the screen and letting you edit them — came out first on the Macintosh. You have to buy extra hardware (high-resolution monitor, graphics cards, mouse and extra memory) to get the equivalent features on an IBM PC or compatible computer.

All of the Macintosh page makeup programs accept text from either Microsoft Word or MacWrite (except MacPublisher, which accepts text only from MacWrite). You can specify the typefonts and type sizes in the page makeup programs if you want, or you can specify some of them (such as italic and bold words, and tab spaces for tables of numbers) in MacWrite or Microsoft Word and carry them over to the page makeup program.

Most of the page makeup programs accept text characteristics (typefonts and tabs) from MacWrite, and all accept unformatted ASCII text as saved from Microsoft Word and other word processing programs. Many also accept text characteristics from Microsoft Word files; for example, PageMaker accepts and uses any tabs, typefont settings and soft hyphens in Word files.

Page Makeup on the PC XT/AT

Neither the IBM PC nor the PC XT displays high-resolution graphics without a high-resolution monochrome monitor and a graphics card. The IBM PC AT displays high-resolution graphics without an additional card or monitor, and most AT compatibles do the same. Some PC XT compatibles display high-resolution graphics because the high-resolution monitor and graphics card are either supplied with the machine or built into the machine.

To run most page makeup programs on a PC XT, you need a high-resolution monitor plus a Hercules or compatible monochrome graphics card. Most of the page makeup programs also require 640K of internal memory in your PC XT. The hardware configuration (Hercules graphics, hi-res monochrome monitor, and 640K) is usually more expensive than your typical Macintosh setup (unless you can find this hardware at bargain basement prices, but watch out — full Hercules compatibility is not always present in the bargain basement graphics cards).

You may not want to go this route for two reasons: cost is higher than the Macintosh setup, and you may not need a WYSIWYG (what you see is what you get) program to do desktop publishing. You can get excellent results using a low cost laser printer and word processing program equipped with the appropriate driver for the laser printer, as described in Chapters 2 and 3. However, you will not be able to merge text and graphics on the screen before printing.

There are three excellent page makeup programs for the IBM PC that provide page makeup facilities comparable to the Mac setup: Personal Publisher (T/Maker Graphics, $185), the PC version of Page-Maker (Aldus Corp.), and Ventura Publisher (Ventura Software, $695).

Personal Publisher is the least expensive of the three, and it requires only a PC XT with 384K, IBM Color Card/EGA compatible and a hard disk. Ventura Publisher is also inexpensive compared to professional packages described in Chapter 7; however, it does require more hardware (Hercules-compatible Monochrome Card). Ventura Publisher offers more features and a better display, and it works within the familiar GEM (Graphics Environment Manager, Digital Research) system for PCs. PageMaker works within the rival Microsoft Windows environment and looks very much like the Macintosh version (described in the previous chapter).

In this chapter we show you how page makeup is performed, using PageMaker as an example. Then we describe the salient features of other page makeup programs.

PageMaker (Macintosh, PC AT or XT)

The Macintosh version of PageMaker (Aldus Corp.) requires a 512K Macintosh or Macintosh Plus, with two floppy disk drives; a hard disk is recommended. The recommended configuration for the PC version of PageMaker is a PC AT with an enhanced graphics adaptor, mouse, hard disk, and 512K of internal memory. Although the PC version of PageMaker will run on a PC XT with a graphics card, the performance is not nearly as good as on a PC AT, for which it was designed. If you prefer to do page makeup on a PC XT, skip this section and read closely the descriptions of Personal Publisher and Ventura Publisher.

Although you can type text directly into PageMaker, you probably will want to use a word processing program such as Microsoft Word, so that the text is retrievable for use with other programs. For captions and text used within graphics, you might want to type directly into PageMaker.

PageMaker provides tools for drawing boxes, circles and several line styles. However, for creating more complex graphics, use Mac-Paint or MacDraw on the Macintosh, or Microsoft Windows Paint (or Windows Draw from Micrografx) on the PC AT. You should use a hard disk to avoid running out of storage space with large documents.

PageMaker for the PC is nearly identical to the Macintosh version. New features include full dictionary-based automatic hyphenation, support for larger publication files, and additional typographical controls, including kerning.

The PC version of PageMaker works under Microsoft Windows (described in Chapter 4), which provides a Macintosh-like graphics environment with icons, pull-down menus, multiple "windows" on the screen, and mouse support.

With PageMaker running under Windows, you can load your word processing program, your graphics program, and PageMaker into separate windows at the same time, and then transfer text and graphics from the other windows into the PageMaker page.

The PC version of PageMaker can accept text from Microsoft Word or Microsoft Windows Write and retain the typefont and style attributes set in those word processing programs. It can also import graphics from Microsoft Windows Paint and Draw.

The Macintosh version of PageMaker is supplied with a special LaserWriter driver program on the disk that is installed for use with the LaserWriter or Linotronic typesetter.

The PC version can print pages on any printer supported by Microsoft Windows, including any PostScript laser printer or typesetter, the H-P LaserJet and LaserJet Plus, and Epson-compatible printers.

Features   The revised version of PageMaker (version 2.0) is not limited in the number of pages per "publication file," as are the earlier versions. The early versions of PageMaker (version 1.x) are limited to sixteen pages per publication file. Some printing presses print sixteen pages at a time in a *signature*, so dividing production work into sixteen-page sections can be useful in preparing the design of each signature.

You can also use separate PageMaker publication files for separately-designed pieces that are sixteen pages or less. For example, you can create a PageMaker file for each article of a magazine or newsletter, or for a portion of a chapter or entire chapter of a book or manual, or for a special section of a document, or for a single page advertisement or multi-page flyer, etc.

The program is designed to follow the steps a designer would follow. You start by defining a layout that will be used for most if not all of the pages in the document file. In the layout you define the columns for text, any rules (lines) or borders that will appear on every page, and any *folios* (page numbers, titles, copyright notices) that are to appear on each page. This blank page is a "master" that you customize for your job. All the elements you set up on this "master" page are automatically placed on each page. Both left-page and right-page "masters" can be created and stored for each publication file. The "master" defines the default (automatic) settings for each page.

PageMaker offers a wider selection of lines or borders than Mac-Draw and includes four double rules — thin and thick lines separated by white space — that can be used as borders, or for boxes. Page-Maker lets you choose the radius of the corner of a rectangle (or box) from a selection of six rounded corners.

You can draw boxes, circles, ovals or other shapes to block off space where text should not be filled in. You can also mark a block to hold text, as in a sidebar (a box of text on the page connected to but separate from the rest of the page elements). You can even make a column of text indent its left or right margin to accommodate a box jutting into the column.

In one session with PageMaker, you can set up columns, add pages, fill columns with text over several pages, adjust text and have it "spill over" into subsequent pages, save the publication file, and print the entire set of pages on a laser printer or typesetter. PageMaker can automatically number each page.

PageMaker hides many of the tedious details of layout mechanics by calculating column widths and letting you place text and graphic elements, without any layout skills required. You can specify the number of columns on the page and the space between columns. Choose rulers to measure space in inches, picas or millimeters; you can change the measurement method whenever you want. PageMaker 2.0 offers more ruler choices.

PageMaker gives you two rulers: one across the top of the page and one down the left side. Dotted lines in both rulers follow the pointer as you move it, so you can fix graphic elements and text blocks exactly where you want them. The rulers show the "zero point" — where the top and the left margins intersect on the page. You can change this zero point by dragging the icon and placing it at any position on the page to use as a frame of reference. The zero point stays where you set it, and rulers adjust when you enlarge or reduce the display, to show you where you are in relation to the zero point.

In PageMaker, the *margin* guide is the same for each page, but the *column* guide can be different for each page. PageMaker employs a "snap-to guide" function that automatically places text or graphic images exactly flush to the column guide. Using this function, you don't need excellent hand-eye coordination to line up columns of text (as with MacPaint or PC Paint). The guide acts like a magnet to attract the edge of your block of text or graphic image to the nearest column guide. You can turn this feature off whenever you don't want elements to be magnetically drawn to the guides.

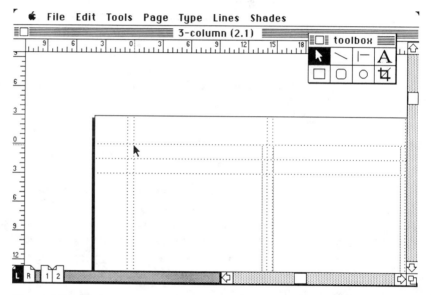

Figure 5-1. Setting margin and column guides with horizontal and vertical rule guides (rulers show pica measurement). The zero point shows where both rulers intersect at the top left margin of the page.

You can also create horizontal and vertical ruler guides anywhere on the page, perhaps for titles, running heads (titles that appear at the top of each page), and folios (running "feet" on each page with page numbers, copyright notice, or whatever). You can hide all guides to see what the printed page would look like (the full-page display resembles a paste-up board on a light table), or you can display all guides for easy placement of text and graphics.

Starting a Layout PageMaker's "Master pages" feature lets you define the overall layout of your publication. When you create a master page containing all the borders, rules, guides and columns, PageMaker copies this information to all pages in the publication file (to a maximum of sixteen pages per file for versions 1.x).

If you create a double-sided publication (recommended if you want facing pages), you are provided with two master pages: one for all left-hand pages and one for right-hand pages. The first page of a double-sided publication is always a right-hand page, but you can start your layout on any page — odd-numbered pages are right-hand pages, and even-numbered are left-hand pages.

You are not restricted to using the master layout for every page, because you can select an option to "turn off" the master page layout for any page in the file. You may want to place on the master page graphics and text that is going to be repeated on each page — such as folios at the top or bottom of each page, or line borders around each page.

PageMaker's automatic page number function can be useful even if your publication is broken into several publication files for production purposes. You can set the starting page number in the Page Setup menu (for example, page number 17 for the start of the second sixteen-page signature).

Since it takes time to develop the master pages, if you plan to use the same design for more than one file, it makes sense to develop one master publication file *with empty pages*, and then make copies of it to use each time you start a new publication file. Create a separate master file for each format you plan to use, and you can save time by using the "Catalog Page" file, or "Book Page" file, or whatever you call your master page files. (This is like having the "boards already lined," if you were doing a manual paste-up, with a different grid for each type of job.)

On the master pages you set the default characteristics, which are carried automatically to each page as you create the page. The characteristics include where the columns are positioned; any rules, lines or blocks; the "snap-to" feature (column guides act as magnets for easy placement of text and graphics); and the "guide lock" (column guides and other guides are fixed, not movable). The default settings on the master pages are automatically copied to each page. You can change any of these settings, including column and other guides, for each page.

You can set up your measurement preference from the Edit menu to be in inches, picas or millimeters. In the Column Guides dialog box, you can type the number of columns you want on the master page, and the amount of space to use for the gap between columns. You can change the columns on each page, or keep the number of columns used for the "master" page. The Column Guides dialog box shows the number of columns on the current page.

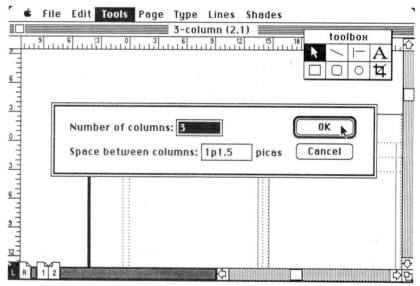

Figure 5-2.   Selecting columns in PageMaker for a typical newsletter page.

Placing Text   You can bring text into PageMaker pages from a word processing program such as MacWrite (Macintosh), Microsoft Word (Macintosh or PC), Multimate (PC) or WordStar (PC). You can bring graphic images into PageMaker pages from MacPaint and MacDraw "PICT" files (Macintosh), or from Microsoft Windows Paint ("MSP") and Micrografx Windows Draw ("PIC") files (PC).

You can also bring text and graphics into PageMaker through the Clipboard and Scrapbook functions of the Macintosh, or the clipboard of Microsoft Windows. This gives you the flexibility to capture data from spreadsheets and charts from business graphics programs. The Macintosh has a built-in Clipboard and Scrapbook feature; PageMaker for the PC works with the Microsoft Windows program, which provides a Macintosh-like clipboard and scrapbook feature.

When using MacWrite on the Macintosh for preparing text for use with PageMaker, keep in mind that the text should begin at the 1-inch mark in MacWrite; if you started the text at the default 1.25-inch mark, the text would then appear on the PageMaker page 0.25 inches indented.

PageMaker picks up entire paragraph indents or block indents when you are placing text within a column, depending on the word processor used. PageMaker also picks up any indents caused by using the Tab key, such as the starting line of paragraphs and elements in a table (from any ASCII text file). However, PageMaker will pick up extra spaces if you typed them into your file to line up the text. The spaces may not fall at the beginnings of lines as you intended, because the lines in PageMaker end at the edge of the column you defined, not on the margins set in your word processing program.

Therefore, use the Tab key in your word processing program to create tab spaces when you need to line up columns of numbers or text, and begin paragraphs. However, don't use tabs to move the text beyond the column width you will use for your typeset columns.

PageMaker picks up these characteristics from MacWrite and Microsoft Word: tab stops, line spacing, alignment, left, right, and first-line indents, and the typefont, style and size. Once you place the text on a PageMaker page, you can change all text specifications (in earlier versions of PageMaker you could not change the size of the indents and tab stops; in version 1.2 you can change them). Place any tab stops using MacWrite or Word — PageMaker will ignore indents and tab stops that exceed the line length defined on the PageMaker page.

MacWrite rulers are not accurate for use with the LaserWriter — the line breaks in MacWrite will not match the line breaks formed by PageMaker using the same column width. One inch in MacWrite is actually 1.1 inches in PageMaker. You can safely ignore your line length in MacWrite — that is, let PageMaker change it to fit its columns — as long as you don't use tabs or indents that *exceed* the intended line length.

Microsoft Word is a better match with PageMaker, because you can set the *leading* (space between baselines of text) in Word for the entire document. MacWrite, on the other hand, has no leading control (other than "automatic leading") and if you want special leading you have to do it within PageMaker.

With Microsoft Word, start your text at the zero inch mark. Page-Maker inserts a tab stop if it encounters a tab character in a Word document. PageMaker also recognizes Word's *discretionary hyphens* and will use them to hyphenate words. Discretionary hyphens (also called *soft hyphens*) are ones you type into the larger words of your document while you are writing or editing it; the software uses those hyphens only if it needs it to break a line properly.

Text files from computers other than Macintoshes can be transmitted to the Macintosh and treated as text-only documents. They can be placed into PageMaker pages. PageMaker uses the typesetting specifications you set in its "Type specs" command from the Type menu. PageMaker puts in tab stops every half-inch. With this feature you can import tables from other applications, such as Microsoft's Multiplan (via the clipboard and scrapbook). PageMaker recognizes the tab characters and lines up each table item in the appropriate column.

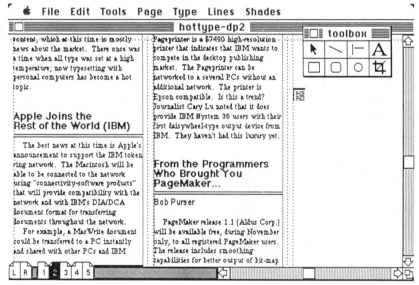

Figure 5-3. Placing text into a PageMaker page (icons in the lower left show the number and orientation of the pages). The Toolbox shows drawing and editing tools.

If you embedded a graphic image in your MacWrite or Microsoft Word document, you can still place the entire document in Page-Maker, but the graphic image becomes a separate item in PageMaker, no longer linked to your text. This lets you place the graphic wherever you like on the page.

To import a text file into PageMaker, choose the Place option in the File menu. This action presents a list of files you can place. Select a file and click the menu to place it, and the pointer will change to a text cursor. You can place the text anywhere on the PageMaker page. The text column aligns itself to the column guide if you place the text cursor within the column.

If the text overflows the column, an icon resembling a window shade, showing a plus sign, appears at the end of the column. You can adjust the window-shade icon to stop the text before the end of the column, or click the plus sign once to get the text cursor again. With the text cursor you can place the rest of the text in another column, or even another page. By continuing this process you can place a lengthy document over several pages, leaving room for graphic elements.

When you add a page, PageMaker shows a new page icon in the lower left corner of the screen. The icon also tells you if the page is a right- or left-handed page. In double-sided publications, odd-numbered pages are right-handed, and even-numbered pages are left-handed. Single-sided publications consist of only right-handed pages.

Importing Graphics

On the Macintosh, you can import graphic images from MacPaint and MacDraw "PICT" files, or paste them directly onto the page from the Clipboard (copied or cut from the Scrapbook). MacDraw images must be saved in the "PICT" (picture) format. Do all of your graphic touchup work in MacPaint or MacDraw first, before importing an image into PageMaker, since PageMaker has no eraser to selectively erase parts of your image.

On the PC, you can import graphic images directly from digitizers (described in Chapter 4), and directly from Microsoft Windows Paint or Micrografx Windows Draw.

The graphic is placed on the page at its original size. Once the graphic is on the page, you can use PageMaker's box tools to create a border, or the cropping tool to crop the edges of the graphic. You can also enlarge or reduce the graphic.

Use the Place command from the File menu to import a "PICT" file (Mac), or an "MSP" or "PIC" file (PC). The pointer changes to a paintbrush with MacPaint or Microsoft Windows Paint, or a pencil with MacDraw or Micrografx Windows Draw. When you click the pointer in a location on the page, the image appears with small "handles" you can use to reduce or enlarge it (figure 5-4).

To get text or images from the clipboard, use the "Paste" command from the Edit menu, as you would in most other Macintosh or Microsoft Windows applications.

Figure 5-4. Placing a graphic image from MacPaint onto a page. Using the "handles" on the image, you can reduce or enlarge it, and compress or expand it.

Changing Elements on the Page

You can shorten or lengthen columns of text, and PageMaker automatically reformats the rest of the text to show the change. Experiment with different text layouts until you are satisfied, and all changes are made on all pages.

To change a column of text, click the pointer anywhere in the block, and the block will sprout window-shade icons on either end. Push and pull the window shades to adjust the text. You can push text from one page to the next, or pull text from the next page to fit on the current page.

You can add text to the page with the "A" tool in the Toolbox. As you type, the text takes on characteristics you specified in the "Type specs" menu from the Type menu. If there is other text next to the insertion point where you are typing text, the new text takes on the characteristics of the older text that is closest to it. You can easily add titles, captions and special lines of text, or make editing changes to text already placed on the page.

For trimming graphics, the Toolbox has a cropping tool. It lets you trim the edges from a graphic image. You can use the "handles" on the graphic image to reduce, enlarge, compress or expand the image.

You can also draw straight lines in any direction without angle restriction, or you can restrict lines to 45-degree and 90-degree angles. The Lines menu shows sixteen line styles, including hairline, dashed line, double line and no line (for drawing filled shapes without outlines showing around the pattern).

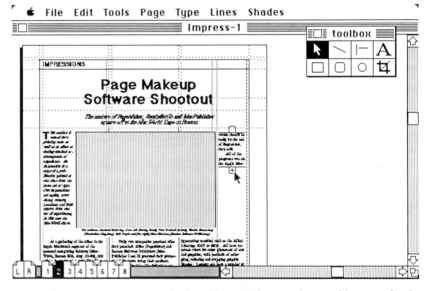

Figure 5-5. Placing text around a box. You can drag a column guide to use for the area next to the box, and use the window-shade icon to drag text through the area.

Squares and rectangles are easy to draw, even with square or rounded corners, as are ovals and circles. You can fill these shapes with sixteen different shadings, including transparent gray, patterns, or no shade (to put a box around text or a graphic image).

To move a block of text, select it with the pointer tool, and drag the text to another place or another page. To move text to another page, place it anywhere outside the borders of the page (the area called the *pasteboard* surrounds the page), then switch pages to change the page (the pasteboard remains the same). Your text or images on the pasteboard will still be on the desktop when you move to another page. You can then move objects from the pasteboard back onto the page you want.

You can also wrap text around a graphic image (see figure 5-5). If the image is rectangular, use the window-shade icon to make the text flow up to the image, then below the image. Then, after dragging a column guide to the area alongside the image, use the window-shade icon to make the text flow through the narrow space. If the image is not rectangular, make the text flow over it, and break the lines using the "A" tool and carriage returns.

Figure 5-6.   PageMaker lets you view two pages at once. You can interactively work with elements on both pages.

Displaying the Page

PageMaker has several display options. You can see the page at the actual size, at 200% enlargement, at 75% reduction, at 50% reduction, or reduced to fit the entire page on the screen. You can also display a two-page spread and work with elements on both pages.

To move an element from one page to another, drag the element to the area outside the page, select the other page, and drag the element from the pasteboard (area outside the page) onto the other page. The

"Reduce to fit" option from the Page menu makes it easy to do this, because you can see a full page display.

Printing the Page   Printing is very easy from PageMaker — you select the "Print" command. To send output from a Macintosh to a LaserWriter or Linotronic typesetter, make sure the "Choose Printer" or "Chooser" accessory (accessible from the Apple menu) is set to the correct output device. ImageWriter pages are not ideal for placement or proofing, but they do give you a general idea of the PageMaker layout. PageMaker composes pages for a particular "target" printer such as a PostScript device — you can print in "draft mode" but the draft printer will try to emulate the target printer.

You can print one or more pages at regular size, or reduce or enlarge the pages. PageMaker can also print "thumbnail" sketches of all pages in a publication.

PageMaker for the Macintosh is shipped to work with a LaserWriter and an ImageWriter. It can also output to any other device that operates with the PostScript language from Adobe Systems, including the Allied Linotype Linotronic series typesetters.

PageMaker prints graphic images on the ImageWriter in Tall Adjusted mode with a resolution of 72 x 72 dots per inch (the Macintosh screen displays 72 x 72 pixels per inch). The LaserWriter prints 300 x 300 dots per inch. Because the LaserWriter's resolution is not an exact multiple of 72 (the screen resolution), the LaserWriter makes a calculated adjustment to graphic images that may distort those images, and gray shadings may develop moire patterns. You might be able to eliminate these problems by reducing the page to 96%. PageMaker can employ a similar "smoothing" algorithm that MacDraw uses to print images with less-jagged edges (at 300 dots per inch).

PageMaker for the PC is shipped to work with Microsoft Windows. It can therefore print to any printer supported by Microsoft Windows, including PostScript printers and typesetters, the H-P LaserJet, and Epson-compatible printers.

Non-standard   PageMaker can print tabloid-size (11 x 17 inch) pages with the special
Page Sizes   "tile" option, which prints the first half of the tabloid page on a piece of letter-size paper. On the Macintosh, to print the second half you move PageMaker's ruler zero point and print again with the "tile" option. This produces the second half, with enough of an overlap to join the letter-size pages together for copying onto tabloid-size paper. On

the PC, tiling is automatic for your selected paper size; however, if the paper size is larger than the page size, the program prints trim marks.

With the tiling feature, you can take anything on the screen and print it at a larger size. Although the different pages have pieces of the graphic that you have to fit together like a puzzle, the tiling feature leaves an extra "lip" of the image to use for matching the pages together precisely.

Summary   PageMaker was the first page makeup product for the Macintosh that we could use to produce magazine pages. The major limitations of PageMaker version 1 are no automatic hyphenation and no kerning; both features are implemented in version 2 and in the PC version. Automatic hyphenation makes it easier to flow text over many book pages and long documents where text is justified to the right margin. Kerning is important for typographers because it is sometimes needed in large titles and subtitles, where the space between letters is very noticeable.

PageMaker does not transfer editing changes made to PageMaker pages to the text file from which text was imported, so you must use a word processing program to make your changes, and then re-pour your text. It helps to use a word processor like Microsoft Word, which also gives you control over *leading* (line spacing), so that you can make one leading change to your Word file before reading it into PageMaker. And you have to be careful how you place text — whether you place it "on the pasteboard" or within column guides determines the line length of the text.

On the Macintosh, PageMaker has more features but is higher priced than MacPublisher and MacPublisher II (Boston Software) and ReadySetGo (Manhattan Graphics). On the PC AT, PageMaker has more features than Personal Publisher (which runs on a 384K PC), and is comparable in price and functionality to Ventura Publisher (which is newer and runs on both the PC and the PC AT). In short, there is no clear winner. A Mac user might want PageMaker because it handles columns of text more easily than ReadySetGo and provides better graphics handling than MacPublisher, although ReadySetGo's blocks are easier for ad makeup, and MacPublisher II is loaded with features. A PC AT user might want PageMaker because it has been around longer than Personal Publisher and Ventura Publisher, on the theory that most bugs have been worked out.

At $495 (Macintosh version), PageMaker it is still much less expensive than page makeup systems that cost over $2000 (some cost over $20,000 and run on much larger computers, yet provide basically the same features). We consider PageMaker to be a standard for page makeup software, by which others will be measured.

ReadySetGo

ReadySetGo (Manhattan Graphics, $125) is a page makeup program with most of the features of PageMaker and MacPublisher, but is less expensive. ReadySetGo is very easy to use, although a bit slower than the others, due to the treatment of columns as boxes. ReadySetGo is excellent for designing very complex layouts with text flowing into areas of different widths.

When you start ReadySetGo, you see a grid on your screen that corresponds to the upper right corner of the page. To move around the page in ReadySetGo, you select the Show Page option from the Special menu, and the program displays a miniature version of the page with a movable window. Move the window to another section of the page, and the program redisplays the grid to correspond to the new position of the window.

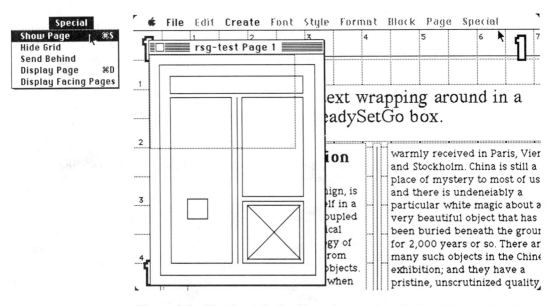

Figure 5-7. The ReadySetGo Show Page option displays the completed page elements.

To design a layout with columns for text, think of the columns as *boxes* — not necessarily boxed with lines, but as rectangular-shaped entities that can be moved and reshaped. The Block menu has a Modify option whose menu changes depending on the type of block you create, but gives you a way to accurately size any block.

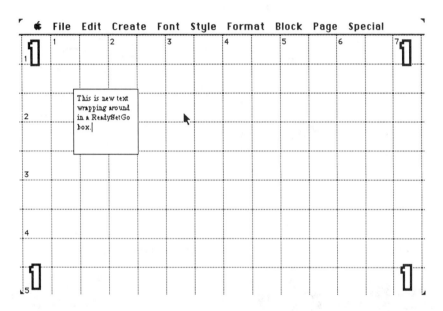

Figure 5-8. ReadySetGo text columns start as empty boxes you can move and reshape.

To create a column of text, you start with the Text option in the Create menu. This produces a small square on the screen overlaying the grid (see figure 5-8).

You can type text directly into a ReadySetGo text block, move the block to another location, and resize the block, and the program automatically reforms the text to fit the block. To move a block, you move the pointer to the upper right corner of the block and drag it into position. To resize and reshape a block, move the pointer to the lower right position and drag it into a new shape and size.

Using a mouse is not as precise as you might want, so ReadySetGo provides a menu for sizing a text block (or any block) using specific dimensions. The Modify option of the Block menu produces the specifications menu shown in figure 5-10.

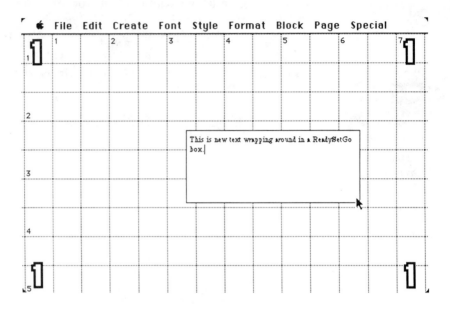

Figure 5-9.   You can move a ReadySetGo text block and resize the block, and the program automatically reforms the text in the block.

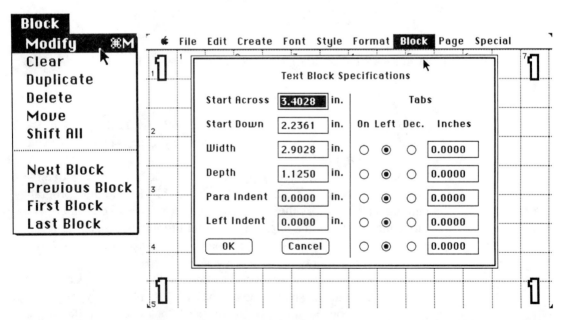

Figure 5-10.   You can define the size and shape of a ReadySetGo text block with precise measurements in inches or picas (inches shown).

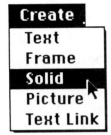

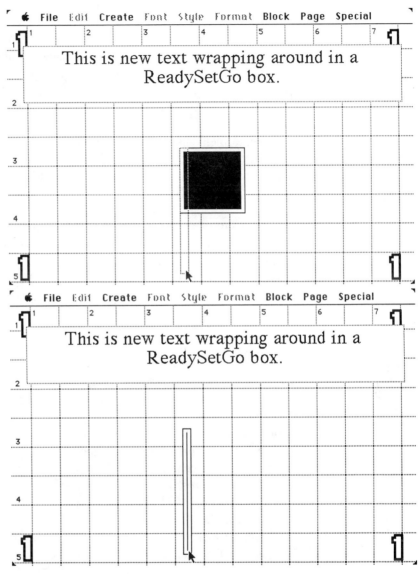

Figure 5-11. To draw lines in ReadySetGo, you define a solid block and then reshape it into a line.

To change the typefont and point size of a section of text, mark the section as you would in MacWrite or almost any other Macintosh program, and select a typefont from the Font menu and a style and point size from the Style menu. The text is automatically reformed to fit in the text block. The Format menu provides left, right, center or justified paragraph formats and line spacing. You can pick the standard single line, one-and-a-half line and double line spacing, or choose Other for a specific *leading* amount expressed in points (72 points to the inch).

To draw a line in ReadySetGo, you create a solid block and reshape it into a line (see figure 5-11). First you choose the Solid option from the Create menu, then you move the resulting solid block into position, and finally reshape the block into a straight vertical line. You can use the more precise measurements on the Modify option in the Block menu to get exactly the line thickness and length that you want.

ReadySetGo provides framed blocks for areas that are to be enclosed within a box. You simply choose the Frame option from the Create menu, move the framed box into place and reshape it to what you want. Use the Modify option in the Block menu (which provides a frame thickness and pattern) to do precise reshaping.

To place a graphic on the page, you create a picture block (picture blocks are marked with an "X" through them until they contain a picture). You can then copy a graphic from the Scrapbook on your system disk to the Clipboard, and from there paste it into the picture box. You can move the picture box to the proper location and then re-size the picture box to see the entire graphic image.

To re-size the image as well as the picture box around it, choose the Modify option in the Block menu. This time, the specifications include a scale across and a scale down, referring to the graphic image. To keep an image's pixel ratio the same but enlarge or reduce the image, use the same percentage (such as 200 for 200 percent enlargement) in both the scale across and scale down specs.

To place columns of text on the page, you start by defining a block for each column. Create a text block, re-shape it with the Modify option in the Block menu, then create a *text link* (choose the Text Link option from the Create menu) to create the next column. Each text link you create is a text box that is linked to the previous box. Continue making columns in this fashion (creating a text link to start the column), and insert new pages if you think you will need them to contain your text.

To place text on the page from a text file, select the first column box to receive the text, then choose the Get Text option from the File menu. The program displays the names of files you can open, and when you click the open bar, text fills the first box. You can modify text in the box — add or delete text, or change point sizes and styles — and after making your changes, choose the Reflow option in the Style menu, and the text reflows through all of the linked boxes.

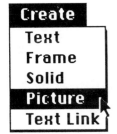

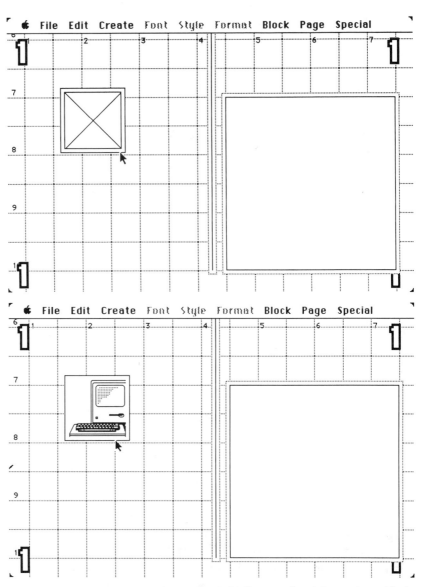

Figure 5-12. To place a graphic on a ReadySetGo page, first define a picture block, then paste the graphic from the Clipboard.

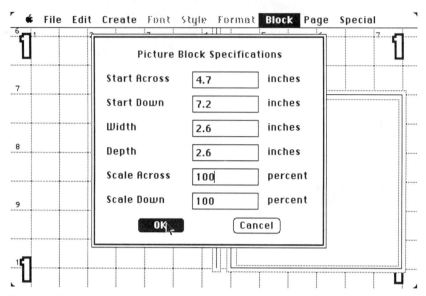

Figure 5-13. You can re-size and re-shape a graphic within a ReadySetGo picture box by specifying a percentage to scale across (horizontally) and scale down.

You can continue to create text links to contain the rest of the text, and reflow the text through those blocks. You have to return to the first block to start the reflow, but this is easy to do from any page — simply choose the First Block option from the Block menu.

If you want to change the arrangement of blocks, you can "vacuum" the text up into the first block with the Vacuum option of the Format menu. You can then rearrange blocks and reflow the text.

You can lay out up to 32 pages in one ReadySetGo file, with up to 100 blocks per page (1000 blocks per file), and up to 30K of text in each text block or text chain.

ReadySetGo is best for designing single-page advertisements, flyers, marketing literature and other short design pieces where columns of text can be any size. It is not as useful as PageMaker for doing newsletter or magazine pages, but it is easier to learn and is certainly less expensive.

MacPublisher I and II

MacPublisher (Boston Software Publishers, Inc., $99) has the distinction of being the first desktop publishing program for the Macintosh. It's also the only one that works on 128K Macs.

You can fit as many as 64 articles and 64 graphic images in a Mac-Publisher publication file, which can have up to 32 pages. You can open articles and images simultaneously as windows on your Mac desktop, along with the layout page.

MacPublisher uses icons that represent standard graphics arts tools. Using a see-through "ruler" (calibrated in inches, centimeters, lines, or pixels) and "scissors," you can measure, cut, and paste blocks of text or pictures and carry run-over text over to another page. A "through-the-lens camera" lets you crop and snap images from the Clipboard (without distortions due to stretching), using graphics from MacPaint, MacProject, MacDraw, Chart, and digitizers like ThunderScan and MacVision.

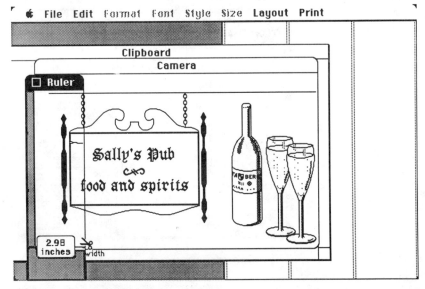

Figure 5-14. MacPublisher uses a see-through ruler, a scissors pointer to cut and paste blocks of text and a camera tool to crop images.

MacPublisher employs an invisible grid to automatically align text and pictures in one-third-, one-half-, two-thirds-, or full-page columns — or in fact, any column up to 48 columns per page. Margins between columns can also be specified in one-point increments. In free-form layout mode, articles and pictures can be placed anywhere on the page — to reposition them you pick them up with the mouse and drag them to a new position. Mix text and graphics on the same line, with precise run-around of text.

Use MacPublisher's text editor to create documents, or you can use text created with MacWrite, Microsoft Word, or other Macintosh word processors. MacPublisher lets you adjust leading (space between lines) and text alignment (left, right, centered, or justified, with letterspace justification). The program also lets you select normal, condensed or expanded characters, ten character sizes (from 8 to 72 point), six styles of text, and ten built-in fonts, as well as dozens of commercially available Macintosh fonts.

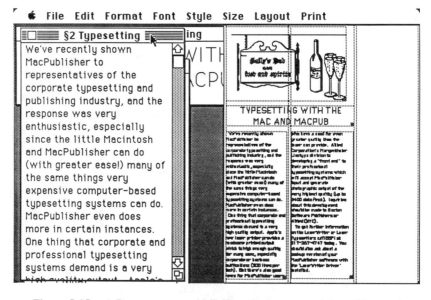

Figure 5-15.   A Dummy page and MiniPage let you test a variety of layouts.

To deal with possible power failures, MacPublisher can automatically save text as it is entered, or you can override this feature for faster performance, and save text as usual using the File menu.

MacPublisher automatically creates a running table of contents, listing each article and picture name, page, and column. A "Dummy Page" option (showing rough layout in blocks at 44% reduction) and a "MiniPage" option (showing the actual page at 44% reduction) let you view your layouts before printing. You can print pages at up to 200% enlargement to improve font quality (then use photo-reduction before printing to reduce the page to final size).

Since MacPublisher and MacPublisher II are relatively small programs, they can run on a disk with a Macintosh system, leaving an external disk free for a rather large publication — 400K bytes can store 96 text pages at 4K bytes per page.

Letterspace Justification

Most of the software that offers justified text on the Macintosh accomplishes line justification by distributing the extra space at the end of a line between the word spaces (enlarging the space character) to fill the line. This includes MacWrite, Microsoft Word, ReadySetGo, and PageMaker. The result is often unacceptably-wide spaces between words.

```
 ┌  🍎  File  Edit  Format  Font  Style  Size  Layout  Print         ┐

   ┌──────────────────────┐   ┌──────────────────────┐
   │      Flush Left       │   │  With Justification On│
   │                       │   │                       │
   │   The most exciting   │   │   The most exciting   │
   │ combination of software│  │ combination of software│
   │ and hardware available│   │ and hardware available│
   │ for the Macintosh in 1985│ │ for the Macintosh in 1985│
   │ was page-makeup soft- │   │ was page-makeup soft- │
   │ ware like MacPublisher│   │ ware like MacPublisher│
   │ and the incredible Apple│  │ and the incredible Apple│
   │ LaserWriter™. The     │   │ LaserWriter™.  The    │
   │ LaserWriter sparked a │   │ LaserWriter sparked a │
   │ new industry, called  │   │ new industry, called  │
   │ 'desktop publishing' or│  │ 'desktop publishing' or│
   │ 'personal publishing.' We│ │ 'personal publishing.' We│
   │ prefer 'MacPublishing' and│ │ prefer 'MacPublishing' and│
   │ like to think of all our│  │ like to think of all our│
   │ users as 'MacPublishers.'│ │ users as 'MacPublishers.'│
   └──────────────────────┘   └──────────────────────┘

 └                                                               ┘
```

Figure 5-16.   Letterspace justification in MacPublisher and MacPublisher II helps eliminate "rivers of white" running between words on the page.

MacPublisher uses a better method called *letterspace justification*. The program widens the inter-character spacing (putting extra points between every character on the line) and also widens the interword spacing, but the spaces between words do not look exaggerated (figure 5-16). Boston Software also offers an automatic hyphenation software package (Mac-Hy-phen) that further improves the appearance of text.

MacPublisher II   MacPublisher II ($150) gives you some additional features. You can view a full-size page as well as two facing pages; with automatic page numbering and continuation lines ("continued on page..."), repeating elements (such as a running head) starting on any specified page, and precise page positioning of text blocks at specific vertical and horizontal screen pixels (locations).

Like PageMaker, MacPublisher II lets you change type style (normal, bold, underlined, italics, outline, and shadow), font, and size within a line. You can open MacDraw, MacWrite, or MacPaint files directly and resize MacDraw graphics, with no distortion (images are not stretched to change the original 1 to 1 aspect ratio). A zoom window lets you enlarge the layout 200% to 900%.

MacPublisher II also offers some features not available in other programs. A type specification box lets you set type characteristics for each article (you can lay out several articles in one publication file), and type sizes can range from 4 to 127 points in 1-point increments.

MacPublisher II also offers "depth justification," which means that leading (spacing between lines) for adjacent columns of text with different numbers of lines, font sizes or styles can be adjusted so that the tops and bottoms of the columns line up exactly to the point.

Use the Facing Pages display to move text and graphics on the right-hand page to line up or otherwise position items relative to the left-hand page. MacPublisher II lets you select any font, style, or size for page numbers and enter any desired folio line of text to appear before the page number, then uses your selections to automatically place page numbers. The resulting folio may be placed at the top or bottom of the page, adjusted left, right, or centered, or indented, by changing entries in the dialog box. Folio lines appear on the MiniPage and MaxiPage and in printing.

Similarly, Page Jumps ("Continued on page nn") can be styled and edited (e.g., "Please turn to page nn") and indented from the side of the column of text. Once selected, whenever text is continued onto another page, Page Jumps are displayed on the MiniPage and Maxi-Page, and printed. The program can insert or remove pages at any location, and even swap any two pages in the layout.

MacPublisher II can produce up to 96 pages per publication file on a 400K dual floppy drive Macintosh. Since the page limit is determined by available disk space, it can produce many times more pages if you use a hard disk.

File Management Unlike MacPublisher, MacPublisher II Article files are ordinary Macintosh "TEXT" files that can be edited or created by any program that can edit "TEXT" files. For example, using the program's "NewsWire" desk accessory, a newsletter or newspaper editor can receive a telecommunicated article and immediately incorporate the "wired" news item into an issue, by simply giving it the same file name as an item already laid out, and deleting (or renaming) the original item.

MacPublisher II has an unusual "Delete..." menu item in the File Menu that lets you eliminate a file without quitting the MacPublisher application and returning to the finder. Choosing Delete also reports in its dialog box the number of free bytes on the selected disk. This is important when trying to print with a small amount of disk space available for the spooled printed file.

Hyphenation *Discretionary hyphens* (also called *soft hyphens*) are invisible hyphens that become visible only when a word breaks at the end of a line. MacPublisher II's discretionary hyphenation is identical to that offered by Microsoft Word and PageMaker, and uses the same key (command-hyphen) to enter a discretionary hyphen in a word. You can bring a Microsoft Word file containing discretionary hyphens into MacPublisher II with its hyphens intact. (However, you do lose Word attributes like font size and style.)

Boston Software offers a $59.95 desk accessory called Mac-Hy-phen that works with MacPublisher II. Mac-Hy-phen uses a 40,000 word dictionary to automatically insert discretionary hyphens throughout a block of text at appropriate word division points. The dictionary method requires room on your disk for a large dictionary file, but this method is far more accurate than algorithmic or statistical approaches to hyphenation. Once a block of text has been hyphenated, it will never need to be hyphenated again unless you add new words to it, even if the text is re-wrapped differently (by deletions, changing column width, font size, etc.).

You can also install Mac-Hy-phen as a desk accessory in Microsoft Word, PageMaker or any other Macintosh software that recognizes the discretionary hyphen character.

Oversize Printing MacPublisher II offers more page sizes for layout than the other page makeup programs for Macs. Five sizes on the ImageWriter (four sizes on the LaserWriter) can be turned into landscape (sideways) orientation as well. Any of the ten (eight on the LaserWriter) resulting page shapes and sizes may be expanded, using the Oversize 200% mode to allow a selection of twenty MacPublisher II layout page sizes.

MacPublisher offers oversize printing of articles to allow the ImageWriter owner to print large size copy and then photo-reduce to achieve font images far superior to the original ImageWriter printed page. This method requires you to cut and paste the article "galleys" onto an oversize mechanical.

MacPublisher II simplifies this oversize feature and extends it to graphics and to the whole page layout. A layout can be doubled in width and height (to a maximum size of 21 x 28 inches). Mac-Publisher II offers the option of printing the resulting layout in pieces, on more than one sheet of paper, and then taping the sheets together to make a large "poster" out of four standard pages.

Another way to improve the quality of ImageWriter pages is to use the 50% reduction mode offered in new ImageWriter software. The same large 200% oversize layout page can be compressed by the ImageWriter and printed on an ordinary size page. The result is twice the dot density and a significant enhancement in image quality.

Text Flow As editorial changes are made in the text of an article, MacPublisher II can automatically flow text forward to carry over text to other columns or other pages, and backward as necessary when text is deleted. This method is somewhat more flexible than the text flow techniques of other Macintosh publishing software and even many minicomputer-based publishing systems, in part because of MacPublisher's page data structure, which uses the location of rectangles to rebuild a page when a change is made.

Other text flow schemes require the user to specify in advance the column guides, which constrain the flowing text on the left and right. To change the width of a text item, you must re-specify the page column guides. MacPublisher II can flow text in this fashion by setting both left and right snap-to guides. But MacPublisher text blocks can be widened (or narrowed) without resetting the column guides of the layout. This is done by manipulating a "mini" size box in the corner of the text block, or by changing width or depth in the Type Spec Sheet (which allows sizing and placing to the point far more accurately than can be accomplished easily with the mouse alone). Text then flows automatically into the new width.

MacPublisher II gains speed and flexibility by allowing text flow to be turned off for accomplishing special editing functions. For example, suppose a block of text on Page 1 contains one or two lines at the bottom of the page (called *orphans*) that would be better moved to the next column or page — but the depth of the article is already correct. With MacPublisher II, you can resize the article to the end of the paragraph with text flow on, then turn off text flow and return the article to the prescribed column depth. Then you can adjust the leading to make the text fill the column depth, either manually by changing leading, or automatically by selecting Depth Justification, without waiting for the screen to be redrawn at each step of the change.

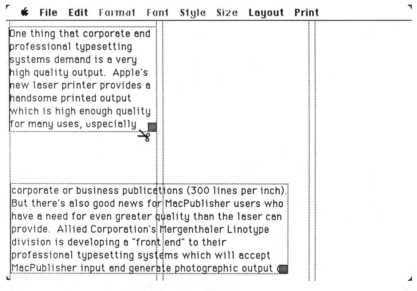

Figure 5-17. Lengthening or widening the column will cause the text to flow automatically with MacPublisher II.

Repeating Elements MacPublisher and MacPublisher II solve the problem of building a page in a different way than ReadySetGo and PageMaker. Rather than building a large page image containing all text and graphic information, MacPublisher creates a page data structure with only the locations and size rectangles for the text and graphic elements and the column grid data for the page. It stores the elements themselves as editable text files and picture files. MacPublisher then rebuilds the entire page whenever it is printed. Boston Software claims that this approach is more crash-resistant because with MacPublisher's

Automatic Save feature, data is almost never lost.

Since the Issue Layout data structures don't really "know" the text or picture information, they are very small files, helping MacPublisher to run in a 128K Macintosh. They also allow MacPublisher to replace the text file contents with new material for the next issue, and have it already completely laid out, with carryovers to the same pages and columns as in the last issue. Once an issue layout has been designed, it is very easy to produce pages quickly (using that layout) with Mac-Publisher.

An additional benefit of this architecture is that MacPublisher can display the Dummy Page, showing the title, and number of lines and characters in each block. Simply clicking on an item on the layout page will bring up the Picture or Type Spec Sheet (Shift-Click) or open the picture or article (Option-Click) for editing of the original file as well as the current layout. Shift-clicking on the page itself brings up a Layout Spec Sheet that lists all the text and graphic elements laid out on that page.

Programs (like PageMaker) that save only page data cannot update text or graphic source files. Crucial last-minute editing changes are therefore saved only with that particular layout, and unavailable when the time comes to use the same text material somewhere else. So if you're publishing a newspaper or a newsletter with last-minute changes and breaking news, MacPublisher II may be your best choice.

To continue the comparison, PageMaker uses the concept of master pages (a left and a right) for laying out items (like folio text, excluding page numbers) that are to be repeated in the same position on every page of a publication. MacPublisher II can repeat any item from the first page on which it occurs to the last page of the issue — but there are no separate master pages. Any item can be designated as a repeating element — to appear on every succeeding page in the same location, or to appear on only the left-hand or only the right-hand pages.

Repeating elements can also be keyed or matched to pages with a "number columns" grid. For example, you can choose to repeat elements on successive pages only if they are also three-column pages. Since MacPublisher II offers up to 48-column/grids, you might consider it equivalent to having 48 master pages.

Repeating elements appear on all the MiniPages and MaxiPages. Like PageMaker's master pages, repeating elements can only be moved on the first page on which they were laid out, and in the Dummy Page view they appear only on the first page.

Type Specifications   A valuable feature of MacPublisher II's Type Spec sheet is the copy description, which immediately informs you about the typographic status of a given article. It contains the standard information needed to "spec" the copy for a typesetter, plus a line and character count, and where the article appears in the issue.

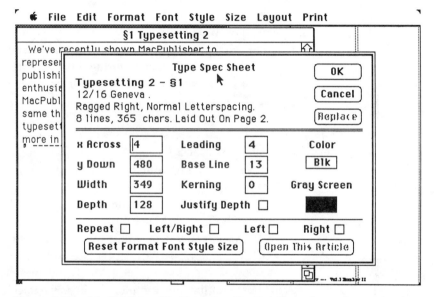

Figure 5-18. MacPublisher II's Type Specification Sheet shows font, style, size, position, width, depth, etc., of an article. Note the Replace button, allowing for substituting a new story in an old layout, and the color capability (ImageWriter II only).

After the title line, the Type Spec sheet shows the type size and leading (line spacing), the type font and style, and the kind of justification used. This spec can be read by a printer or typesetter as meaning, for example, "This article is set 12 points on 20, in Helvetica bold italic, ragged right."

Users no longer need to know this kind of arcane terminology if their publishing is all done "in house," but it is nice to know that all the technical terminology is provided by MacPublisher II if the time comes to work with a typesetter.

Kerning   MacPublisher II is the first Macintosh WYSIWYG page makeup program to offer *kerning* (forthcoming versions of PageMaker and others will also have it, and JustText has always offered it). Kerning means moving certain letters closer together or further apart for a better "look" — for example, tucking the letter "a" under a preceding capital "T". MacPublisher II allows both do-it-yourself manual kerning and automatic kerning of selected letter pairs. The letter pairs are stored in a MacPublisher II resource file that can be edited by sophisticated users who have special kerning requirements.

Kerning is especially critical for printing large typefont sizes on the LaserWriter, because of the way the LaserWriter prints letters in conjunction with other letters, and especially because programs tend to expand the space character during justification. Manual kerning restores a level of control to the typographer, since individual letter pairs can be kerned manually, both inward and outward, until the LaserWriter produces the desired typographic effect.

Rulers MacPublisher uses a see-through ruler, which automatically reads out the value in inches, centimeters, pixels (points), or lines of text when the mouse is clicked at a location inside the ruler. This Desktop Ruler, which can be moved around anywhere on the MacPublisher desktop, has been retained in MacPublisher II and augmented by somewhat more conventional rulers along the top and side of the layout page (MaxiPage), and inside Article, Picture and Camera Windows.

The new Rulers, like those of MacDraw and PageMaker, can be set to inches, centimeters, or picas/points. The Rulers have gray lines (crosshairs) which "track" the movement of the pointer to facilitate measurement. Unlike rulers in most of the other page makeup programs, the Desktop Rulers can also be made transparent (like MacPublisher's moveable Ruler), to provide a less obstructed view of the text or graphic information you are measuring.

One additional option is a continuous "readout" of the pointer position, measured in points from the upper left corner of the active window.

Rules and Borders Creating Rules and Bordered Areas is a special problem for the page designer, since it may be time-consuming to prepare and import graphics from existing Macintosh software. It may be easier to prepare such graphics with MacDraw, using its large palette of fill patterns; its rulers that make it easy to place lines and rectangles; and its "group" attribute, which combines several graphic objects into a single picture element that can be placed as a unit, duplicated, and copied through the Clipboard to other applications, such as MacPublisher and Ready-SetGo.

The MacPublisher II Graphics tool can create custom rules and borders from very simple lines to decorative borders that approximate Art Deco in appearance. The designer can turn on from one to three "pens," each of which can be any width, to create an enormous variety of horizontal or vertical rules or bordered rectangles. The corner radius can be set to any value, and the rectangle can be changed to a perfect circle.

As with MacDraw and PageMaker, the resulting graphic can be filled with a pattern (see figure 5-19). MacPublisher II has more fill patterns in its palette than MacPaint, MacDraw and PageMaker combined — 99 patterns in all, including 9 shades of gray. (PageMaker offers five shades of gray, MacDraw offers six.)

You can use complex fill patterns with up to three pens set to any of the 99 fill patterns to make decorative borders, including dashed lines if you use a vertical bar pattern in a horizontal rule. MacPublisher also has a transparent NONE pattern for showing anything placed underneath it.

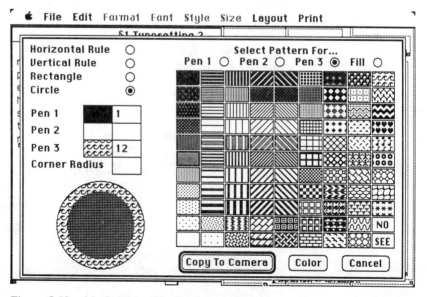

Figure 5-19.   MacPublisher II's Graphics tool patterns — 99 patterns in all, including 9 shades of gray.

Color   MacPublisher II's Graphics tool incorporates Macintosh color information, recognized by the ImageWriter II equipped with a multi-color ribbon. Any of the three pens and the fill patterns can be separately assigned one of eight colors (Black, White, Red, Green, Blue, Yellow, Cyan, and Magenta).

You can copy the resulting multi-color graphic into the MacPublisher "camera," where it can be sized or scaled (using the rulers in the camera window or the Camera Spec box for precise results) to a desired size or shape. Circles can be made into ovals, rectangles into squares, etc. You can make further adjustment in the exact point width and depth after laying out the graphic using MacPublisher II's Picture Spec Sheet dialog box.

With MacPublisher II you can also assign a specific color to any text or graphic element. Headlines can be printed in red, body copy of Articles in green, etc. You can add a single color to images imported from MacPaint or MacDraw. MacPublisher II's color procedures follow Apple's Macintosh guidelines precisely, so that when a multi-color MacPaint document is imported into MacPublisher, it will print out in the original colors, overriding any MacPublisher II color.

Templates   Boston Software also sells "Layouts for MacPublishing," a disk ($95) containing standard templates for newsletters and other documents. You can load a template into MacPublisher and start laying out a publication without spending time learning the design expertise normally required to do layouts.

Personal Publisher (PC XT or AT)   One of the best buys for page makeup on PCs is a program that handles graphics superbly without sacrificing the ability to handle text. Personal Publisher (T/Maker Graphics, $185) can fill up to 100 pages, with text flowing from one page to the next so that changes made anywhere in the text cause the subsequent pages to re-form the text automatically. Personal Publisher can also place on its pages graphics from various sources (even MacPaint files).

The program runs on an IBM PC XT, PC AT or compatible computer, and requires the IBM color card, the Hercules Monochrome or Color card, or an EGA color card, and 384K of RAM. As requirements go for page makeup programs, these requirements are the easiest and least expensive to comply with. T/Maker also provides one hundred fonts with Personal Publisher, which can print on PostScript printers such as the LaserWriter, PostScript typesetters such as the Linotronic, and laser printers such as the H-P LaserJet.

Adjusting the Baseline

Personal Publisher is both a word processing program and a finishing tool for designing and printing pages. It lets you play "what if" with text and graphics until you are satisfied with the final presentation. You can set the number of columns (1-4) and flow text into them, then change the column by stretching its *baseline* into position. The text automatically re-flows through the new column layout.

The *baseline* is a concept T/Maker borrows from typographic history. When you learn to write at school, you are taught to place your letters on the page so that they rest on the baseline. Blocks of type use a standard baseline, that descenders on letters drop below. If you don't use enough vertical space from baseline to baseline (*leading*), then the descenders on the first line may overprint the ascenders on the second line. Personal Publisher displays the invisible baseline with "handles" so that you can adjust the leading and length of each line by moving the baseline (figure 5-20).

Figure 5-20.   With Personal Publisher (T/Maker Company) you can change the line length and leading by moving the baseline.

The design makes it possible to control leading even when you are mixing large and small characters on the same line. The Ripple selection lets you adjust leading when you insert a larger character onto a line with less leading. There is also a general kerning function that tucks characters closer together, but the program does not yet have true kerning pairs.

Text and Graphics

You can use Personal Publisher to edit text, or any word processing program that can generate a regular ASCII text file. You can flow text around graphics, and *overprint* text on graphics for special effects.

Personal Publisher requires no graphic environment program such as Windows or GEM. Personal Publisher provides a Macintosh-like environment with icons, pull-down menus and mouse support. You can use either the Mouse Systems mouse or the Microsoft mouse, or skip the mouse and use the cursor control keys to move around the page. The cursor control keys are based on the numeric keypad, with 5 as the home position, 8 as up, 2 as down, 4 as left, and 6 as right.

Personal Publisher accepts PC Paint files and others that are in the "PIC" file format (such as files from Micrografx Draw). You can use any paint or draw program that can output "PIC" files to create and add graphics to your layout pages.

T/Maker Company also publishes ClickArt for the Macintosh, a library of public domain clip art images, so the company made Personal Publisher compatible with MacPaint files and font-compatible with the Macintosh.

With Personal Publisher on your PC, you can use an AppleTalk interface card such as the PC MacBridge (Tangent Technologies) to transfer MacPaint files to your PC. You can also dial into CompuServe with a modem and retrieve hundreds of free MacPaint "binary" image files to use on your PC with Personal Publisher.

Automatic Text Flowing

Personal Publisher can flow text automatically throughout each page of the document. You can turn this feature off if you don't want to change the rest of the pages, and any extra elements that overflow off the first page are saved in a temporary buffer. If you turn off the automatic text flow, you can then move or delete text and graphic elements on that first page, to create enough room to add the elements saved in the temporary buffer back onto the page.

The text is in full-scale view most of the time, with Personal Publisher showing only a small portion of the page on the screen. The program has a "Show Page" option to show a full page; however, the program shows "greek" (slang for unreadable text that is displayed only for placement) and graphic images that are distorted because the PC screen does not have a 1-to-1 aspect ratio of pixels (see figure 5-21). The screen display is better with high-resolution monochrome cards such as the Hercules.

Figure 5-21. Personal Publisher's "ShowPage" option shows the entire page reduced to fit into the screen window.

Typefonts The program optionally supports LaserWriter typefonts (PostScript typefonts from Adobe Systems), so you can do page makeup on your PC and print the result on the LaserWriter.

Personal Publisher also supports the Hewlett-Packard LaserJet typefonts, such as the A and B cartridge screen fonts (containing the Helvetica, Times and Courier fonts), and other laser printer fonts.

To get best results on the LaserJet, you select a LaserJet font rather than a Macintosh font, otherwise you get jagged letters. Personal Publisher's font menu lists the names of the typefonts, plus an icon that identifies the font as a LaserWriter, LaserJet, or other laser printer typefont. You can select the appropriate fonts for the printer you use.

All of the screen fonts are displayed at a resolution of 72 dots per inch, but are printed at higher resolutions, depending on the printer.

Summary Personal Publisher offers more features and is easier to use than many of the other page makeup programs. The program offers excellent graphics integration and an easy way to flow text around graphics and over several pages.

Personal Publisher doesn't offer the high-end system features, such as automatic page numbers, headers or footers. You can place headers and footers, but you must do them by hand, because there is no tool to automatically place them.

The basic package, configured for an Epson, Okidata or compatible dot matrix printer (using Macintosh typefonts) is $185. With the LaserWriter or LaserJet driver, the complete package is $335. Click-Art images are $50 each package, with a large library to choose from.

Personal Publisher fits the needs of those who have documents that are 20 to 30 pages in length or less. The typical newsletter, brochure, report, small manual, or mailing piece can be produced easily with Personal Publisher. The program can accommodate 100 page document files, but performs best with smaller files.

Ventura Publisher (PC XT or PC AT) The most feature-oriented page makeup program for the PC is Ventura Publisher (Ventura Software, $695). The program runs on the IBM PC XT, PC AT or compatible computer with either a standard IBM Color Graphics Adaptor and color monitor; a Hercules or compatible monochrome graphics card and high-resolution monitor; or an IBM Enhanced Graphics Adaptor (EGA) or compatible card with a color or monochrome monitor. The program requires 512K of memory and the storage capacity of a hard disk.

During the installation process, the program configures itself to your specific peripheral devices (screen, printer and mouse), through use of a short series of menus presented on your screen after you first type the name of the installation program. Ventura Publisher can be installed for the Hercules Monochrome Graphics Card, the IBM Enhanced Graphics Adaptor, or standard IBM Color Card. Each of these graphic cards provides different display resolutions, and the Enhanced Graphics Adaptor can provide color.

Ventura Publisher works from within the GEM system software

from Digital Research, which is bundled in the package. The GEM (Graphics Environment Manager) software lets the PC behave like a Macintosh, with icons, pull-down menus, and graphic paint/draw programs. (You can purchase the GEM Desktop or other application programs to add to your system if you wish to use them, but they are not required.)

GEM and Ventura Publisher both work best with a mouse. You can use the Microsoft, Mouse Systems, Summagraphics or Torrington mouse (Microage computer store franchise sells Torrington brand under the Microage label).

Ventura Publisher uses whatever typefonts you have available in your laser printer or typesetter, such as PostScript fonts or cartridge fonts, and the program knows what fonts are available, based on what printer you choose in the configuration menu.

Various laser printers are supported, including the H-P LaserJet and LaserJet Plus; PostScript printers, such as the LaserWriter and Laser-Writer Plus; PostScript typesetters, such as the Linotronic series; and Epson-compatible printers. The H-P LaserJet requires use of one of the font cartridges with *proportionally-spaced* fonts. The LaserJet Plus can use either the cartridges or, for a wider variety, the disk fonts.

Using the Program

You can start the Ventura Publisher application from the GEM desktop by clicking its icon, or from the PC-DOS command line by typing its name. The main screen area is a window into your page, with scroll bars on the right and bottom margins of the screen that you use to move the window around on the page.

The small window on the top left of your display shows four icons that you can select, one at a time. These icons represent the four main functions available in Ventura Publisher: Select, Layout, Text Edit, and Format. You select a function by pointing to the icon and clicking the mouse button (if you have a mouse with more than one button, Ventura Publisher uses only the left button).

Stylesheets

Ventura Publisher has many of the powerful features found in professional page layout programs, but the program was designed so that non-professionals would be able to use it. For example, a graphic artist can put together a "stylesheet" for a newsletter using Ventura Publisher. Then a secretary could prepare the newsletter with Ventura, selecting and reformatting each paragraph with formats defined in the stylesheet. The program can automatically reformat pages using the information in the stylesheet.

The stylesheet can have all the page formatting information stored for a particular document style. For example, one variable in page design is the number of columns you want on a page. Ventura Publisher lets you set up your page to have from one to four columns. This choice, plus other design considerations (such as typefont and size, tabs, page breaks, line spacing, indents and rules) can be saved in a stylesheet which can be called up and used again and again. You can save (and modify) stylesheets under any filename you choose, with a ".STY" filename extension.

You can create your own stylesheets, and use (or modify and use) the stylesheets in the Ventura Publisher package. Additional stylesheets are in development.

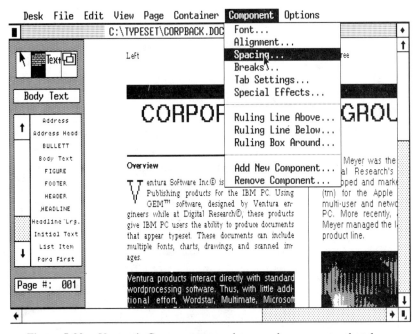

Figure 5-22. Ventura's Component menu lets you change paragraph styles.

Automatic Layout Stylesheets automatically format each page. Each stylesheet contains up to 64 style types. To apply a style type to an individual paragraph, you select the paragraph with the mouse, and then select the style type from a list displayed in the selection box on the screen. A "paragraph" in this sense is defined as a word, paragraph, or page, with two successive returns defining paragraph boundaries.

As soon as the style is selected, the paragraph — *and the entire document* — is immediately reformatted. The program can reformat pages very quickly.

The layout format automatically repeats to the next page, unless you change the format. Different articles can be placed on the same page, each with different formats (different number of columns, etc.), and the articles can be continued anywhere on any other specified page — useful for newsletters, newspapers, magazines, etc., where you need more than one story per page, and you need to continue the text to someplace else in the document.

The Layout function lets you create "containers" to hold formatted text or graphics. You can define several containers on the same page, and set parameters for each, such as margins, number of text columns, and rules.

Stylesheet text settings can be overridden for any selected block of text. This text can be set to boldface, italic, underline, subscript, superscript, small caps, strikethrough, all lower or upper case, or all initial caps.

Most of the design elements that were automatically set by the stylesheet can be changed later by selecting actions from the pull down menus. You can play "what-if" with your layout until you like the design.

Special Features The program can set ragged-right, ragged-left, centered or justified margins. It has the kind of automatic hyphenation and justification you would find on more expensive systems. The program uses the hyphenation algorithm refined by Donald Knuth for his T_EX typesetting language (described in Chapter 7) and a dictionary of exceptions to the rules.

You can set automatic page breaks with running heads and footers, and you can override the column controls for headlines (or titles) that are set across a multi-column page.

Special features include bulleted lists, first line of paragraph indents, and automatic feathering (to line up two side-by-side vertical columns so that they rest on the same baseline).

You can typeset a "Big First Character" (also called "dropped initial cap"), which sets the first character of a "paragraph" (defined above) as a large character inset into the text. The body text is indented for the first two lines of the paragraph so that the big character is set into the column, and the left margin is vertically aligned. You can then pull down the Component Special Effects menu (figure 5-23) to change the font and size of dropped initial caps to whatever final result you like.

You can adjust the automatic line to line and paragraph to paragraph spacing. You can also set up to three rules (lines) with different weights (thicknesses). The rules can be above, below and around a text or graphic element as a box.

Page break controls include line, page, and column breaks before and after paragraphs, and which side to break paragraphs (for left- or right-hand pages). Left/right margin settings act as vertical tabs, handy for indenting whole paragraphs. You can set up to sixteen tabs per paragraph (includes leaders), defined as right, left, center and decimal tabs.

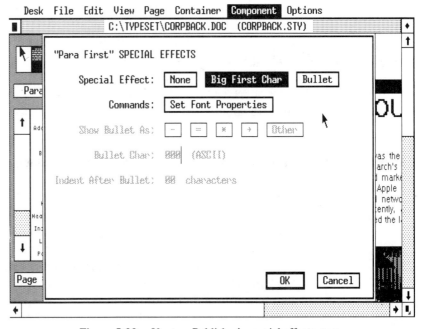

Figure 5-23. Ventura Publisher's special effects menu.

Viewing Your Page

To view your progress in designing your page, you can pull down a menu that gives you four viewing choices. The normal size (100%) provides as close to WYSIWYG as you can get on a PC — adjusted for each different type of graphics card, so that the screen is as close as possible a match to the printed page. The 200% magnified view shows text in a large size for editing, and graphic images for placement. The full page display, which "greeks" the text to resemble a design rough or "dummy", shows the whole page on screen at once, so you can view the design at any time, without having to print the page until you are satisfied with your results.

The fourth display choice is facing pages, where two facing pages are displayed to fill your screen, so that you can see how two pages that will be a pair (left and right, or facing pages, in your final document) will look together before you print them. They are also "greeked," but you can see placement to see if your margins across pages are even, and judge whether the pages are balanced in other ways.

You can select to turn on rulers (inches or picas) to help with measuring margins, lines, graphics, and you move about on the page with left/right and up/down scroll bars. Usually you will want to look into a window on the page at the same size as your printer produces (8½ x 11 or 11 x 17). Working at this actual (100%) size, you can easily scroll around to the position you want, or you can select from the Page menu to view the page at 200% (zoom in for a magnified look), or reduced to fit the full page (or facing pages) on the screen.

If you plan to print your final copy in color, you can see on the screen the effects of changing colors. Eight different colors and eight textured backgrounds can be used in each article, each scanned image, and each graphic image.

Advanced Layout Tools

You can set up your article to have automatic page numbering, with a choice of arabic numbers, upper or lower case roman numerals, or alphabetic "numbering" ("a" is one, "z" is twenty-six). Page numbers can be included in headers and footers.

The program can set different headers and footers for left and right pages, and section headings can be automatically included in the header or footer, formatted automatically to be justified according to your preferences (left, center, or right justified).

One problem in layout is what to do with *widows* and *orphans*. If you have a line isolated at the bottom of your page (orphan) or a line that ends a paragraph isolated at the top of the next column (widow), the line looks out of place, and is distracting to your eye. Ventura Publisher has adjustable widow/orphan control, and a "keep with next" feature that can be used to force headings and subheads (or titles) to be placed on the same page with the paragraph that follows them, so you won't end up with orphan titles.

You can set automatic column balance so that each column is the same length, and ends at the same point on the page. This feature is useful for text on the last page of a chapter that would otherwise be placed in one long and one short column. Instead, the columns are shortened and lengthened to the same baseline. The Container menu offers the Container Balance option to balance however many columns you have in a container to have an even bottom margin length.

For longer pieces of text, Ventura Publisher provides automatic flowing and formatting of text across multiple pages. For example, three articles that are each two columns wide can begin on the same page, and each can continue to different pages and/or columns (this feature is needed by most newspapers).

Text and Graphics

Ventura Publisher can read text saved in a straight ASCII file created with any word processing program. Spreadsheets can be read into the program if they are in the ASCII text format.

If the file was created with Microsoft Word, WordStar, or Multimate, the text file is actually opened by Ventura Publisher, and any editing or formatting changes you make to the document will also be saved in your text file. When you edit the file later with your word processing program, you will be working on the new version of the file.

This means that changes you make to the text in your layout are saved automatically as changes to your text file, so you are always working with the same (latest revision) version of your text file, whether you read/change the text with Ventura Publisher or your word processing program.

To place your text, select a page or container by pointing to it with your mouse, then select the text file from those shown in the selection list on the screen. When placing new containers on the page, text is reformatted to flow around the container. You can place either text or graphics inside any container.

The Text Edit function lets you insert text at any point. The entire document is automatically reformatted as text is added or deleted. Individual blocks of text (and graphics) can be moved by selecting Cut, Copy or Paste from the Edit menu.

You can read scanned images (graphics, logos, etc.) into your pages. Datacopy, Microtek and Dest scanners produce images that can be brought into Ventura Publisher documents, where they can be moved, sized (reduced and enlarged), and cropped to fit. Scanned images at a low resolution can be improved (scaled to a higher resolution) by reducing them after you bring them into your page layout.

Art created using GEM Paint, GEM Draw, and other GEM programs (GEM Graph, GEM WordChart) can be moved and sized and placed in your Ventura Publisher documents.

The program uses GEM's VDI (Virtual Device Interface) to give full output resolution independent of screen resolution, except for scanned images, which are printed at a resolution dependent on the scanner (original resolution depends on resolution capability and setting of scanner) and scaling factor (size down or reduce for higher resolution, or size up or enlarge for lower resolution — but when you enlarge, the dots get bigger as well as further apart).

Printing Pages   Printers range in output resolution and typefonts. Ventura Publisher prints to the Epson/IBM MX-80 and FX-80 and compatible dot matrix printers, Epson-compatible laser printers, the IBM Proprinter, the H-P LaserJet (and add-on font cartridges) and LaserJet Plus, and the Apple LaserWriter as well as all other PostScript laser printers and typesetters.

As the GEM system software supports new printers, so will Ventura Publisher, since it relies on the GEM printer drivers.

Summary   Ventura Publisher is the first personal computer page makeup program in the under-$1000 category to offer both WYSIWYG page makeup and the stylesheet approach for lengthy documents.

Each chapter can be up to 100 pages long. Each time you change automatic settings, the program reformats the entire document with lightning speed. When you add, move or delete graphics or text, the document is also reformatted. The reformatting is faster (the longer your document, the more you will appreciate the speed) than any other program we've seen on the PC, and also faster than PageMaker on the Macintosh.

The program is useful for just about any desktop publishing application, from designing one-page advertisements to 100-page manuals. The program excels in producing the lengthier documents because the stylesheet approach makes it easy to define a page format and copy it to hundreds of pages.

The program is fast in reformatting because it doesn't actually store the text and graphics with the page layout. By manipulating pointers to the text and graphics files, the program composes each page over and over but does not have the time-consuming task of storing and retrieving text. Consequently it is easy to have changes made to the text in the page saved in the original file.

Compared to both the page makeup programs in this chapter and the professional programs in Chapter 7, this program is the best buy. It packs the most features into a useful structure that lets you handle both single pages and multi-page documents with precision and simplicity.

CHAPTER SIX

Design and Production

Half the money I spend on advertising is wasted, and the trouble is I don't know which half.
— John Wanamaker

Where to Begin To create an attractive and readable publication, or an effective advertisement or marketing piece, you need to think about visual communication techniques. No matter how simple a design problem seems to be, you should be able to answer five essential questions about your publication or piece:

1. *What* is your objective (what is it you are trying to achieve)? Do you want to entertain, inform, impress, or sell something? Be specific — supply answers like "I want to sell records" or "I want to explain how to use this piece of farming equipment." Forget for a minute how it will be published or presented — concentrate first on why you want to publish it and what results you want.

2. *Who* is your message aimed at? Can you define the audience or reader? Again, be specific — "The reader is a twelve-year-old girl" or "The reader is a farmer who already knows the price of tomatoes in Des Moines." You have to know what your reader wants to read, if only to attract attention to your message.

3. *Why* does your message need to be published? "The record won't sell without a powerful message, sensitive to the interests of pre-teen females," or "There is no way a farmer could use this piece of equipment without instructions." If you can answer this question without a doubt in your mind, you will come up with an effective design.

4. *Where* does your message belong? "In a teenage fantasy magazine" or "in a manual packaged with the equipment." If your message belongs on TV, don't waste time designing a newspaper ad. (Your answer to this question will depend on the answers you gave to the other questions.)

5. Finally, *how* are you going to produce and convey the message? "In a colorful print advertisement in a glitzy tabloid" or "In a bound manual of around fifty pages, in a size that fits the equipment's existing packaging." This is the last question because it depends entirely on the answers to the ones before it. The answer to this question is the foundation on which you build your design effort.

Design must attract readers, entice them to continue reading after they read the headline or title, and provide a structure and hierarchy for the information that helps readers understand the message. You've heard of the need to "invite the reader into the page" but you should also be careful not to let the design get in the way of the text. On the other hand, if your text is not comprehensible without graphics, the reader may become annoyed; if the text itself is barely legible, the reader may become hostile.

In very few cases does a reader absolutely have to pay attention to a published piece; therefore, you must write and design the piece to offer something in return for the reader's time. Designers and text writers must work together to produce something that will communicate effectively.

The theory is all well and good, you might say, but how do you go about designing your marketing piece, your newsletter or magazine page, your book page, or your manual? Start with answers to the five essential questions described above. Then look for an idea if you don't already have one. "Borrow" an idea if you want to test the effect — copy the format from a newsletter or magazine that deals with a different subject but in a similar manner, or try to match your competitor's marketing piece, or test layouts from numerous books and manuals.

Then look at the hardware and software described in this book, and see what production method matches your needs. Start with *typesetting capabilities* and any four-color needs. Usually the design hinges on what you can afford in typesetting and four-color processing.

For example, your design may call for very large type in a headline used in a full-page advertisement in a large-circulation consumer magazine. Readers come to expect a high-quality ad in such a magazine, so you have to consider the style and weight of the letters, whether or not you need *kerning control* (adjustable spacing between letters), and whether or not you can afford a four-color ad (the process costs more and the magazine usually charges more), a two-color ad, or a black-and-white ad.

Your answers to the questions about typesetting will help you decide which software to use and on which computer to use it. Your answer to the question of color graphics will help you decide whether or not to design the ad with a four-color graphic, a black-and-white graphic with gray tones or spot color, a black-and-white halftone photograph, or just black-and-white line art.

You might work backwards, from the equipment you have to what you can produce with it. Here's an example: we chose PageMaker for the page makeup and typesetting for an issue of *Desktop Publishing* magazine. Since there is no provision for automatic hyphenation or kerning in the version of PageMaker we use, we chose a page design that used ragged-right columns without a lot of hyphenation. These design criteria came out of our choice of typesetting methods.

If you commit to a typesetting process with limitations, you are usually stuck with those limitations in your design, but you may also come out ahead in cost and in quality control. PageMaker made it possible for us to "pour" text into pages easily, without the need for paste-up, and produce typeset magazine pages more quickly than before. Ragged-right columns saved us hours of typesetting time and money.

This chapter is about learning some layout and production tricks that can save you time and money. It is not a crash course in design, because there are many excellent books that provide such information, and they are listed in the bibliography. However it does touch on many of the basic production techniques, typesetting and printing terms, and design considerations.

Press Limitations   When you start the design effort, consider limitations of the printing presses available to you (and what you can afford). Ask a printer how the presses work. A surprising amount of what a graphic designer does involves working around the limitations of printing presses. Ask for a copy of mechanical specifications for your publication from the printer you plan to use.

Cost is a major factor that controls the page size. Paper comes in only a few standard sizes, and if you do not use a standard size, the paper must be cut from an oversized sheet or roll of paper (this additional step costs extra).

You may not be aware that many low-budget printing presses cannot print to the edge of a standard-size sheet of paper. If you try to print the entire sheet, the edges will be blank. The area that prints is called the *image area*.

Some presses print to the edge of the paper and beyond ("bleed" off the page). If you intend to bleed your image, in addition to the image area, you must know the *live matter area* dimensions. To be on the safe side, do not put important information (such as type and graphics) near the edge of the paper (outside the live matter area), because low-cost presses can't print exactly on the same spot on each sheet. Anything positioned too close to the edge might be off the page on some of the sheets.

Trimming also affects the "live matter." Often magazines are printed on oversized sheets of paper, folded, and then trimmed to size. Rather than being limited by the single sheet printing press, you must plan for the accuracy of the trimming machine. Many mechanical trimmers cannot trim precisely the same spot on every copy. Therefore, you must keep your copy and images away from the edges of the page, unless you intend to bleed them. Ask your printer how much variation to expect. Older web presses can vary by up to ⅛ inch from copy to copy, allowing for the inaccuracy of the trimmer.

Another term you need to know is *bleed*. If the image goes to the edge of the paper and beyond, the ink is said to bleed off the page. The printer will tell you how big you must make the bleed area. If the bleed area is not large enough, some sheets may not bleed off the edge if the printing and trimming is not precise. If the bleed area is too large, the ink can begin to build up on the rollers of the printing press, causing other problems in the press run. Usually a web press requires ⅜ inch (¼ inch is ideal, plus ⅛ inch variation for bad trimming) "overwork" for bleeds on all sides to guarantee the result.

Some print shops have preprinted sheets that show their recommended publication size, the image area, the "live matter" or safe area, and/or the maximum size that the printing press can print. Or ask for a sample of a similar job, and use a ruler to measure the image-area dimensions.

Many instant-print shops cannot print an image larger than 7¾ x 10½ inches on a regular-size piece of paper. This limitation is partly the result of the action of the "gripper," which grabs the paper at the top or bottom and pulls it through the printing press. If your image is partly tucked under the gripper, that part will not be printed, so design your page to leave space for the gripper.

Overall Page Layout

The Apple LaserWriter and many other laser printers print only an 8 x 10.9-inch image, and some xerographic copiers cannot print an image larger than 8¼ x 10⅝ inches on a regular piece of paper.

Most page layouts call for text to be presented in one or more columns. When designing a multi-page document, divide each page into a grid of columns, with the left page a mirror image of the right (as a starting point; you can always change it if the design doesn't fit your needs).

It makes sense to pick a column measurement used in other publications that are similar to yours, because readers are used to reading columns of that size. Columns are usually measured in *picas* (one-sixth of an inch increments) so that it is easy to translate a printer's point (½ of an inch) into picas (12 points to the pica). Most page makeup programs provide a "preference" menu for you to choose increments for your on-screen ruler to be in inches *or* picas.

If you don't have a typical column width to guide you, a good rule to follow is to make your columns as wide as the lowercase alphabet typed twice, so pick a typestyle and size, type the letters a through z twice, and then measure the resulting line. This is the recommended column width for that typestyle and size.

The reasoning behind this rule is that if the columns are too wide, the reader's eyes will have to do too much work and will get tired. If the column is too narrow, the reader has to scan too many lines.

You also need a *gutter* (white space) between columns so the eye will know that it has reached the edge of the column. If you have too little space, fast reading becomes difficult, but if you have too much space, you will waste valuable page space.

Gutter *rules* (straight lines) reduce the need for white space between columns. How much is a matter of judgment, but you should pick a style that works in another publication similar to yours.

Right margin text justification in a column affects the amount of white space around the column. When you are reading quickly, the smooth edge of justified text on the right is easier to see than a ragged edge, and therefore you need less white space. Unfortunately, justified text is often harder to read than ragged-right text, especially in narrow columns, because of the uneven (proportional) space between words.

Page layout involves an infinite number of choices. Although none of them are absolutely right or wrong, some are better than others in attracting readers. The advantage of using a page makeup program is that you can play "what if" and produce models for others to see and give you feedback. You can try many different page layouts until you're satisfied.

Figure 6-1.   Sketching your publication's page layout before starting PageMaker. The final trim is the paper itself, and the image area is the outer box. The inner box is the border, and inside this box are boxes showing columns for text.

Using PageMaker for Production

Before you create a PageMaker publication file, you should have a basic idea of how the publication should look. You need to know the *image area* (the area where all text and graphics should be placed), and what design elements you will use (borders, page numbers and folios, graphic elements, and so on).

The first thing PageMaker wants to know is the image area. You might find it easier to work with the sample from the printer and a ruler, to calculate by hand the dimensions and placement of the borders and text for your publication before you start to use PageMaker. Perhaps it makes sense for you to use a piece of 8 ½ x 11-inch paper to represent the final trim dimensions of your publication (the final trim is where the paper will be cut to make your publication). Most newsletters are 8½ x 11 inches. If your publication is smaller than 8½ x 11 inches, draw a box to show the final trim dimensions.

Draw a box on the page to represent the image area (the image area is always within the final trim dimensions). If you intend to use a decorative border, make the border the size of the image area or smaller. If you are going to put page numbers outside the border, leave room for the number within the image area. Nest a second box within the borders of the first box and place your columns of text and images within this inner box (see figure 6-1).

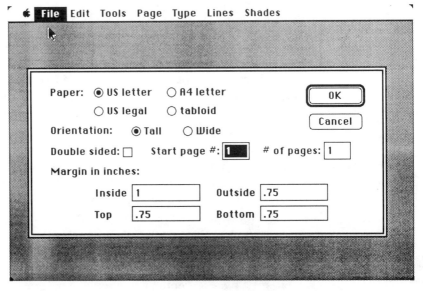

Figure 6-2. Starting a publication file in PageMaker: specifying the margins of the page. You can use picas, millimeters or inches.

You can select pica, millimeter or inch measurements in the Preferences selection of the pull-down Edit menu, and you are ready to open a new document — select New from the File menu. Page-Maker displays a menu asking for the outer margins of the page (figure 6-2). Measure from the edge of the paper (the trim size) to the innermost box.

Once you have finished with the page setup, select the Column

Guides menu and type the number of columns for the master page, and the amount of space to use for the gap between columns. Use about 0.25 inches for the column gap (also measured as "1p6pt" for one pica and six points, if using pica measurements). You can change the columns on each page, or keep the number of columns used for the "master" page. The Column Guides menu always shows the number of columns on the current page.

Standard Page Sizes

If you want to publish a small newsletter or one-page flyer, contact a local instant-print shop and ask them for information about printing such a flyer — what kind of press they have, and whether you should leave a ¼-inch or ⅜-inch blank area around the edge of each printed page (the difference between the trim dimension and the image area). You may also need to leave a margin for the press gripper on one side of the page.

If your newsletter or flyer is a standard paper size (8½ x 11 inches), you can use the default PageMaker settings for the image area. These are: 1 inch from the inside (right edge on left-hand pages, left edge on right-hand pages), ¾ of an inch from the outside (the reverse of the inside), and ¾ of an inch from the top and bottom edges. PageMaker can print on 8½ x 14 inch paper with these settings as well.

If you are not sure of dimensions, or you are designing something that is not 8½ x 11 inches, determine your image area as it should appear on the page printed by the laser printer. The LaserWriter and LaserWriter Plus can print up to 8 x 10.9 inches. You can use a wide orientation (also known as *landscape* orientation) or the usual tall (also known as *portrait*).

When PageMaker asks for the margins, measure from the edge of the paper to the image area, using a ruler with decimal fractions of inches, or pica or centimeter ruler. If you are doing a one-page flyer, click the double-sided option off, as shown in figure 6-2. This gives you one master page for all pages. If you are doing more than one page, click on the double-sided option to select left and right master pages.

Columns and Borders

Next, select the Column Guides menu and define two columns (or three columns, or up to ten columns), with at least a 0.15-inch gap (preferably a 0.25-inch gap, or 1 pica and 6 points) between columns (see figure 6-3).

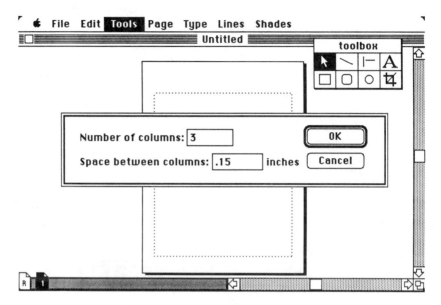

Figure 6-3.   Selecting columns in PageMaker for a typical newsletter page.

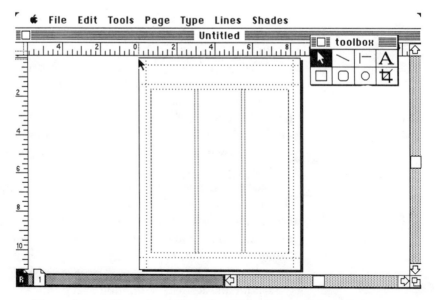

Figure 6-4.   Adding ruler guides in PageMaker for a typical newsletter page.

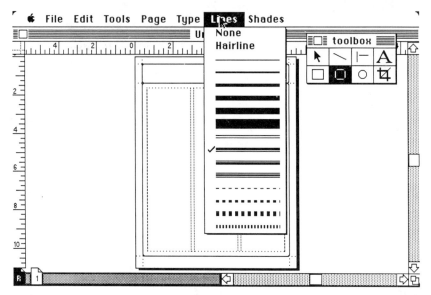

Figure 6-5. A border can be drawn on the master page using the straight or rounded box tool. You can then set the line thickness of the border.

You can display rulers while working on a master page or any other page. You can put ruler guides anywhere you like (ruler guides are for placement of text and graphic elements — the "snap-to" feature makes placement to a ruler guide very easy). For example, you can use a ruler guide for the headline, one for the bottom of text, one for the page number line, and two for the outer margins to show where a border could be added.

Use the straight or rounded box tool to draw a border around the page, as shown in figure 6-5. You can select the line thickness for the entire box in one step.

You can use boxes, shading, rounding, and other options of Page-Maker to create special effects on the master page or any other page of the publication file. If you're doing a one-page flyer, create the borders for the headline on the master page. If the publication will have more than one page, place only the items that you want to repeat on the master page and put the heading box on page one only.

Save the master page definition as a publication file so that you can use the same design for new publications without having to redefine the master page (figure 6-6).

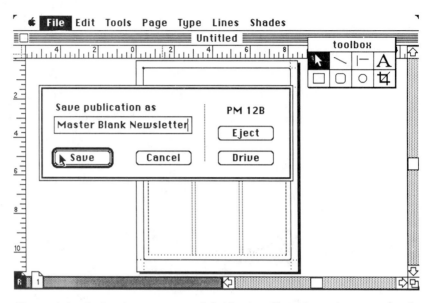

Figure 6-6. Saving the master page definition in a file, to be used as a template for more flyers or newsletters.

Postcards and Business Cards

Postcards and business cards are easy to prepare with PageMaker. Ask your local instant-print shop about printing postcards. They will probably tell you that they can print four on a single sheet of heavy 110 lb. index stock and then cut them apart.

Draw an outline of the postcard on 8½ x 11-inch paper to get the dimensions of the trim size (use a real postcard as a template). If your postcard is too big to fit the text and graphics of all four on one laser printed page, you can draw one and then cut/paste four copies of it onto a board for your printer (you must do it this way if the laser printer cuts off part of the text or image at the edge of the page).

Draw boxes within your trim size to indicate a border around the image area (if you want one), and another to indicate the area where text and graphics will be placed. Use these measurements when you start a new publication with PageMaker (see figure 6-7). You don't need column guides unless you plan to use more than one column.

The master page (figure 6-8) shows the ruler guides for the outer trim, the border, and the image area. You can use the middle ruler guides to create a box border. Boxes can have straight, rounded, oval, or circular corners.

In figure 6-8 you can see the border has fancy straight lines with rounded corners. You can also put tick (crop) marks to show where the postcard will be trimmed, as well as instructions for the press operator and trimmer in a little box on the same page (figure 6-9).

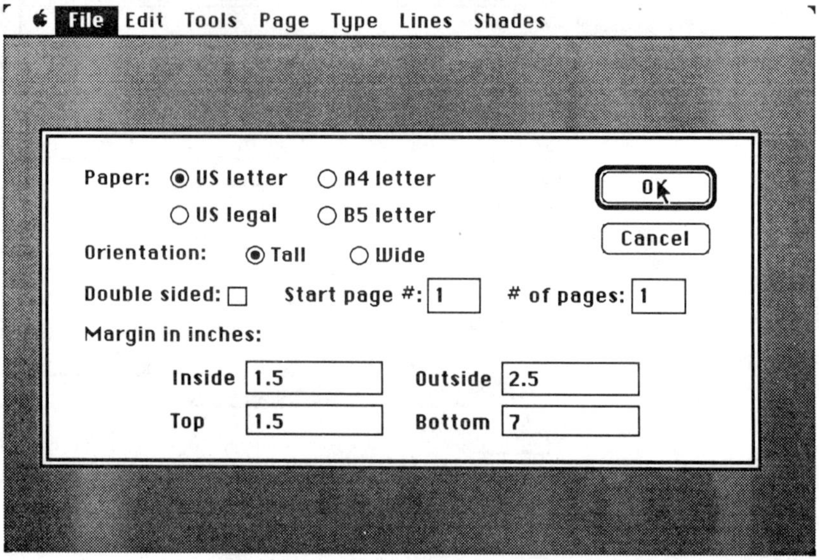

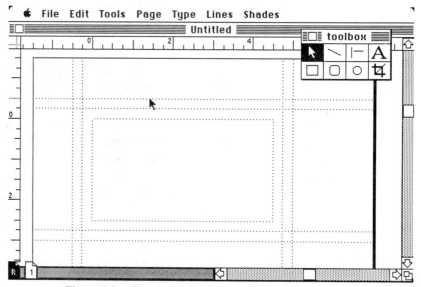

Figure 6-7. Sample PageMaker margin measurements for a postcard.

Figure 6-8. Sample PageMaker master page for a postcard.

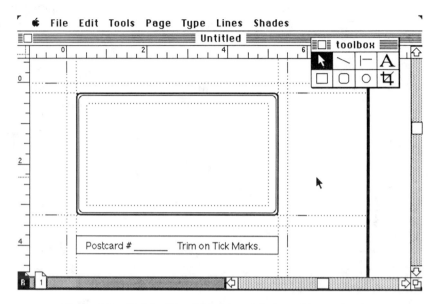

Figure 6-9. Finished PageMaker template for making postcards.

Print shops usually print business cards two at a time on a very small piece of card stock and cut them apart. Others put ten business cards on an 8½ x 11-inch piece of card stock. The trimming charge is higher with the second method but the total cost (and the printing charge) is usually lower.

You can create one business card template and make multiple copies of each business card on the laser printer, then cut/paste the copies onto 8½ x 11-inch paper for printing.

Draw a box on paper representing the trim size, and another representing the image area (you won't have much room for a border, and the trimming is less accurate than with postcards).

When you start a new publication with PageMaker and it asks for the margins, measure from the edge of the page to the inner box (see figure 6-10). You don't need the column guide option.

On the master page you can add ruler guides to show the outside of the card, and move the zero point to the corner of the card.

Templates such as these (defined master pages with a blank starting page) are becoming available from professionals who use PageMaker (third-party sources), and such templates (for newsletters, brochures, etc.) are planned from Aldus Corp. You can open a template with

PageMaker and start placing text and graphics immediately, or change the master pages to add more elements or subtract some.

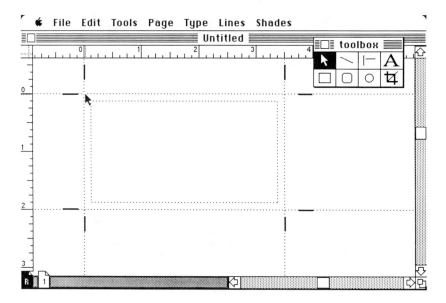

Figure 6-10.   Sample PageMaker margin settings for a business card.

Sample Page Layouts

Most newsletters and U.S. magazines are standard in trim size (8½ x 11 inches) and in image area (7 x 10 inches). A popular width for the image area is 6⅚ inches, or 41 picas, leaving 1/12 of an inch on either size of the page for a border rule (if any). This arrangement makes it very easy to measure a two-column page and a three-column page, using the same basic grid, as shown in figure 6-11.

Within a 41-pica safe area you can place two columns that are 20 picas each, and have a one-pica gutter. You can produce a publication that mixes two- and three-column pages of the same width (using three columns of 13 picas with one-pica gutters).

If you want more than three columns, it might be easier to define a safe area width of 39 picas, so that you can place four columns of 9 picas each with one-pica gutters, or five columns of 7 picas each with one-pica gutters.

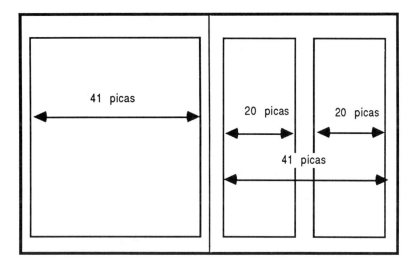

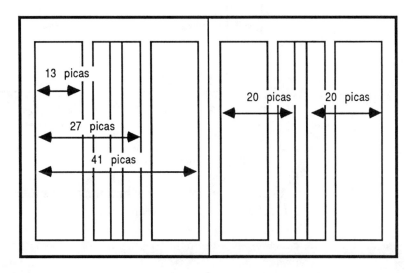

Figure 6-11. Layouts for one-column, two-column and three-column pages for newsletters and magazines, with measurements in picas (a pica is one-sixth of an inch, or 12 printer's points).

Headlines and sub-heads can span several columns, and you can wrap text around graphic images that are larger than the boundaries of the columns. Start with a consistent column layout and then design graphic elements that bend the rules for overall attractiveness. Check the bibliography for books on magazine page design.

Flyers and Advertisements   Flyers (and broadsides) are usually a standard 8 ½ x 11 inches and designed to look like one-page advertisements or magazine pages. Brochures can be almost any size and shape, depending on how they are folded. An easy way to decide what size to use is to get samples from a printer.

The simplest folding methods are done with 8 ½ x 11-inch, 8 ½ x 14-inch, or 11 x 17-inch paper. The most common folds for brochures are the eight-page map fold and gate fold (figure 6-12).

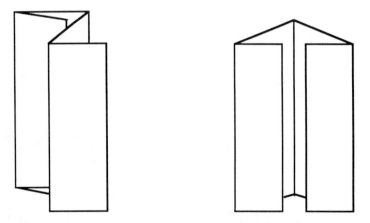

Figure 6-12.   An eight-page map fold (left) and gate fold for brochures.

The type of fold you choose should be one that can be handled by the printer's machines, because hand folding is expensive.

Because there are so many different ways to lay out information for a brochure or flyer, there are no typical page layouts. However, you can't go wrong if you design a page layout that is similar in style and exact in measurement to one that was successfully printed by your printer.

Single-page magazine ads (and two-page spreads) usually follow the same rules as magazine pages — a safe image area of 7 x 10 inches, perhaps with an image bleeding on one side, two sides, three sides or all four sides, extending out beyond the trim size.

Theories on good design for advertising are plentiful, but one tenet of nearly every theorist is that the design of the advertisement should grab a reader's attention immediately. This is usually accomplished with a headline or image that "grabs" you and brings you into the page.

At that point, once you get their attention you shouldn't bore the reader with unnecessary words. Get right to the point, or lead up to it in such a manner that the reader is engrossed. Some theorists say you should design the ad to look like a page of editorial content, on the theory that the reader will be fooled into thinking it is editorial copy, at least at first (and if you have their attention you can sell them a product, even if they're insulted by your approach).

This can backfire on you, of course — nearly every technique can backfire on you if not implemented in a way that makes the ad effective. There are no rules on ad design except that the absence of a rule is the rule. But there are plenty of guidelines, the best being actual examples of ads that work.

There are magazines and newsletters with regular feature columns that critique advertising by the design experts. See the bibliography for a list of such publications.

Some guidelines are common sense: don't use too many images or large type headlines, just enough to grab the reader. Don't use a typefont that is hard to read or illegible (more on typefonts later). Don't use a muddy photograph or a complex drawing unless it grabs the reader for some reason. Go ahead and insult the reader, but only if you think the idea will sell products.

Although publishers may design their magazine pages as inexpensively as possible, advertisers in those magazines usually have experts design their ads; after all, ads take up costly space and are supposed to directly generate income. Therefore, consult with a communications or design expert before finalizing your ad design, and make sure your ad looks as good as it possibly can.

Book and Manual Pages

Books and manuals have a different purpose: to present a lengthy amount of information in a consistent and readable fashion. Book and manual designs are usually very simple but effective in presenting information from front to back that is easy to refer to by means of headings and sub-headings. Designs take into account chapter titles, headings, sub-headings, figures (areas with line art or photographic images) with figure captions, charts, running heads (descriptive chapter title and/or heading at the top of each page), and page numbers.

The best example we can use of a book layout is in your hands. This book's text was prepared with personal computers and typeset by personal computer. The column width is 26 picas — and the design has running heads (book title on even pages, chapter title on odd pages) with page numbers, a layout with a narrow left column for headings, sub-headings, figure captions and small illustrations, and a wider text column. This layout lets us use different size figures — ones that span both columns, ones that are contained in the wide text column, and small ones that can fit in the narrow left column.

Our book layout was designed to fit a certain size book. Books come in many different sizes, but generally the column width of text should not be longer than 70 characters — you can make the point size larger if you need wider columns.

Manuals that are 8½ x 11 inches in trim size can be designed with the same layout used for two-column magazine pages: 20 picas each column with a one-pica gutter (total safe area: 41 picas). However, manuals usually need the same reference elements found in books: chapter titles, headings and sub-headings (sometimes numbered in manuals), running heads with descriptive titles, and page numbers.

Typefonts and Styles

The first rule is to choose the most readable typefont, style and size. This advice might seem obvious, but many newcomers to desktop publishing want to use the fanciest type in the weirdest sizes. Just because you have 100 typefonts available to you doesn't mean you should use all of them. Use only two or at most three, plus the italic and bold styles.

It helps to know what kinds of typefonts are known to be effective in the kind of publication or piece you are designing. For example, books are usually set in Times Roman (as this one is set) or a similar font, such as Baskerville or Bookman.

The font named Baskerville, designed in the late 18th century, is a transitional font, neither old nor modern style, while Helvetica (the typefont used in many advertisements) is contemporary, designed in the 20th century. Helvetica is a sans (without) serif typefont (*serifs* are small curves added to the edges of letters).

Most contemporary typefonts are sans serif, and are designed to be used in advertising, reference and clinical reports, technical books, signs, and headlines. A sans serif font is usually clean, uncluttered, and communicates the message quickly.

Serifs on a well designed font are not merely for decoration — they perform the useful function of leading your eyes into the letter, so are thought to make reading more comfortable. Typefonts with serifs are often used for setting the text of articles, magazines, books, and lengthy documents.

As a new font is designed either from scratch, or using a rediscovered style from the past, it is usually trademarked by the maker. However, once the name is copyrighted, other manufacturers of fonts design similar fonts with similar names and make minor changes to the design so they won't look exactly alike, and they don't violate the copyrights.

For example, Baskerville is the font name used by Mergenthaler, Compugraphic, Harris Composition Systems, Dymo Graphic Systems and Varityper, while Alphatype calls a very similar font Baskerline, and MGD Systems calls one Beaumont.

For a font designed in more recent times, you see the effects of one company copyrighting a font, which means they own the rights to the name. Thus, a font similar to Mergenthaler's Helvetica is called Helios by Compugraphic, Newton by Dymo Graphic Systems, Geneva by MGD Systems, Vega by Harris Composition systems, Megaron by Varityper and Claro by Alphatype.

Century, designed for the magazine *Century* (1881-1930) by L.B. Benton, is a classical serif typefont that is considered one of the easiest to read. It is often used to set the text in books. The Apple LaserWriter Plus has a version called New Century Schoolbook. Mergenthaler, Harris Composition Systems and Dymo Graphic Systems call it Century Schoolbook, while it is called Schoolbook by Varityper, Century Text by Alphatype, Century Textbook by Compugraphic, and MGD Systems calls it Cambridge Light.

Times Roman (a serif font) is variously known as English, Times New Roman, and London Roman, and usually includes mathematical symbols (a bonus not found in many other text fonts).

For a decorative use, you might want to choose a decorative typefont, such as Egyptienne, Dresden, American Typewriter, Park Avenue, Vivaldi, Ringlet, P.T. Barnum, Stencil, Romantique or many others (some are available for the Macintosh or PC print formatting programs). Do not use a decorative typefont for lots of text — they are best used as headlines.

Many decorative typefonts for personal computers have the "jaggies" (jagged edges) because they are not PostScript fonts at 300 dots per inch, but Imagewriter fonts printed at 75 dots per inch. You get sharper dots with a laser printer, but the same number of dots. The typefonts that print at 300 dots per inch are typically Times Roman, Helvetica, a special Symbol font, Courier (typewriter font), Avant-Garde, Bookman, Century Schoolbook, Palatino, Zapf and Zapf Dingbats (another symbol font), with new fonts being designed (in PostScript) by Adobe Systems (Palo Alto, CA).

Styles and Families

You can find typefonts on dot matrix and laser printers, typesetting machines, special purpose headline machines, and even on mylar sheets in a rub-on (Letraset™) form. The same basic design can go by different names, but expect to find slight variations in design from manufacturer to manufacturer, even if the name for the typefont is the same. You may be able to "match" type, but sometimes you will find that you have to change the point size, or even the spacing between letters to get the best match. Getting a good match also depends on how popular a typefont is; Times Roman is easier to match than other less popular fonts.

Typefonts can be presented in "families," where regular (or medium), bold, and italic styles are grouped together. Other font styles can include bold italic, outline, expanded or extended (Eurostile Bold Extended), condensed (as in Avant Garde Medium Condensed), oblique (slanted, as in Futura Extra Bold Condensed Oblique), backslanted, light (American Typewriter Light), extrabold (Folio Extrabold Outline), and even such characteristics as BAUER BODONI TITLE (a font that offers only uppercase letters), or a single font such as Arrow®, designed in only one version, and a registered trademark. The Arrow typefont is popularly seen on Arrow brand men's dress shirt packaging.

Symbol fonts usually have all the symbols you'd need, plus large symbols divided into two or more characters. For example, you can typeset a Mastercard symbol by typing its left side and then its right side, in proper sequence, so that they overlay each other to make one complete image. Other symbol fonts are for mathematics, architectural icons, medical icons, and punctuation symbols in other languages.

You can create your own special symbols by *overstriking* (spacing back over a character you just typed and overlaying a second character on top of it) and combining characters from the same fonts. Combining two characters from two different fonts to create a new symbol or character may or may not be possible, depending on the capabilities of your system, but most systems allow you to overstrike two characters that are on the same font.

Type Size and Leading

Establish a consistent pattern for changing type sizes. For example, use a large size for titles, another smaller size for sub-titles and headings, a smaller one for sub-headings, and a regular size for body text and running heads. Choose a size for your body text that is not too small or too large.

Type size in America and Britain is most often measured in *points* and *picas*. A pica is one sixth of an inch, and a point is one seventy-second of an inch. There are 12 points to a pica. Agate lines, used to measure column depth in newspapers, are 14 to the inch. You can easily find a ruler that includes points, picas, inches and agates, and such a ruler is a handy reference for converting between measuring systems, as well as for measuring. Try your local office supply store, or a printing/graphics supply shop.

A Line Gauge is another useful tool for measuring type, and the most complete one we have seen is copyrighted and available in *The Graphics Master* (volume 3) from Dean Lem Associates, PO Box 46086, Los Angeles, CA 90046. The Graphics Master line gauge and ruler measures centimeters, pica and elite typewriter, 6-12 point (picas and half picas, marked off on a 6 point and 12 point scale), agate, inches and 7, 8, 9, 10, 11, 13, 15 and 17 point sizes, plus it includes a centering ruler in picas and inches.

Type sizes are usually measured in points — both height of the letters and the space above and below the letters (the space above and below the letter is included in the type body size). When you use a typefont that has lowercase letters with descenders (like g and y) or ascenders (like b and k), they may butt up against the bottom or top of the type, and in some fonts they may extend beyond the top and bottom of the type size.

The x height is the distance between the baseline (the imaginary line that characters rest on top of) and the top of lower case characters such as a, e, s or x. The cap (or capital) height is the distance between the baseline and the top of an upper case character. In some typefonts, some capital letters such as L extend higher than the cap height of other capital letters like A. The descender line (below the baseline) is the lowest point reached by letters like g, q and p.

To avoid such problems as overprinting, you can specify blank space between lines (called *leading*), usually specified together with the type size. For instance, you might choose for your body text a Times Roman 10 point type with 12 point leading, also expressed as Times Roman 10/12pt., or "ten on twelve point." If you don't specify any leading, the default leading is assumed to be the same as the point size. We use 11/13pt. for the main text font size in this book.

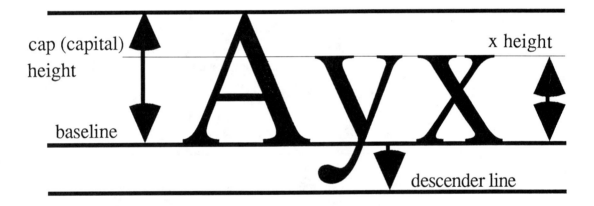

Figure 6-13. Measuring capital letters and small letters.

Depending on which font you choose, you may have extenders and descenders on your letters touching or overlapping if you choose leading the same as the type size. This may also make blocks of text too dense for easy reading. Using a leading size that is one or two points greater than your type size avoids the problems of lines jammed on top of each other, and increases readability.

If you are using a large type size of 40 points or more, and your extenders and descenders are not too long (their length can vary greatly from font to font) you probably won't need more than one extra point of leading (41 points) between lines, and default leading the same as the type size (40 points) might work well. If you have more than one line of bold type at this large size (a headline, for instance), you may want to increase the leading to 42 points to better separate the two lines.

Popular point sizes and leading for the main text of a book, magazine or newsletter include 10/12pt, 10/11pt, 9/10pt, 9/11pt, 11/13pt, 12/14pt and 12/13pt. Experiment with variations to decide which methods work best for you. A copyright notice or other fine print is often set at 6/6pt, or 6/7pt, because 6/8pt opens up too much space between lines.

A rule of thumb used for type size and line length is that the line should be no wider than twice the type size. A ten point type size means the ideal maximum readable line length is 20 picas. The minimum line length is equal to the point size, therefore an 8 pica line length is too short for 10 point type.

Special Typesetting Features

For special effects or fine tuning, you may want to adjust the space between a typefont's characters or the space between words. When you are using a typesetter, laser printer or dot matrix printer capable of proportional spacing of characters, the space between characters is calculated by the computer. If you don't like the spacing you get, you may not have a choice in the matter with dot matrix and laser printers, but you certainly have a choice in typesetters.

Kerning is the most popular adjustment to character spacing. Kerning is the process of tucking one character underneath the arms of another, larger character, so that the characters don't appear to be too far apart (see figure 6-14).

Publishing Tools

Publishing Tools

Figure 6-14.   Kerned letter pairs vs. un-kerned pairs.

You can also adjust the interword spacing — the space calculated by the computer between words placed on a justified line of text. The interword spacing on most daisy wheel printers is so bad that people turn off the justification feature of their word processing programs. However, dot matrix printers can do interword and intercharacter spacing that is more acceptable, and laser printers are even better. Typesetting machines offer controls to fine tune the spacing.

Art and Photo Reproduction

Graphics and color or black-and-white photos can give your publication or piece a professional look. Color photos and graphics are much more expensive to produce — around $300 or more for each color image just to prepare it for printing — but black-and-white photos and line art are not as expensive to reproduce.

Scaling or *sizing* is the term used for reducing or enlarging an image without changing the relation of the dimensions. You can roughly scale an image by drawing an imaginary line diagonally across the image and extending the line to the top corner of the area where the image is to be placed. To specify a percentage reduction or enlargement, use a proportional sizing wheel available from any artist's supply store.

Photographs and line art are rarely in the same size or proportion as the space they should fit into on the page. To make an image fit, you might have to eliminate certain areas of the image — this is called *cropping*. Some page makeup programs have a cropping tool for eliminating the outer edges of graphic images brought into the program for placement on a page. If you are doing manual placement of images, or supplying negatives, you should cut a piece of tracing paper equal to the original size of the image (or make a copy of the image on a copy machine), attach the tissue on top of the image, and mark on the tissue overlay the areas to crop out of the picture. If the image has borders, draw fine lines in the borders to use as crop marks.

Taking Photos

For newsletters and inexpensive production, use black-and-white photos. Digitizers can reproduce photos for printing without the process of halftoning, described next, but the quality is poor compared to halftones.

You can get good results with Tri-X black-and-white film and a 35mm camera with a 24mm super-wide-angle lens or with a 75-200 telephoto-zoom lens. Take the film to a photo lab that specializes in black-and-white film processing, and ask that the film be developed only (and ask for a contact sheet — rather than getting regular prints, which are much more expensive). The total cost for the film, developing, and contact sheet should be about $10.

After looking at the contact sheet, pick the photos you want to use for publication. Mark the contact sheet to show how you want the photos cropped, and take it and the negatives back to the same photo lab. Be sure to ask for glossy prints. Each print will cost about $2.

Halftones   Photographic prints and negatives are *continuous tone* images — they have gradient tones from black-to-white. In conventional letterpress and offset lithography, tones cannot be reproduced by varying the amounts of ink. To get gray tones, the printer prints tiny dots of solid black that are so small they look gray. Before you can print a continuous tone photograph on a printing press, you must convert it to a mass of very small dots. The process of converting a continuous tone image to an image comprised of dots is called *halftoning*, and the dot image is called a *halftone*.

When you have the prints you need, take them to a graphic-arts camera firm (not a photo-camera shop) for halftoning. Specify the amount of enlargement or reduction you need, and whether you want a screened print or negative (screened print is less expensive, but a negative will give better results).

To make a halftone, the camera operator uses a screen and special film. By using different screens, you can alter the density and pattern of the halftone.

The density you need depends on the printing press. Newspapers, for example, require dots to be much farther apart (less dense, prepared with a coarser screen). This is because the newspaper printing press is optimized for speed rather than quality, and the type of paper is too rough to reproduce closely-spaced dots without running (plugging) the ink together. Magazine presses, however, can usually handle denser halftones (produced with finer screens).

The coarseness of a screen is measured in lines per inch. Newspapers typically need a 65-line or 85-line screen. For advertisements, commercial work and magazine pages, you use screens with 120, 133, 150 or more lines per inch. For full-color work you use 133 to 200 lines per inch. Pattern screens may also be available that produce results that resemble effects you can produce with digitizers.

The dot screens give best results.

There are two ways to do halftoning: expensive negative halftones (for high quality) and less expensive screened print halftones. As long as you get your printing done at a commercial print shop, a quality instant-print shop, or a quality copy center, you will get excellent results with the inexpensive method of reproducing photos.

The simplest way to reproduce black-and-white photos is by making a positive halftone or, as it is more commonly known, a *screened print* or a screened PMT. Once you've made the screened print, you trim it and glue it in place on the finished page before you give it to the printer. The printer then takes a line shot of the entire page, which includes the halftone.

When you need screened prints, go to a specialist rather than a print shop. Some commercial printers can make screened prints from black-and-white photos, but not all have the skill or special equipment to do a quality job. Surprisingly, many print shops charge more for screened prints than graphic-arts camera services, since they produce so few screened prints. Graphic arts services can offer advice about which type of screened print to use for the printing process and printer.

A small screened print costs from $4 to $7. If you have more than one photo, however, you can save money. For example, if all of your photos have similar shading (the same range of gray tones) and need the same amount of enlargement or reduction, you can save money by ganging them up onto one large sheet of paper, and have a single screen print made of all the photos at once.

Unless you are doing it as a special effect, be sure that the printer does not screen an already-screened print, because this causes moire patterns to appear in the image (dots overlayed upon dots).

The more expensive but high quality method is to create a negative halftone image rather than a print. The dots in a negative can have a much greater resolution, resulting in a more dense image than a screened print.

The printer makes a line shot of the entire page with black areas where photos should be, and "books" (or "strips") the halftone negative into the page negative (physically tapes it). The page negative is then used to make the plate for printing.

The extra cost of the negatives and the metal plate is rarely justified for newsletters, business reports, fliers, manuals, and the like, but is essential for quality advertisements, magazine pages and books.

One inexpensive trick you can try without halftoning is *posteriza-*

tion — turning a continuous tone photo into blobs of solid black-and-white. Use a copy machine to create posterization effects.

Experiment with different copy machines — some produce different effects than others. If you do not have a good copy machine, take your photo to a print shop or graphics-camera business and ask for a stat (also known as a PMT or velox), which is an extremely-high-contrast photographic reproduction that costs about $5.

Figure 6-15.   A halftone image, screened at 85 lines, with a section enlarged 200%.

Preparation for Printing

The elements that make up the printed image must be assembled on a clean, stable surface (usually *artboard*), but you can also use thick, smooth white paper. The final product that you hand to the printer is called *camera-ready art*.

To get the best results, keep your camera-ready art as clean as possible, and place the elements on the artboard as squarely as possible (use a T-square for alignment). The artboard should have the appropriate corner marks and registration marks printed on the outer edges; if it doesn't, ask your printer to help prepare the artboard.

Production Planning

The most important production tool is your schedule. Without adequate planning your production process can become a nightmare. There are many paper tools — charts, calendars, and such — and there are personal computer tools that can plot events using the highly-acclaimed Critical Path Method (CPM). Milestone (Digital Marketing Corp, $99) is an excellent project planning tool for the PC, and Mac-Project (Apple Computer, $125) and Micro Planner (Micro Planning Software, $495) are two for the Macintosh.

The design step of the creative cycle should occur simultaneously with the writing step, so that when both are finished you are ready to start production. The design and writing step should take into consideration any photos, graphics and other special effects that are part of the message.

The production cycle can start as soon as you have the written material, ready for typesetting, and a finalized design. Typesetting and page layout must occur next, followed by preparation of the artwork and final camera-ready preparation. All of these tasks have to be scheduled to finish at the right time — when the printer needs the material for the timely press run.

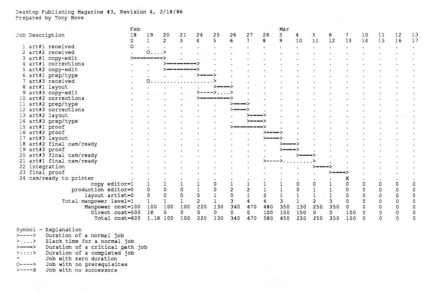

Figure 6-16.   Milestone for the PC shows the critical path for a project with each task and its associated costs.

By using a project management tool such as Milestone or Mac-Project, you can identify each task in the project and its logical position in the sequence of tasks. Some programs can keep track of direct costs and labor costs for each task and present a budget for the project.

Milestone displays a critical path analysis on your PC screen and lets you ask "what if" questions with the tasks. You can change the duration and deadlines of individual tasks without having to redraw the schedule by hand. Each time you insert a new task into the critical path, the entire schedule is computed again.

Milestone shows you which activities are critical and which have slack time, based on subsequent tasks that depend on them. The program can keep track of costs as well, including the cost of labor (called "manpower") and direct expenses relating to each task.

Milestone prepares CPM reports showing cost estimates, and a project calendar with each task and associated resources shown in its logical position in the cycle. At $99 it is the best buy for PC users who want a CPM project scheduling package that is easy to use.

MacProject, for Macintosh users, provides an on-screen scheduling function and "what-if" function for tracking any size or type of project. The program is simple and easy to use, but lacks the ability to model more than one project schedule at a time.

Micro Planner is a more sophisticated package for the Mac that tells you when your resources are over or under utilized, and how best to allocate resources given your priorities. An on-screen modeling function lets you test different solutions and play "what if" with project schedules. Micro Planner can store and compare five different scenarios on the Mac screen simultaneously. Micro Planner is harder to use and costs $495 compared to MacProject at $125, but is well worth it if you are doing serious project planning on a Mac.

Selecting a Printer

To start your process of selecting a printer, call at least ten printers and give a brief description of the job to find out whether the printer has the equipment to do it. If they think they can do the job, they will start asking you questions. You can answer them in writing and ask for a print quote.

If you don't want to spend lots of time learning the printing terms, or getting competitive bids, you can use a print broker, but you could end up paying more. The economies of using a broker over doing it yourself depend on whether the broker can stall payment until the job is completed. A good print broker not only provides the best service at the best price, but also can defer payment until the job has been completed to your satisfaction (COD is standard terms the first time you use a printer or print broker). The broker acts as agent for your business, using his/her good credit rating to guarantee the best service.

If you choose to do it yourself, you may save some money on the overall job. You may have to supervise the press run (do a "press check"), but this ensures that you get what you want. You should brush up on printing terminology by reading some of the books about production and printing in the bibliography, especially the *Pocket Pal* from the International Paper Company.

CHAPTER SEVEN
Professional Composition

I am the voice of today, the herald of tommorrow... I coin for you the enchanting tale, the philosopher's moralizing, and the poet's visions... I am the leaden army that conquers the world — I am TYPE.

— Frederic William Goudy, *The Type Speaks*

Advances in Composition

Most of the desktop publishing products for PCs have evolved either from word processing programs for personal computers, or from professional typesetting software for larger computers.

There is a deliberate cross-over and blending of technologies. For example, the newest typesetting programs, from established vendors of large computerized typesetting systems, borrow their command set from the popular WordStar program. They imitate WordStar to get sales from personal computer users who already know WordStar. Meanwhile, vendors of word processing software for personal computers are enhancing their programs with commands borrowed from large computerized typesetting systems. They are trying to get sales both from personal computer users who need more power from their word processing program, and from professionals who understand the typesetting commands.

Computers have been running typesetting machines since the early 1970's. Before personal computers became popular, typesetting was an operation that required computer specialists. The term "keyboarding" came into usage to describe how text was entered into the large computer system for typesetting. More than just typing, keyboarding meant the use of a special keyboard equipped with keys for typing symbols and paragraph endings, and the use of special software codes that control the appearance of the typeset text — the line length and leading, the typefont style and size, and the format of each paragraph.

The typesetting software evolved into programs that could perform advanced word processing functions, such as the find/replace function that can search for a word, partial word or phrase throughout a text file and replace it with another word, partial word or phrase. As these programs became popular on DEC and Wang minicomputers and IBM mainframes, versions of them started to appear on PCs.

T$_E$X (pronounced "tech," as in *technical*), a typesetting system suitable for setting complex mathematical and scientific equations in text, was one of the first typesetting systems to migrate down from the world of Unix systems (mostly DEC minicomputers and Sun workstations) to the PC.

Typesetting equipment manufacturers are starting to offer complete typesetting systems (ranging from $20,000 to over $100,000) that use PCs as "front ends" (computers controlling the typesetter or feeding data to another computer that controls the typesetter). They are not inexpensive nor do they fit on desktops, but in some cases the software is available for PC users who simply want to do the text editing and preparation on their PCs, and use a service for typesetting.

For example, MagnaType offers a word processing program called MagnaWord for PCs that is similar to WordStar but offers typesetting codes for use while writing and editing text. You can take your MagnaWord documents over to a PC-based MagnaType typesetting system for output.

Another major advance in the typesetting technology is the integration of graphics on the electronic page before typesetting. Nearly every full-page composition system over $50,000 offers graphics integration with optional digitizing equipment. The Interleaf system, which runs on Sun workstations, is an excellent example of a professional composition system that integrates digitized and computer-drawn graphics and typeset text in a fully-featured pagination system. The Interleaf system is mentioned briefly in this chapter, even though at $46,000 for the minimum configuration it is on the extreme high edge of desktop publishing.

Most if not all of the professional typesetting and page composition packages offer an automatic hyphenation and line justification function, called *h&j*, that either runs in the background while you do something else (because the h&j process is time consuming), or runs at an acceptable speed due to software optimization. Automatic hyphenation is essential if you want right-justified columns; without it your interword spacing looks terrible, because the system has to use a lot of space to justify each line. The hyphenation is usually performed with a combination of algorithms and a dictionary of exception words that do not fit the algorithms (called an *exception dictionary*). The accuracy of the automatic hyphenation is one of the many features you judge a system by. The best way to judge accuracy is to run sample text through the system to see how it hyphenates.

Some of the software programs described in this chapter are borderline desktop publishing products because they are so expensive (ranging from $1000 to over $50,000). However, with the exception of the Interleaf system, they all work on personal computers that can fit on a desktop, and they all work with inexpensive laser printers. JustText ($195) is the only program in the chapter that is priced reasonably as a desktop publishing program; the others are priced more for professional typesetters.

Professional Page Composition

Professional typographers require more typesetting control functions than the page makeup programs in Chapter 5 offer. They also require a degree of compatibility with older and current typesetting machines such as the Alphatype CRS, the AM Varityper 6400, the Autologic APS-5 and Micro-5, the Merganthaler 202, the Compugraphic 8400 and 8600, and Allied Linotype typesetters.

No doubt the publishers of less expensive page makeup programs are making improvements that will challenge the position of the professional packages mentioned here; but for now, these packages are popular among professionals and are useful, although they are priced almost out of the realm of desktop publishing. All of them provide a WYSIWYG display of the text and graphics and page makeup features.

PagePlanner

Suitable for lengthy books as well as one-page ads, PagePlanner ($3995 from PagePlanner Systems) provides an easy way to bring WordStar text into a full-page layout system with something like a WYSIWYG display. You won't see the actual words on the full page display using an IBM PC XT or compatible, but you can get the optional PagePlanner monitor which uses a 68000 processor for displaying pages. PagePlanner is a page typesetting system — it does not handle graphics but lets you indicate areas where graphics would be placed, and lets you draw lines and boxes. In addition, the supplied AdSet program lets you flow text around non-rectangular areas set aside for graphics.

PagePlanner presents its functions in two menus: one for ad layout and one for books and long documents. Both modules give you full-page layout with headlines, rules and boxes. You lay out the grid for a page, and then you can "pour" text into selected areas. The program can display the entire page, with text areas filled with a pattern rather than actual words. Information about typefont size and the dimensions of the page appear on the left side of the screen, and the depth of the file is calculated in lines as well as in inches or picas and points. You can "toggle" back and forth from page view mode to text view mode.

PagePlanner supplies a conversion utility to convert WordStar files into PagePlanner format, while preserving the WordStar print formatting commands. Text from other word processing programs can be brought into PagePlanner, but formatting commands are not retained.

PagePlanner can automatically hyphenate and justify the text, but only *before* you pour the text into position on the page. If you find any errors, you have to return to the original text file to edit and rehyphenate/justify the text, then repour the text into position on the page.

PagePlanner requires an IBM PC XT with 512K bytes of RAM and a Hercules-compatible monochrome or IBM EGA graphics card (a card is optionally bundled with the package for users who don't have a graphics card — as well as a high-resolution black-and-white monitor). For an extra $4000, you can buy PagePlanner with a completely-outfitted, PC-compatible ITT PC equipped with a ten-megabyte hard disk and 640K of RAM.

PagePlanner can print on the Epson FX or MX printers (for draft purposes) and produces output for the Allied Linotype 101 and 202 typesetters, the Compugraphic 8400 and 8600, the AM Varityper Comp/Set and Comp/Edit systems, the Autologic APS-5, the Laser-Comp, the Compugraphic EditWriter, and the Linotype CRTronic 150, 200 and 300 typesetters.

SuperPage and Type Processor One

The SuperPage five-disk package from Bestinfo ($7000) provides WYSIWYG page makeup for multi-page documents, integrating both text and graphics (such as digitized images from the Datacopy scanner). Type Processor One, a forerunner to SuperPage, is a less expensive alternative ($4995) that can handle only one page at a time, without graphics. Both packages run on an IBM PC XT or compatible.

Type Processor One uses markup commands similar to conventional typesetting, but is limited to one 8 x 11-inch page, and each page is stored as a separate document. Type Processor One can draw rules and boxes but cannot edit graphic elements. When you pour text into positions on a page, the program shows where the cutoff occurs in the text file so that you can find your place to pour the subsequent text into the next page.

Type Processor One is designed for producing forms, display ads and brochures. It provides leading in ½-point increments, and kerning (using your cursor keys you can kern letters closer together).

SuperPage is similar to Type Processor One, with additional features to handle multiple-page documents. With SuperPage, you can set up headers and footers with right and left pages. You can design page formats with rules and boxes, and use them as templates for documents. You can flow text from a word processing program into areas mapped out on the page, using automatic settings for typefont, type size, leading, paragraph spacing, vertical justification between lines and paragraphs and above subheads, spacing between words, kerning, and orphan/widow control. SuperPage can flow text over many pages, and any changes made on one page cause the program to readjust all of the subsequent pages. It can also supply "Continued on page ..." lines at the end of each page.

SuperPage can wrap text around irregular shapes and incorporate digitized images from the Datacopy scanner. You have the option of using a 10 x 7-inch monitor available from Bestinfo that can show full pages with readable text.

Bestinfo provides additional optional programs for use in multiuser or network systems. Typedit, a $500 word processing program, includes job tracking and file management. Typesat ($6995) has all the features of Typedit plus automatic h&j (hyphenation and justification) running in background mode for faster results. You can use Typesat by itself or in conjunction with SuperPage.

SuperPage prints on the IBM Graphics Printer and the Epson FX line of printers for preview drafts, and on popular laser printers including the H-P LaserJet, QMS printers, Imagen printers and the Xerox 2700. It can also drive typesetters from Linotype, Compugraphic, Autologic, AM Varityper and Itek, and prepare output for other composition systems, including Atex, Penta, CCI, AKI and Quadex.

SuperPage and the rest of the software requires at least one IBM PC

XT or compatible with 512K RAM, a ten-megabyte hard disk, a high-resolution monochrome black-and-white monitor, and a Hercules or compatible graphics card. Type Processor One requires the same setup with only 256K RAM.

DO-IT   Studio Software's DO-IT package ($2495, plus $995 per output module and $495 for a hyphenation dictionary) provides near-WYSIWYG page makeup, using icons, pull-down menus and a mouse, on an IBM PC XT or compatible. DO-IT's icons are familiar to graphic artists — a T-square for positioning, a stat camera for making copies, and a blue pencil for defining columns of text and areas for graphics. DO-IT is strictly for one-page or two-page ads, flyers and brochures — the program does not automatically flow text from one page to the next.

DO-IT's advantage is its typographic capabilities at the lower price. You can set the maximum and minimum spacing between words, select automatic kerning, wrap text around graphics and automatically hyphenate words using a 40,000-word exception dictionary.

You can set up format elements in DO-IT for different level subheads and other elements in your text. You prepare the text using any word processing program, putting the labels for your format elements in the appropriate places in the text. DO-IT provides a table for setting typefont sizes and line widths to use for each element. You then define a page with boxes showing areas of text, using the format element labels to indicate which text element goes in which box.

DO-IT lets you zoom in to see the text and graphics layout or display the full page on the screen. DO-IT does not have the ability to draw images or handle graphics, but you can draw boxes and define areas where graphics would be placed on the page.

The program lets you view two pages of text on the screen at once. For data sheets, newsletters, organizational charts and brochures, DO-IT may be worth its price. However, for publishing books, DO-IT doesn't really do it, because additions or corrections that cause elements to overflow or run over onto the next page will not automatically adjust the rest of the pages in your document. DO-IT can place text from any word processing program that can save text in a standard ASCII file, including Multimate, WordStar and DisplayWrite 2.

Studio Software provides optional output drivers for DO-IT that can print on the Apple LaserWriter and any PostScript device, including the Allied Linotype PostScript typesetters. DO-IT can print to a variety of output devices such as H-P and Houston Instruments plotters. DO-IT has drivers for the H-P LaserJet, Imagen laser printers, QMS Lasergrafix Series printers, Xerox 2700 and other laser printers. DO-IT also has drivers for the Alphatype CRS, the AM Varityper 6400, the Autologic APS-5 and Micro-5, the Compugraphic 8400 and 8600, and Allied Linotype typesetters.

DO-IT requires an IBM PC XT or compatible with 640K RAM, an 8087 arithmetic co-processor, the Hercules or IBM color graphics card, and a hard disk. You can improve the display with an IBM Enhanced Graphics Adapter.

Figure 7-1.   Studio Software's DO-IT.

Interleaf and High-end Systems   The Interleaf system is the state-of-the-art for WYSIWYG corporate publishing systems. The system comes with 86 megabytes of data storage, a 20-megabyte cassette tape backup unit, a 19-inch monitor, the Sun workstation Unix system, and an eight page-per-minute laser printer (Imagen), all for $46,000. The system supports PostScript, Interpress and Dataproducts, and uses Sun, Apollo, or Digital Equipment workstations. The software includes a complete text editor and processor, or you can use a PC and transfer the text into the system.

For page makeup, the Interleaf system includes automatic real-time

time pagination, the American Heritage dictionary for hyphenation, a graphics editor that can create, shadow, box and duplicate images, plus a clip art library. Charts are drawn from spreadsheet data in 40 different styles of pies, bars, and surface charts. You can rotate a graphic object, crop it, flop it, do pixel editing, and compress scanned images for more efficient storage. The system can handle continuous-tone data photos and change densities. For example, you can do a 55-line screen for a laser printer or an 88-line screen for a typesetter. You can also make a negative.

The Interleaf system's capabilities are matched by newer competing systems from XYvision, TeXset, Compugraphic and Xerox, most of which are more expensive.

Professional Typesetting

The most accurate and fully-featured typesetting programs are not WYSIWYG, because the features they provide are not easily depicted on the screen. For example, JustText and others let you do precise kerning, control interword spacing, and do automatic hyphenation that is very fast. These functions are either very imprecise on the screen, or they slow down the operation and are deemed not necessary.

For example, typesetting a book would take a lot longer if you used a WYSIWYG page makeup program to design each page. Some of the WYSIWYG programs (such as Ventura's Ventura Publisher) combine screen viewing with quick hyphenation and pagination, but most do not.

For many book publishers, the following non-WYSIWYG programs are perfect for the job. For mathematics and science textbooks, you may want to use T_EX, which was designed by a mathematician and approved by the American Mathematical Society.

JustText

JustText (Knowledge Engineering, $195) is a program that runs on the Macintosh for typesetting text and graphics on the Apple LaserWriter or any other PostScript laser printer or typesetter, including the Allied Linotype Linotronic 100 and 300. JustText was created by a book writer (William Bates) who wanted to use his LaserWriter for typesetting his books. We found JustText so useful that we used it to typeset this book.

To understand why JustText had to be created, you have to understand why the LaserWriter produces better output from some programs than from from others. Page makeup programs and word processing programs that send output to the LaserWriter have to work with a language called PostScript, a page description (text and graphics) and printer control language (developed by Adobe Systems of Palo Alto, CA).

The Apple LaserWriter is driven by a PostScript interpreter residing in the memory of the LaserWriter. Application programs like Microsoft Word and PageMaker send PostScript commands to the PostScript interpreter in the printer. With PostScript commands you can unleash the power of the LaserWriter and produce graphics and special effects like rotated or stretched letters, or precisely-kerned letters. However, most of the Macintosh application software packages do not utilize the powerful PostScript routines to their full potential.

One important feature of JustText is the ability to pass PostScript commands directly to the printer to get special effects. Another is automatic hyphenation that uses a dictionary or logic to hyphenate (a feature that is still missing in most page makeup packages). JustText has a kerning code to perform very precise kerning (changing the spaces between characters), and it will use ligatures (two-letter combinations, such as "ff") in Times Roman and Helvetica typefonts.

The Macintosh screen is not precise enough to provide the kind of WYSIWYG environment that professional typographers want. It is useful enough in many desktop publishing applications, but not necessarily in the typesetting of books, because it is slow.

Professional typographers are used to the non-WYSIWYG approach of putting typesetting codes in text files — the codes are a simple programming language that controls the output precisely. JustText was created for professional typographers and graphic artists, and for anyone who wants a lot of control over the LaserWriter. The familiar-looking typesetting codes (familiar to typographers, that is) may seem a step back into the stone age, but JustText converts them to PostScript commands that control the output very precisely.

The JustText codes are typed into your text file with ticked brackets — for example, the code {`f5`} stands for "change to Times Roman bold." You don't use a mouse or pull-down menu to click on "bold" — you simply type the code. The program also has special features, such as typing a Command-**B** (the shortcut in MacWrite for changing to bold), which produces {`f5`} in your text.

JustText codes are a boon to those who have text files already clogged with such codes — files from word processing programs such as

WordStar or Word Perfect. You can use JustText to find each word processing code and substitute a JustText code. The job can be done much faster than if you had to delete the word processing codes and click-on a Macintosh font for each instance of a typeface change.

```
{pn1}{c1,636,108,108,516}
{cj1}{a60}
{f5}{l18}{p14}CHAPTER ONE{qc}
{a18}
{f5}{p30}{l34}Overview of Desktop{qc}
Publishing Tools{qc}
{a24}
{f6}{p11}{l13}
Production is not the application of tools to materials, but logic to work.{qc}
{f4}— Peter Drucker{qr}
{a36}
{f4}{p11}{l13}
{ys}{c1,636,204,108,516}{yr}{c2,366,108,108,192}
{cj2}{yr}{rl}{f5}{p12}{l14}{lw0.5}
Applications{qr}
{b9}{br7}{cj1}{yr}{xc2}{f4}{p11}{l13}{xr}
Remember the last time you prepared some text to be typeset?
Did you spend a lot of time on the preparation and proofreading,
and also a lot of money on a vendor's service, without much
control over the schedule?  Would you prefer to do the
typesetting in your office, see the results immediately, and make
corrections at no extra charge?  Wouldn't you rather use an
inexpensive personal computer so that you only have to type the
text once, and have the computer do all the proofreading?
{ql}{em}The essence of desktop publishing is this: saving time,
gaining a measure of control, and ultimately saving money by
doing it yourself.  What makes it possible is the "trickle down"
theory of applied technology: fantastic devices for processing
words and pictures are now becoming affordable for personal
computer users.
{ql}{em}Laser printers have been in use for several years, but they
used to cost over $50,000.  Today's desktop laser printers are in
the $1,500-$24,000 range.  They resemble office copiers, use regular
copier paper, and are easy to maintain.  They provide near
typeset-quality output.
{ql}{em}There are revolutionary advances in graphics production on
personal computers.  You can produce camera-ready art in an
instant, and prepare color images for color separation and
printing.  Digitizing machines ($500-$5000, formerly $50,000) can
convert an image into digital information that can be edited on a
personal computer screen and printed on a laser printer.
```

Figure 7-2. We used JustText to typeset this book. This is the first page of Chapter One.

You can add JustText codes to your text files using any computer and any word processing program, or you can use JustText on a Macintosh (with an environment similar to MacWrite). Substitute JustText codes for word processing codes using any word processing program, or use JustText's find and paste command, which uses the Clipboard to paste new text to substitute for the "target" text.

One great feature of JustText's find/substitute function: it can find one or more carriage returns and tabs and substitute other codes for them. JustText can then "filter" all carriage returns in the file and turn them into "quad left" codes. Quad left is a typesetting term for setting a line of type flush to the left margin. Each paragraph and single line should end with a quad left code.

JustText handles quotation marks superbly. It automatically translates the double quote character (which is straight up and down) into curling double quotes for the beginnings and ends of quotes. It does this with a simple dual-state software "toggle" that uses opening and then closing quotes and is reset at the end of a paragraph (a quad left).

Set up the page parameters (such as line length or column width), and the parameters take effect for the rest of the pages until you change them (with JustText codes). This makes it very convenient to typeset a book whose pages are nearly identical in format.

The page setup codes we used to typeset pages of this book are shown in figure 7-2. The JustText codes define the columns and typefonts.

JustText automatically shifts to the next column if it is at the end of a column, or to the next page if it is at the last column of a page. You can force JustText to start typesetting in the next column, or jump to a specific column by specifying a column number in the column jump code. You can also jump to the next page with the page break code.

You can jump freely among columns on the same page by first saving the vertical position with the {**ys**} code, then jumping to the other column. To restore the y vertical position, use the {**yr**} code. You can also use the "lowest y" code to move text below other text that was typeset as a variable-length table.

JustText has a right and left margin indent, a both-margin indent, an indent-on-text code (indent an offset computed from any point in the text), and a hanging indent code. There is also a hanging bullet code for doing simple bulleted lists.

Tables can be set with items centered, flush left, or flush right within up to ten tab columns, and columns can be defined using picas and points. You can also draw boxes around tables. It is surprisingly simple to draw boxes around columns and sections of text. You can directly control the line weight in decimal point sizes. You can also draw a box automatically in the current line weight around the column specified or the current column.

A preliminary version of "art wrap" is available in version 1.09 of JustText. It lets you wrap text around artwork from MacPaint files in two ways. The "paint include" code used in your text file tells JustText to ask you (in a dialog box) for a MacPaint file. The MacPaint image is then included in your output at 100% (original) size, registered one-half inch above the bottom of a standard 8½ x 11-inch page; any text left to be typeset on that page is wrapped around the area of the artwork. You get a one-pica border around the artwork.

Another way is to define a bounding box using Bates' LaserTools utility, and convert the MacPaint image to a PostScript-language text file to be "included" in your text file. When JustText encounters the "include" code (to include any PostScript file or named file), it respects the boundaries of this bounding box when it typesets the text.

JustText is useful by itself, but LaserTools, available with JustText, is another gem worth having if you want precise control over printed graphics. LaserTools is a set of graphic image converters that turn images from MacPaint, ThunderScan (Thunderware) and MacVision (Koala Technologies) directly into PostScript files that can be edited as text files (the text is in the PostScript language).

LaserTools can position an image anywhere on a page, including bleeds off the page, because it bypasses Apple's Quickdraw conversion routines to get a larger page area. LaserTools can enlarge, reduce, or "flip" images horizontally or vertically, rotate images by degrees, or crop images. You can also define a bounding box around an image and convert it for use with the "art wrap" feature of JustText.

The automatic hyphenation alone may be a reason for using JustText, since only a few page makeup programs have automatic hyphenation. JustText let you turn hyphenation on or off with codes in the file. To hyphenate, JustText first checks to see if the word is one of the buzzwords used in computer terminology that has an upper-case letter in the middle of the word — if so, it hyphenates there; otherwise it searches an exception dictionary, and if not found, it uses logic. You can add to the exception dictionary, and you can also use discretionary hyphens ("soft" hyphens typed into words, so that the hyphen is used if the word falls at the end of a line).

Features like a large initial capital letter code with automatically-computed point size of the letter, and easy box-drawing codes, make JustText easy enough to design full pages. It is especially useful if you repeat design elements (boxed columns, same-size columns).

ScenicWriter   ScenicWriter (Scenic Software, $995) is designed for producing many-page documents, manuals and books where the ability to define a format for all of the pages gets the job done much more quickly than designing pages on the screen. ScenicWriter does not provide WYSIWYG page makeup nor graphics editing (except rules and boxes). As with JustText, you don't see what the page will look like until you print the page, but ScenicWriter's page formatting commands are very similar to the print formatting commands in WordStar.

You can use ScenicWriter as a word processing program or as a program to format and process text written using other word processing programs. Formatting is accomplished with embedded WordStar-like codes that can do multi-column layouts. The package can produce an index and table of contents, with backward and forward cross-references that are automatically adjusted when you add or delete text. ScenicWriter can also handle chapter headings and footnotes.

ScenicWriter is great at handling multi-level, nested indents. The program also offers a macro capability to repeat functions over many pages, which is the only suitable method of typesetting hundreds of pages. However, ScenicWriter does not yet have automatic hyphenation or kerning (both features are scheduled for the next revision of the product).

MagnaType and MagnaWord   MagnaType (Magna Computer Systems, $8500) is designed for PC XT and AT or compatible computers with at least 512K and a hard disk. The program controls a typesetter or laser printer as a "front end". The company also offers MagnaWord ($2500 by itself, $3500 on a network), a WordStar-like word processing program with all the features of MagnaType except actual typesetting. The setup is primarily for MagNet ($4000 itself or $3500 with MagnaType), which is a network of up to eight PCs that can share a typesetter. Each network node could have a copy of MagnaWord for word processing, with the typesetting station running MagnaType.

With MagnaType you can write and edit text as well as typeset text; you can also use any word processing program (such as WordStar or Multimate) to create and edit the text, then transfer it to MagnaType.

MagnaType uses five methods of automatic hyphenation — an expandable exception word dictionary, up to 99 user-defined secondary dictionaries, a temporary dictionary (for one job), discretionary (or "soft") hyphens typed into the text while editing, and logic algorithms. The automatic hyphenation and justification computation (h&j) can occur in a background multitasking mode so that you can continue to typeset and edit text.

You can set up to 1500 automatic kern pairs and four levels of white space adjustment (interword and intercharacter spacing). You can typeset multiple columns (up to 40) and specify column widths in proportional units, picas or points. MagnaType handles indents on both left and right margins with skewing, so that you can create special effects such as text in the shape of a triangle or diamond.

MagnaType can drive the popular laser printers and such typesetters as the Linotype Linotron 202, the Linotronic 300, and the Compugraphic 8400 and 8600. A special version of MagnaType that is less expensive ($5250) prepares output for PostScript devices (including the Apple LaserWriter) by converting MagnaType codes to PostScript. MagnaProof ($1500) is also available to drive the LaserWriter or any other PostScript device in a "proof" mode.

Thank you for your interest in MagnaType,® the only production-oriented front end system with full typographic aesthetics on a micro computer.

MagnaType is capable of outputting to most major typesetters, as well as all Postscript® compatible devices, like the Apple LaserWriter.® Nothing you have ever seen on this laser printer can compare with the output on MagnaType. As a matter of fact, this letter was produced on the Apple LaserWriter using MagnaType Software.

Figure 7-3. MagnaType sample output.

Math Typesetting

The typesetting language T$_E$X was designed by Prof. Donald Knuth of Stanford University to be an elegant way of describing mathematically oriented text. The elegance of its design makes it a very nice language to use for typesetting complicated constructions. Until recently, T$_E$X has only been available in universities and research laboratories that have mainframe computers.

However, now there are two versions of T$_E$X for the PC: MicroT$_E$X (Addison-Wesley $495) and PCT$_E$X (Personal T$_E$X Inc., $279, plus $100 for dot matrix printers; plus $300 for laser printer drivers). PCT$_E$X is bundled with the Corona LP 300 laser printer for $3395, and a screen preview option (requires Hercules card and high-resolution display monitor) is $250. T$_E$X is also available for the Macintosh (MacT$_E$X from FTL, $750).

T$_E$X gives you more control over the appearance of your text than any other language on micros and is well suited to book production and other complex documents. Like JustText, the program does not display a WYSIWYG screen, but uses typesetting commands imbedded in text for more precision and for production of large amounts of text where page-by-page layout would be too time-consuming.

T$_E$X offers such power typesetting features as automatic hyphenation, line and page-break control, and macros (a list of commands for formatting blocks of text automatically), but is best known for its power in creating mathematical equations. For example, there are standard mathematical symbols built in. You can specify superscripts of superscripts for exponential equations, with higher superscripts getting progressively smaller. Letters can come out in italics and numbers come out in roman, and other standard mathematical conventions are followed automatically.

The T$_E$X Metaphor

In most every other typesetting language, you are limited in your control of the typesetting machine. When you put out a letter or a word, it could be thought of as being printed on the paper at that time, and at the current position. Once a letter is placed, that is that. You can't go back in and adjust the line-breaks if you don't like the way it came out the first time — not automatically.

The best mathematical typesetting has always been done by hand, with precise little blocks of type stacked together in rows. Once a complicated assembly, like a mathematical display, was put together, it was treated as a unit, and allowed to "float" within the surrounding frame (the "chase") until everything that would go on the page was present. Then blocks of wood called "furniture" and metal shims called "lead" (pronounced *ledd*) were used to fill up the space and mechanically hold everything in place. The final "lock-up" was done by steel wedges ("quoins") that ratcheted past each other when their connecting gear was turned with a wrench.

This is the metaphor used by Knuth to design T$_E$X: little blocks within larger ones, floating within the space of the page until everything was in, and only then locking it all in place.

How T$_E$X Creates Pages

In T$_E$X, the blocks and furniture become "boxes" and "glue." By allowing glue to stretch and shrink as necessary, T$_E$X has all the flexibility of traditional hand-set type. It is just as easy to center a block of type vertically as it has always been to center type horizontally.

By waiting until everything is present to "lock-up" the page, you are able to do, in T$_E$X, all kinds of things before typesetting the page. For instance, T$_E$X treats a paragraph as a complete unit. Other systems fill up a line, hyphenate it if necessary, and then set it and begin the next line. They never look back. T$_E$X reads in an entire paragraph, and decides where the best line breaks are. "Best" is based on minimizing the number of hyphenations, avoiding adjacent hyphenations, minimizing the looseness of individual lines, and minimizing the difference in tightness and looseness between adjacent lines. Thus the end of a paragraph will influence the way lines break at the beginning. After all, that is the way it is done with hand-set type.

The lines of the paragraph, once broken, become boxes separated by vertical glue. Depending upon the rest of the page and the design parameters that have been set, that glue may be allowed to stretch ever so slightly, to make the bottoms of adjacent pages even, or move a section heading onto the top of the next page. Again, this is the way it is often done with hand-set type.

This construction of paragraphs illustrates T$_E$X's recursive nature. Each character is a box, with height and width dimensions. A horizontal stack of those boxes, separated perhaps by glue, is a line. A vertical stack of those boxes is a paragraph. A larger vertical stack is a column of type. A horizontal stack of columns, separated by glue and possibly vertical lines, is the text on a multi-column page. That box of columns, stacked vertically with a header box above and a footer box below, is a completed page. The rules for stacking boxes, and for floating them within the available space, are the same at each level (with minor variations for vertical and horizontal stacks).

In T$_E$X, all spaces between boxes consist of a springy *glue*, which can *stretch* and *shrink* and has a *normal*, relaxed size. By varying these three parameters, one can specify maximums, minimums, and the relative importance of various parts of the space surrounding the type.

One of the primary reasons for using a typesetting system like T$_E$X, rather than a WYSIWYG system, for doing books and manuals is that all of the design decisions can be made up front, as part of the language design or in the format definition of a particular document. Once the design and format definition are complete, hundreds of pages can be processed without having to make design decisions on each one.

Design specifications, such as having a minimum number of lines of a paragraph at the top or bottom of a page, can be enforced by building stretch into the glue between paragraphs, before section titles, around figures, and so on. This gives the flexibility needed to avoid layout problems like widow lines while allowing the bottom baselines on pages to match.

T$_E$X builds forward until it has passed the point where anything more can fit onto the current page (usually stopping at the end of a paragraph). It then looks backward to find the "best" place to break the page, balancing considerations like widow lines, section titles, and the amount of stretch required, and spews out one page of data. Then it returns to gather more material for the next page.

T$_E$X Features   T$_E$X has a number of features designed specifically for mathematics typesetting. One is *math mode* — letters are in italic while numbers are in roman fonts, and superscripts on superscripts are in progressively smaller fonts. T$_E$X takes care of all the details of font size and character position. For instance, the limits on an integral symbol (if you know any calculus) belong in particular positions, while the limits on a summation are placed differently. If your expression would look better with a different convention, it is easily changed. The T$_E$X syntax for each of them is identical, making it easy to type and to read.

The entire concept in T$_E$X of boxes and glue is derived from the requirements of constructing math formulas. Putting parentheses around a complicated expression comes easily when the size of the expression is a natural part of the nested-box construction.

Another feature, *alignments*, are used to set tables, charts, mathematical matrices, and anything else that needs to have constructed elements lined up either horizontally or vertically. Again, the concept of alignments grew out of the need to be able to typeset matrix expressions in mathematics.

Another feature is *macros* — a sequence of instructions defined by one word you use to execute them. The purpose of macros is to make the text, and the author's intent, clearer by putting the technical details out of the way. Being able to define macros makes it possible to do "top-down" programming in T$_E$X. At any stage in the process, you can simply make up a new macro name that conveys the intent. That macro can be later defined in terms of other macros, some of which may themselves not yet be defined.

T$_E$X is not the best typesetting language for all applications. It is particularly not suited to production typesetting, where all the decisions have been made already, and the typist's job is simply to get the material into the machine in the right order, watching out for those circumstances that require special handling.

T_EX is well suited to the task for which it was originally designed, providing a way for authors of complex, technical books to code a manuscript that is readable (and therefor editable) and yet can be source material for elegant typesetting.

PC T_EX requires a PC, PC AT or compatible computer with 640K RAM and DOS 2.0 or later and uses 5 megabytes of storage on your hard disk.

MicroT_EX requires a PC AT, PC XT or compatible with 512K RAM and DOS 2.0 or later, and uses 4 megabytes of storage on your hard disk (if you install all the fonts).

During the initial system installation, you may be prompted to insert MicroT_EX disk 3 in drive A, even if it is already present. The second prompt is a result of the separate font installation procedure. To continue, simply press < RETURN >.

It is a good idea to set a path to the \tex subdirectory, along with any other paths you may have. This precautionary measure can save you difficulties if you tend to work in numerous directories. To set such a path, type path c:\tex.

* GRAFTRAX and GRAFTRAX^{PLUS} are registered trademarks of Epson, Inc.

Figure 7-4. MicroT_EX sample output.

T_EX for the Macintosh

T_EX is also available on the Macintosh from Addison-Wesley, and a more complete implementation is available from FTL Systems Inc.

FTL's MacT_EX ($750) includes all of the features of standard T_EX, plus PLAINT_EX, LaT_EX and INITT_EX. In addition, MacT_EX for the Macintosh typesets text in all 35 LaserWriter typefaces, with complete control of columns and math fonts for proper typesetting.

FTL's implementation goes beyond other T_EX software in that it allows graphical information such as photographs and drawings to be merged with the typeset text. FTL has plans for a special image editor called *DarkRoom*, which can take a digitized photograph and perform image processing functions on it. The altered picture can then be merged with the T_EX text for printing.

Another feature of MacT_EX is the ability to preview the typeset text on the display screen. This allows documents to be proofread without printing them. You don't need a LaserWriter to run T_EX this way — it is also possible to print a draft image of the typeset text on the

ImageWriter dot matrix printer.

MacT$_E$X, like JustText, does not do PageMaker-style WYSIWYG page layout. However, it does allow you to preview the document on the screen. It uses the emerging de facto standard of desktop publishing — PostScript, considered to be one of the richest languages for graphics layout. Companies such as DEC (Digital Equipment Corp.) are now incorporating PostScript into their high-resolution printers. Other major companies are considering making PostScript the standard for their document production. Some publishing houses already accept author-typeset text in PostScript for direct printing of their books.

What made the LaserWriter especially attractive was that Adobe Systems also came to an arrangement with Allied Linotype and International Typeface Corp. (ITC), two of the largest producers of typefaces and typographic equipment in the world, such that their typefaces could be incorporated into all PostScript-driven printers. The new LaserWriter Plus contains 35 Allied and ITC typefaces, which gives Macintosh users the same degree of flexibility as professional print shops.

Putting T$_E$X onto the Macintosh appeared to be the next logical extension of the Macintosh/LaserWriter combination. You can use the Macintosh/LaserWriter combination for draft work and the final copy can be printed directly on PostScript-compatible Linotronic 100 or 300 phototypesetters and produce phototypeset text. This means that a version of T$_E$X for the Mac would be more powerful than many of the systems that drive hundred thousand dollar phototypesetters, making it a viable contender for the corporate publishing market.

But before the Davids of desktop publishing take on the corporate electronic publishing Goliaths and the entrenched typewriter/typesetter/paste-up cycle and bring desktop publishing literally to every desk, a few developments are required. We look at some trends and possible future developments in the final chapter.

AFTERWORD

Small opportunities are often the beginning of great enterprises.
— Demosthenes (343 B.C.)

One small opportunity came our way in early 1980, when we first discovered WordStar running on a sturdy CP/M microcomputer system. Having worked with minicomputers for several years, we fully appreciated the power of the micro and its word processing software. Minicomputers were already driving typesetting machines in 1980; as technical writers, we were already immersed in typesetting for the sake of quality control in producing technical documents. For us, word processing was where publishing began, and typesetting along with paste-up was the bottleneck where schedules were never met.

With microcomputers we could produce much more material in the same amount of time. The act of writing also became easier. As we accumulated disk volumes of writings and honed our skills (learned to type fast and organize files), we found ourselves capable of producing a complete magazine on a timely basis, as well as several books.

As the machines were pressed into a higher service than just word processing, they immediately showed their weaknesses. There were gaps in the standard ways to connect equipment from different manufacturers, so that you couldn't just transfer data from a personal computer to a typesetter without solving some data conversion nightmare.

People pushed word processing technology beyond its limitations into the world of graphics and professional presentations. The architects of computer systems responded to their needs by working on low cost desktop publishing systems. There are two major trends in the use of information that are affecting their design decisions for better and for worse.

257

One is the ever-increasing role of paper in the presentation of information and in our everyday transactions. As laser printers arrive in the office, they show that the job of producing a newsletter or marketing brochure is as easy as printing an office memo. Knowledge workers can mix graphics and text and draw up a document for publication within minutes. People are wondering why they never had this capability in their personal computers before.

The other major trend is electronic publishing and the storing of information by electronic means. As a computer user, you have access to services (via a phone and modem) that can put on your screen electronic entertainment as well as useful information like the Official Airline Guide for flight schedules and fares.

Businesses and professions are storing information electronically to be more efficient in retrieving it. The paper file cabinets are being replaced by disks, and paper archives are being replaced by removable disks, tapes, compact disks and other computer-compatible media.

Part of the promise of electronic publishing is electronic mail. Industry pundits ballyhoo'd the benefits and drawbacks of such systems, but the systems are very much in demand in corporations that need to have swift inter-office transfer of paperwork. Reporters use it to file stories. Insurance salespeople use it to transmit data for new customers. Engineers and scientists have been using it for years to communicate results and hypotheses. The police use it to catch crooks.

We used it to write this book. With part of the writing team on one coast and part on the other, we used MCI Mail and CompuServe to communicate quickly and efficiently with hundreds of vendors and experts nationwide and in other countries. Without it, we would have taken twice as long and the information in this rapidly changing new field would have been out of date.

Electronic mail links computers so that you can share your data. Since a copy of this electronic paragraph can be made in a wink of an eye, imagine how easy it is to copy the data from a form, or a story from a reporter's electronic notebook.

For presenting technical or detailed information, paper is still the most effective and useful medium. However, storing, retrieving and archiving the information is more efficiently done in the electronic medium. The two media are becoming more compatible as a number of technical advances bring more power and flexibility to desktop publishing programs:

- Larger screens will let you see an entire 8½ x 11-inch page on the screen and be able to read the text in the typefont and size you selected.

- More memory will make it possible to process more pages at a time, and at a faster rate, with memory-resident spelling checkers, thesauruses and other writing tools at your fingertips.

- Data compatibility across networks of different personal computers, minicomputers and mainframes will preserve your investment in your data.

- Data storage devices (magnetic disk and tape cartridges, compact disks and laser discs) give you access to all your files at once, without having to sort through many disks, and provide an efficient method of archiving information redundantly to reduce the possibility of losing it.

Specific advances in desktop publishing will affect the way we create documents. By the end of 1986, we're likely to see a more powerful, much faster Macintosh that will show a complete page on the screen at the proper size. You'll be able to read the text in the typefont and size you selected and see full-size pictures. The new Macintosh will probably work with any PostScript device: dot matrix or laser printer, plotter, film recorder, etc. This means that images can be scaled (enlarged and reduced) before printing and printed with high-quality smoothing on any PostScript device, not just the Laser-Writer.

Desktop publishing will move into the news rooms of smaller newspapers, commercial newsletters, and corporate in-house publishing departments. "Multi-author desktop publishing" will evolve, with the capability to interface with local area networks, mainframes, and electronic mail services. Authors of documents will be able to transmit documents across networks for review and revision by others, who in turn will transmit updated information across the network.

The IBM PC family will acquire faster processors, lower-cost memory, and higher-resolution displays. More powerful PC software will emerge to challenge the Macintosh dominance of desktop publishing. The PC software will have the advantage of the large installed base of PCs and better access to corporate data bases. Apple Computer and its third party developers will strike back with faster, more powerful Macintosh computers and AppleTalk network products that will link Macintoshes into powerful information systems and into mainframes and PC networks.

Products like JustText and T$_E$X for the Mac will evolve into full desktop publishing tools that combine WYSIWYG page layout capability with typesetting controls, a variety of fonts, and graphics for printing on PostScript laser printers or typesetters. These software products, which will take advantage of faster, larger-memory, higher-resolution Macintosh, PC, and other computers, will rival million-dollar corporate electronic publishing systems. These products will also make it easier to create foreign-language character sets and associated page-makeup software, bringing desktop publishing into a broader international arena.

More memory and 500-megabyte CD ROM compact-disk storage devices will make it possible to process more pages at a time, and at a faster rate, with memory-resident spelling checkers, thesauruses, and massive library reference materials at your fingertips. CD ROM promises to be an electronic publishing medium for maps, graphic data bases, catalogs, volumes of technical information, and knowledge-based expert systems.

Systems for translating word-processing text and graphics images across networks of different personal computers, minicomputers and mainframes will make it easy and fast to access information regardless of where it's located or what form it's stored in.

Higher-resolution (480 dots-per-inch and higher) laser printers will appear by the end of 1986, along with page makeup software and versions of the Macintosh and other computers to drive them, bringing desktop publishing systems closer to typesetting quality. Color lasers will probably appear by the end of the decade, and prepress production will be computerized, with high-quality, low-cost digital color separations.

There is also a downside to desktop publishing: a plethora of badly-designed newsletters, brochures, ads and ad naseaum. It happened with the electronic spreadsheet phenomenon — innumerable business plans with slightly inaccurate financials. It is well known that the word processing phenomenon fanned the fumes of bad writing. Read a few computer manuals to see how easy it really is...

You can avoid this problem by following simple design rules: don't mix too many different typefaces, don't use very thick lines for boxes and rules, keep your margins just wide enough for ease of reading, and distinguish clearly by size the hierarchy of titles, headings and sub-headings.

You save money by doing production yourself, and gain a measure of control over the schedule, so you can therefore spend some time learning about design. The computer makes it child's play to draw straight lines, angles, boxes, and simple graphics. Or have it designed by an artist, and then produce it on your equipment together with the artist. Desktop publishing equipment makes it easier for graphic designers to use their skills for a client more quickly than before. The lower cost makes it easier for businesses to afford a designer to set up the page makeup template.

There has been immeasurable progress made in publishing technology as a result of the maturing of the personal computer industry. The compatibility among computer equipment makes it possible for you to use the local copy shop for typesetting. The technology can put inexpensive self-publishing tools on every desktop, in every office, school, church, and organization, and eventually in every home, as common as typewriters are today.

This is an exciting, fast-moving time in the history of communications, as pivotal as the Gutenberg press and the first radios and TV sets. Over the next several years, the landscape of copy centers, office and home computers, and other familiar information machines and services will evolve into powerful desktop publishing systems. And over the next decade, desktop publishing will evolve into a new media, yet to be named and invented. Yet the information will be stored in digital form, ready for the next wave of the desktop publishing revolution.

GLOSSARY

Typesetting and Layout Terminology

Be not the slave of words.

— Thomas Carlyle

achromatic — literally without color. Sometimes used to refer to material, especially printed material, that is entirely black and white.

agate — a measure of size used in typesetting. There are fourteen agate lines to the inch. Classified ads are traditionally measured in agate lines or in agate inches, which is agate lines high times inches wide.

air — white or unprinted space in a layout or on the finished reproduction. Insufficient air may make a piece hard to read or grasp, but too much can also be distracting.

align — on a typesetting system, to line up the top, left, right or bottom edge, as specified. The most common type of alignment is base alignment, where the bottom reference line of all characters lies along a single line.

alphabet length, width or **size** — the width of a complete lower case alphabet in a given type size and style. Most often used to compare various types. The size will often be given in points or picas (printer's measure equal to $\frac{1}{72}$ and $\frac{1}{6}$ of an inch).

apex — part of a character where two lines meet at the top; for example, the point on an "A".

area composition — the process of fitting the units of text and photos or other graphics onto the original of a page that will be printed or otherwise reproduced. It is the electronic equivalent of what graphic artists call design and "paste-up."
  Some systems accept specifications for text and graphic elements and show the result as boxes of the resulting size, while the best units will actually show a rendition of the type and a few even of the graphics (though both will be a bit stylized, due to the limited resolution capability of the video screen). See also **composition and markup** for more details.

arm — a part of a letter that extends horizontally or diagonally up, as the two top parts of a capital "Y" or the top stroke in a "T".

art — in graphic arts usage, all non-text material.

ascender — the part of a character that reaches up from a distinct main body of the letter towards the top of the line. For example, the upper half of the left vertical line making up the small letter "b" is the ascender.

backslant — letter forms that slant top to left (which is the opposite from the way italic characters tilt). They're used primarily for special effects.

banner — a large headline or title. Originally, it meant a headline that extended across the full page, but it is now used to indicate any large head. Note the difference with a "flag," which is the name of a publication as shown on the front page or cover.

bar — a horizontal line segment comprising part of a character, as in the central line in the "H".

base alignment — on a typesetter or printer, a mode specifying that the normal lower reference edge of all letters should be horizontally even in a line of mixed sizes or styles. This mode is also called **baseline alignment**.

baseline — a reference point used for the vertical alignment of characters. Except for characters with descenders (such as "y"), it is normally the line crossing the bottom-most part of the character.

big — type that occupies more than the average amount of its point height. Typically, it has small ascenders and descenders, with larger main letter bodies.

Black Letter — a general term for a broad family of typefaces with dark, angular made of both thick and thin lines. The various Old English-looking types are now the most commonly used.

bleed — in page layout, type or pictures that run over the edge of the paper with no margin. Bleeds are more difficult to print, and may be more costly.
   In commercial work, bleeds are most often done by printing on an oversize sheet or roll of paper, and then trimming the pages back to the desired size. Many electronic imaging systems cannot print completely to the margins. See also **live area**.

block — as a style for text layout, set with no indentations (but usually with extra spacing between paragraphs). As a style for overall page layout, arranged so text and art occupy compact rectangles instead of extending in narrow or irregular arms.

block letter — a letter created with equal stroke weights (widths of the lines) and simple curves. Ideally, this is what should be produced in response to "Please print."

blowup (n) or **blow up** (v) — an enlargement, most frequently of a graphic image. Also, used as a verb meaning to make an enlarged image. In electronic imaging, the process is often called "scaling up" the image.

body — the main text on a page or spread of several pages. Occasionally, in a layout containing art by no main text, the main art in contrast to the headings, folios (page numbers) and so on. Naturally, the body is usually set in the body type.
   In editorial work, "body" is the main text of a work (in contrast with the captions, charts, and front and back matter).
   In typesetting, "body" is the unit that carries each letter of type. While on traditional hot (metal) type this was the actual piece of lead alloy, for cold (phototype) this is a box (often imaginary) surrounding the image. See also **body size**.

body size or **body height** — the total height used for a particular typeface, measured from the top of the tallest ascender or capital to the bottom of the lowest descender. It is normally given in points (a graphics measure of size equal to approximately $1/72$ inch).

body type — the type used for the main text of a piece of typeset material. Usage rather than definition determines what is the body type, but some typefaces are designed for this use and are more readable for longer runs of text. Generally, this means type up to 14 points in size.

boldface — printing done in a similar style to standard letters, but made to appear darker, with thicker, more pronounced strokes. Most type styles have a companion bold face. Boldface is used for emphasis, and for adding visual massiveness to a section of type. Sometimes written as bold face.

bowl — a circular part of a letter, such as in a letter "b".

box — a section of text marked off by rules (lines) or white space, usually because it is slightly tangential to the main text. Longer boxed sections in magazine and newspaper stories are called sidebars.

broadside — originally a term for a work printed on one side of a large sheet of paper. It is now often used for any work printed on an oversize sheet, whether or not both sides are printed.

budget — the total editorial (art and text) material for a publication or issue. Depending on who is looking at it, the budget may be limited by available space or available copy.

c&lc — short for caps and lowercase, an instruction for how material should be formatted. In this style, which is commonly used for headlines, the initial letter of each word in set in caps, the rest in lower case.

c&sc — an abbreviation for caps and small caps, a style of typesetting using a set of uppercase but smaller forms in place of lowercase letters.

CAM — an abbreviation for "composition and markup," the process of setting material in type and specifying the arrangement of type on the page. The first generation of computerized typesetting systems only allowed composition (the setting of type), but more recent ones allow the use of codes, menus or programs to change type size, font, and placement.

Interactive CAM terminals show the result of the specifications on a video screen, while less advanced systems merely show code symbols for activating these special functions on a typesetting unit.

camera-ready — in general, material that is ready to be printed. While originally it meant material that was ready to be photographed and made into a metal plate from which the actual printing is done, some of the emerging printing technologies do not require this step. The term has thus come to mean a graphic, picture or page which is all done and ready to be reproduced.

"Camera ready" is also used to refer to the output of word processing programs, text formatters, typesetters, and other devices — pages that are output in a form ready for reproduction. Preparing these pages may include aligning the text, furnishing page numbers, supplying headings, and dividing the text at the proper page boundaries.

"camera ready" photographs are ones that are already converted to the patterns of tiny dots needed for printing (halftones) instead of containing grays or intermediate tones.

cap line — an imaginary line connecting the top of the letters in an particular font. The distance from the cap line to the baseline is the cap size.

caps — short for capital letters, the familiar uppercase form of the letters of the alphabet.

caps and small caps — a style of lettering that shows what would be capital letters in their normal form, and what would be small letters as capital letters of a slightly smaller size.

Many purists in the graphic design field insist that the small caps for this use should be specially designed to go with the capital letters, and there are typefaces which have fonts of caps and small caps. But with the advent of digital and photographic typesetting equipment, small caps are normally created by using a smaller size setting with the same typeface.

caption — the line or lines of text that accompany and identify a figure, photo or other illustration. Books and technical material in shorter form often use numbered captions. A figure may also have a title, and there may be text or call-outs in the figure as well. However, some printers and layout people loosely refer to all lettering on an illustration as the captions.

Caslon — one of the popular type designs in the oldstyle family. Caslon has good contrast between thick and thin strokes, and pointed serifs. It is widely used for books and other text.

character count — referring to a block of text, the number of characters. In graphic arts, spaces are counted but usually not other non-printing characters. In information processing, both printing and non-printing characters are usually included.

In typesetting, the "character count" is the number of characters on a line. The count is used to estimate the total number of lines or pages that will be occupied by a text of a given number of characters.

close up (pronounced "cloze up") — the proofreader's instruction to reduce the amount of space between words, either in general (to "tighten up the line") or at a specific marked point.

cold type — type produced without using metal characters. Some purists insist that only type produced by typewriter-like impact methods (strike-on) qualifies as true cold type, but usage is moving towards including both direct and photographic methods.

column — in the laying out of pages, a vertically-running section of a page. Composition experts distinguish between a column, which is the normal vertical area specified in the format, and a "leg" of type, which is the actual area occupied. In some designs, a leg can be set wider or narrower than a single column.

column inch — a measure of area used by newspapers and magazines. A column inch is one column wide by one inch high. Column inches are calculated multiplying inches high times columns high. Most publications charge advertisers either by the column inch or by fraction of a page. Since page and column size varies, this is not an absolute measure.

column rule — a vertical line, usually rather thin, used to separate columns of type.

comp — as used in graphic arts, short for comprehensive layout. This a mock-up of the final product made by sketching in the headlines, blocks of text, and illustrations all in the correct size and position. Some newer page layout systems can produce a sort of automated comprehensive, using blocks or wavy lines in place of the planned text.

compose — to set material into type.

composition — both the setting of type and the arranging of the type on the page.

composition and markup or **composition and makeup** — the process of setting type and then arranging it on the page. Some typesetting systems can set whole pages at a time, while on others each column of type must be set and the result pasted together.

Composition refers to setting of type or the arranging of type on the page. Markup is specifying how big the type should be and what style or darkness of letters. And makeup is the assembling of the text, headlines, borders and pictorial elements (or spaces for them to go in) into the correct positions.

compositor — a person or company who sets type. However, more often the person, machine or company setting type is referred to simply as "the typesetter."

comprehensive layout — a mock-up of a printed piece showing all type and pictures in rough form but in the right size and in the correct position. See **comp** for more details.

condensed — a style of type that takes less than the normal amount of width. It is used when more letters must be squeezed into a limited space.

Traditionally, typefaces (styles of type) have been designed as families, including a normal and a condensed style (and in some cases and expanded style which uses more space than normal). Many recent systems do not have a separate condensed face, but instead produce it by squeezing the corresponding normal type.

Some phototypesetting systems can actually narrow each letter, either electronically or through use of special lenses. And many word processing systems and almost all phototypesetters can output normal letters with less than the normal space between them.

constants — layout elements that remain the same in all issues.

continuous tone — an image that has grays or shades of color. Continuous tone images cannot be reproduced in that form by most printing methods, which either place ink or tone at a given point or do not. Furthermore, imaging techniques based on digital methods rarely can produce intermediate tones. Consequently, images with gray tones must be broken up into small dark and light areas or series of dots, a process that is called screening. See also **halftone**.

copy — in publishing and typesetting, copy is material that is to appear in the piece being produced. In the more narrow sense, copy is the textual material, and art is the pictorial part, but both words are often used more generally to include all the elements needed for a project.

copyfitting — the estimation of the size of material that is going to be published or printed and the provision of the requisite amount of page space.

crop — in both computer graphics and graphic arts in general, to select a part of an image by cutting off portions from the edges. Cropping is done to eliminate unwanted detail, allowing more attention to be focused on the remaining image. In most cases, the remaining portion is enlarged to fill the space previously allocated to the full image.

In graphic arts, cropping is also used to fit a selected part of an image into a defined space without enlarging or reducing the original dimension.

cursive — applied to typefaces, ones that resemble script handwriting, with connected strokes and curved lines. Two of the more popular are Lydian and Brush. Most people do not find them suited for large blocks of text, but instead use them for titles, displays, and so on.

Cursive faces are used to add a touch of formality or artistry to printed pieces such as invitations and announcements. But since many of the characters must come in several forms to connect their beginning and end stroke with adjacent characters, they are more difficult to use.

cut — in graphic arts, originally a separate piece of wood or metal carrying a picture for use in printing. Now, this term is more loosely used for any artwork or picture.

cut and paste — to remove material from a document and place it at another location or in another document. It is the analogous operation to taking a paper copy of the document and cutting it apart and pasting it back together in another order.

dash — One of the several different characters consisting of a short horizontal line, such as "—". Most people think of the dash simply as a long hyphen, and on a typewriter or computer printer, a dash character is made by printing two successive hyphen characters. But in typeset material, the dash family includes the hyphen ("-"), the en dash (–), and the em dash (—).

dead matter — a printer's term for material that is no longer needed. It can apply to either the original copy, to type, or to typeset material. For example, most newspapers consider their input copy, galleys, and any non-repeating finished pages dead matter after the last edition of the day has been printed.

dedicated keyboard — a entry station that produces the code sequences for one particular model of typesetting machine.

descender — a part of a letter that extends below the main body, as in the tails of the small "y", "g" and "j".

digitized type — type stored as digital dot or stroke patterns, rather than as photographic images. If the dot or stroke density is high enough, the result can look quite clean and crisp, while still offering the cost savings and flexibility of digital computer storage and processing.

discretionary hyphen — a special hyphen character placed in word processing and typesetting files that marks where the word can be broken with a hyphen at the end of a line. If the word doesn't need to be broken there, the hyphen is not printed.

display type — in typesetting, larger type than that used for the text of a piece of work. Depending on the circumstances, this would typically be type of 18 points (¼ inch) or larger.

double truck — a layout or element that goes over a double page spread, including the gutter (the area between the pages).

dummy — in graphic arts, a mock-up of a project, made either for planning and approval purposes or to serve as instructions to the typesetter.

dynamic balance — a layout that is not symmetric, but has elements of equal weight on each side or region.

Egyptian — a term for styles of typefaces with square serifs and uniform stroke widths. Clarendon is one of the best known.

electronic paste-up — the combining of graphic and text elements electronically, instead of physically cutting and pasting together pieces of paper. So-called "page makeup terminals" or page makeup software may offer this capability, but not always including the ability to use externally created elements.

em — a printer's term for a square unit with the edges equal in size to the point size (height of the line of type). It gets its name from the letter "m", which is usually about as wide as the type size. Em measures are most often seen as specifying the width of a column or the size of an indentation.

em dash — a dash that is one em long (equal in length to the type size, or about the same width as a letter "M").

em or **em quad** — in typesetting and word processing, a space character with a width that is theoretically equal to the height of a capital letter of type. It is also approximately equal to the width of a letter "M", from which it gets the name. Depending on type styles, the width may be slightly more or less than the definition.

en — the printer's unit of measurement that is half as wide as the current line size. It gets its name from the width of the letter "N", which is commonly about half as wide as a capital letter is high. En measures are most frequently seen in specifications for the length of dashes and rules (lines) and for spacing.

en or **en quad** — in typesetting and word processing, a space character with a width that is theoretically equal to half the height of a capital letter of type. It is also approximately equal to the width of a letter "N", from which it gets the name. Depending on type styles, the width may be slightly more or less than the definition. An en space is generally wider than the space used between words in unjustified copy.

en space — a space one en wide, or about half as wide as the point size of the type. Note that a 2-en space is not 2 ens wide, but ½ en wide, a 3-en space is ⅓ en, and so on.

expanded characters — characters of more than the normal width. On computer dot matrix printers, they are made by printing each column of dots twice, creating a character twice as wide. In typesetting, the expanded characters of a typeface may be specially designed with slightly wider bodies than normal, or with phototypesetting machines they may be created using a special lens or optical system.

extra bold — type that uses even heavier and darker strokes than boldface, and therefore is much darker than the normal medium type. Some type styles are designed with extra bold weights, but many electronic composition systems can create one on request.

face — short for typeface, a collection of letters and other characters in a given style. The typeface of a printed piece affects not only the readability, but also the attractiveness and the psychological tone.

family — a group of variations on the same basic typeface, such as the normal medium face, boldface, light, italic and various permutations. Some electronic composition systems can create an entire family from a single basic pattern, but purists insist that each must be designed individually for best appearance.

figure space — a space equal in width to a numeric figure (usually an en, which is half the point size in width). It is used to line up columns of figures.

filler — material used to complete a page, usually of little consequence.

fillet — a round corner connecting the serifs to letters on old style types.

flag — the stylized name of a paper or publication shown on page one. The masthead, however, is the listing of the personnel and business information often given on the editorial page, the table of contents or some other inside page.

flat — in printing, a group of negatives mounted on paper and ready to be used to make a printing plate, or camera-ready copy mounted and ready to be photographed.

float — to allow an element of the design to move around on the page. For example, a floating flag is a publication title that appears in different positions on the front page in different issues.

floating accent — an accent that is created separately from the main character and then placed over or under it. Only some composition methods can handle floating accents, while others must instead supply any accented letter as a special character.

flush — in referring to the formatting of text and illustrations, to align with a specific reference line. Unless otherwise stated, the line is the left margin. See also **flush left, flush right, full flush**.

flush left — material aligned along the left margin, or an instruction to align material that way. Flush left is the normal style for handwriting and typewriting, and is often used for typeset material with either ragged (uneven) or justified (equal length) lines.

flush right — material aligned along a right margin, or an instruction to line up material that way. Occasionally, lines of text will be set flush right for ornamental use, but in this culture it is considered harder to read.

font — a complete set of the characters in one typeface and size. Now that electronic systems can create derivative images (such as expanded, italic or bold) from a single set of stored characters, some users count each complete set as a font while others count only the original images.

foot — the bottom of a page.

footline — a repeating line at bottom of pages, often containing the publication name and date or issue.

foot margin — the margin at the bottom of the page. Depending on the user, it may mean the space following the bottom of the body copy, or the space after the folio and any footlines.

form — in printing, a group of pages printed together and then folded and cut into the final leaves. Most commercial printing is usually done this way. Because of the geometry of folding, forms are most often 16 or 32 pages, but occasionally other sizes are used. Since most books and magazines are organized as forms, the economics of publishing often dictate that a work be cut down or extended to a multiple of the form size.

format — as applied to publications, books, reports or other documents, the overall size, layout, typestyle and ordering of the material.

free page — a page that is not done in the usual design format.

full bleed — an illustration that reaches the edge of the page on all four sides. See **bleed** for more information.

full flush — in typesetting, formatting material even with both margins (left and right justified).

full measure — in typesetting, a line set to the entire line length. Also called flush left and right.

galley — a copy of typeset material, arranged in columns instead of made up into pages. Galleys are the normal output of typesetting systems that do not allow page makeup during typesetting, and of hot-type (metal type). Traditionally, the first round of proofreading is done on galleys, so any preliminary copy of typeset material furnished for proofing is sometimes called a galley.

galleys — originally, a printing term for trays of type and for copies of typeset material made by hand for use in proofreading the copy before the actual press run. Now, often used to mean any draft copy which is furnished to allow proofreading or revision.

Garamond — a popular type style, widely used for books and other text. It is an oldstyle type, with pointed serifs and decided contrast between thick and thin strokes.

geometric layout — an arrangement resembling a simple geometric shape, such as a square, pyramid or triangle. The term is sometimes used for layouts that imitate the shape of letters.

ghost hyphen — another term for a **discretionary hyphen**, a specially-coded hyphen that shows up if a word is broken at that point to end a line, but otherwise does not print.

golden rectangle — a rectangle with proportions that from classical Greek times has been thought optically pleasing. Roughly, the ratio is 3 to 5 for the sides (close to 1 to 1.618 in decimal).

goldenrod — the material on which the negatives of type and artwork are assembled to make use as the image for making a printing plate in some processes.

gothic — a group of typefaces with no serifs and broad, even strokes. News Gothic is perhaps the best-known gothic.

gutter — the area between the normal printed area of two facing pages. It is possible to continue material across the gutter, but this requires precise registration and binding.

The "gutter" is also the area between the first printed character and the edge that will be bound in a book or report. In most cases, this is the left margin. "Gutter" is also used to describe the area between two columns of text.

H&J — short for *hyphenation and justification*, the process of setting text into lines and adding any needed codes and hyphens to make the words fit.

hairline — a thin defect in a letter, often noticed only as fuzzy type rather than as a specific break.
A "hairline" in a type style with various width strokes is the thinnest of the strokes.

halftone — the technique of showing shades of intensity by using differing combinations of tiny full-intensity dots. This is the method used to reproduce tones in most kinds of printing, since the printing process can only deposit or not deposit ink at any given point. A gray tone, for example, might be represented by fine black and white dots, with the black covering 50% of the area.
Halftones are produced photographically by taking a picture of the continuous-tone copy through a special etched screen. Electronic systems that do this step are also becoming available. In general, the finer the screen (specified as a greater number of lines), the more detailed the image, but the smoother the paper must be for adequate reproduction.

hanging figures — a style of numerals often used with older type styles that had parts of certain digits extending below the baseline. More modern typefaces instead use **lining figures**, which look cleaner because they all line up at the baseline.

hanging punctuation — punctuation that carries over into the normal margins instead of staying entirely within the edges of the type area. Hanging punctuation, if done well, is often considered more elegant because it keeps a more precise visual edge on blocks of text.

hard hyphen — a hyphen that is meant to be shown whether it would fall in the middle of a line or at the line end.

head — short for headline, a title or other line at the top of the page or section of text that is set apart and usually made larger than the text.

head margin — the interval between the top of the page and the first printed character.

Helvetica — perhaps the most popular typeface in the sans serif class (typefaces whose strokes don't end in added small cross pieces). Helvetica uses very even stroke widths, simple designs, and rounded features.

hot type — metal type, named hot type because it was produced by melting the metal. Hot type technologies are being increasingly replaced by cold type, which uses photographic or electronic processes to create an image.

imaging area — the area on which an output device can place a mark, most often expressed as the bounds of a rectangle. On most electronic printing and imaging devices, this is smaller than the full sheet of paper, resulting in a "live area" smaller than the page size.

initial — a letter larger than the normal text size, used to start a paragraph, chapter or section. Initials may be plain or ornate, and extending above the line (raised) or below (dropped).

italic — a type style that is designed to reflect some of the elements of handwritten script. Italic typefaces slope toward the right and have rounded lines (but not all oblique typefaces are italic). Most typesetting systems have individually-designed italic faces to match their roman (normal upright style) faces, but some newer systems create italics by applying a transformation to their standard fonts.
Some dot matrix printers can print italics on command, but normally material that would be set in italic in printed material is underlined in typewritten material (and similarly, the proofreader's marking to indicate italicized text is a single line beneath the text).

justify — to align text along a margin, or along two margins. In normal practice, text is always left justified (lined up evenly at the left margin), but typeset material is usually both left and right justified (done by adding extra space as necessary to make the right side line up as well). Typewritten material is usually left justified, but ragged (non-justified) on the right. Numerical information in tables is set right justified. When neither side is specified, justification usually refers to full justification (both left and right sides).

kern — as applied to type, the part of a letter that hangs over beyond the space normally given to that character (for example, in some type styles the tail of the "y" reaches back under the previous character). The term is also used to refer to the process of decreasing the space between certain letter combinations (such as "Ta") that look better when part of one letter sticks out into the other letter's space. Most computerized typesetting systems can kern letters on command, and many automatically kern specified letter combinations.

layout — the arrangement of the text and pictorial elements on a page. Usually, layout refers to the conceptual process, rough diagrams and instructions to the typesetter and art department. "Makeup" is the actual electronic or physical page assembly.

leader — connecting lines made up of dots, dashes or some other character used to tie together parts of composite elements. One commonly-seen use is in the phone book, where a dot leader connects the subscriber name or address to the phone number.

lead, leading (note: pronounced as the name of the metal) — the space added between lines of type to provide additional separation. Usually, it is specified in points (each point = approximately $1/72$ of an inch or $1/12$ of a pica).

letterspacing — in typesetting, the addition of small spaces between letters within words to make the total line length come out to a desired value. It is sometimes used when the addition of normal amounts of space between words is insufficient to make a line come out to the desired size. Most experts say that letterspacing creates ugly lines, and should be used only in emergencies.

ligature — a combination of two (or more) letters, treated as a single unit for typesetting. The most common is the "ff" and the diphthongs (such as "oe"). Most computerized typesetting systems can produce the equivalent by kerning (overlapping the normal character spacing between the letters). Older hot metal typesetters often had a set of common ligatures. Strictly speaking, by the way, the ligature is the actual connection between two characters, but common usage applies it to the character combinations rather than the added connecting lines, which in fact are now often omitted.

light or **lightface** — type styles that use strokes that are thinner or not as dark as the normal medium typeface. Light types are not as frequently used as mediums or bolds, but many electronic typesetting systems can produce a light face on request.

line art — illustrations containing only blacks and whites, with no intermediate tones (or similarly bi-tonal arrangements of other colors). Line art can be reproduced without the screening or patterning step most printing processes need to produce a range of tones.

lining figures — numerals that line up at the baseline and rise to equal heights, rather than the oldstyle hanging figures where some numerals extended below the baseline.

live — as applied to typeset material or the computer files that produce that material, still needed or in use.

live area — the part of a page available for printing. Because of either design choices or the limitations of equipment, it may not be allowable or possible to include elements stretching completely to the page edge. Full-page imaging devices, such as laser printers, often have an "imaging area" slightly smaller than their maximum paper size.

logo — originally short for logotype (meaning a combination of letters or a drawing treated as a single character), it is now used to denote a company or institutional symbol or the stylized rendering of their name. Most corporate logos are trademarked. Sometimes, popular logotypes are offered as images for typesetting machines (and on special daisywheels for word processing systems). Many newer electronic typesetting machines can accept digitized logos or even digitize their own.

markup (also **mark-up**) — the process of adding instructions to copy or the actual formats and control codes to a computer file so some person or machine will format the output in the correct way. Marking up copy used to require a great deal of skill and experience, but it is much easier on interactive systems that immediately show you the results of each instruction on the screen.

mechanical — the complete original image ready for reproduction, with all elements positioned precisely where they will be on the printed page. In many types of printing, however, any photos are only indicated on the mechanical, with the actual images added during the printing plate-making process. Mechanicals have traditionally been made by pasting up individual elements, but some types of electronic composition now produce a unified full page image. During layout and makeup, the mechanicals of full pages or spreads are often referred to as "flats."

modern — in speaking of type styles, refers not to our current age, but to what was modern in the early nineteenth century. Modern typefaces are some of the most commonly used text faces, including such well-known styles as Times Roman and Bodoni. Typically, modern faces have good contrast between thick and thin strokes, and thin, straight serifs.

monopitch — referring to type, a style in which all characters take up the same amount of horizontal space. Although most typewritten material is monopitch, almost all typeset material uses proportional spacing.

mutt — a typesetter's term for the em space. It's claimed that "mutt" and "nut" respectively are easier to distinguish than "em" and "en", but there may be other reasons for this use of argot.

oblique — referring to type styles which have their principal axis at an angle to the vertical. Italics are the most commonly seen variety, but not all oblique typefaces are italics.

Old English — a typeface that was designed to resemble the older handprinting style used in England. It is an dark, angular type, technically a member of the family called Black Letter.

oldstyle — a broad family of typefaces characterized by wide, round letters, fairly even line widths, and sloping serifs. Some of the more well-known oldstyle faces include Caslon and Garamond.

on — referring to typography, the size of the total space from one line to the next, including the type and any additional leading (spacing). For example, 10 point type with 2 points of extra leading is referred to as "10 on 12."

optical center — a point where text or graphics that should be visually centered in the vertical direction are aligned. It is generally taken to be about ⅗ of the way up, or more precisely at the top of the shorter leg of a "golden rectangle" whose longer leg is the vertical dimension of the page.

pica — a printing-industry unit of measure, equal to approximately ¹⁄₁₆ of an inch. There are 12 points to a pica. Pica measurements are often used for the width and sometimes height of page areas and columns of type.

pi characters — special characters which are not part of the normal character set or font, but that are added for special text. Typical examples include mathematical symbols or special accents.

plate — the metal, paper or plastic sheet containing the image to be placed on the printing press.

At this point, most methods of electronic composition and layout still produce a final paper "mechanical" or film negative, which is made into the plate by a photographic process.

point — a measure of size used in layout and typesetting. One point is equal to one twelfth of a pica, and approximately equal to one seventy-second of an inch. It it most often used to indicate the size of type. Typical point sizes would be 10 points for typewriter characters and most text in books, 48 for everyday newspaper headlines, and down to 6 or 8 point for legal notices and "fine print". Note that most type styles include some space between lines and thus letters are not quite as high as their nominal point size. See also **body height**.

positive — an image that keeps the same tonal orientation of the original, such as black letters on a white background. Many photographic processes produce negatives, but electronic processes can usually produce either positive or negative images on command.

proportional characters — characters designed so that some characters, such as "m", take up more horizontal space than others such as "i". Proportional characters pack more information into the same space, are easier to read, and look more like typesetting than do constant-width **monospaced** fonts.

quad — to align a block of type to the center, left or right, originally by adding spacing material as needed. Now, the same function can be done by directly aligning the material on most systems.

ragged — said of type where the successive lines do not all start or end at the same position. When not otherwise specified, ragged lines are only ragged on the right while flush (even) on the left.

reduce — to make smaller in size. The opposite of **blow-up** or **enlarge**. Reductions are usually specified by percentage, meaning a reduction to half size is specified as a 50% reduction.

reverse — to change the tonal orientation of an image, making the darker elements lighter and the lighter darker. Most electronic imaging systems can do this by command, but photographic processes are usually fixed as either reversal or positive processes. Note that to physically reverse the spatial orientation of an image is instead known as "flopping" or "reflecting" the image.

roman — the style of letters with upright main stems, in contrast to italics and other oblique letters that have stems set at angles. Roman types are the normal variety in most Western languages.
  "Roman" is also a class of type styles based on the lettering style used by Roman scribes. It has good contrast between strokes and pointed serifs.

sans serif — type styles that do not have serifs (extra strokes on the end of the lines making up the letters). These are more modern looking, but many people find them hard to read in large blocks of text.

screen (v) — to take images that had continuous tones and break them up into patterns of tiny saturated dots, with the darker tones represented by larger or closer dots. Screening is a necessary step for most printing technologies, which cannot directly print intermediate tones. See also **halftone**.

series — the complete size range of a typeface.

serif — a small cross-stroke or ornament at the end of the main strokes making up a character. Most older types have serifs, and many people find typefaces with serifs easier to read. However, sans serif (without serif) types have a cleaner, more modern appearance.

set size — the width of a portion of type of a given point size (height). Typefaces with wider set sizes take up more room for the same content.

set solid — type formatted with no leading (extra space) between the lines. Normally, type is set with extra space, so typically 10 point type might be set on 12 point.

showing — display of the various type fonts and ornamental elements available from a system or compositor.

slug — an identification line showing which story a section of copy or typeset material belongs to. Slugs are usually placed at the top corner of submitted copy, and at the top line of any galleys. A "slug" is also a line or phrase giving the name of a department or section in a publication. Also called a "departmental slug." For example, "Reviews..."

small caps — a set of capital letters equal in size to what normally would be the lowercase letters for that typesize and style. Small caps are normally used in **caps and small caps** formats in place of lowercase letters.

soft hyphen — a hyphen character that has been specially coded so that it is only displayed if the formatting and copyfitting puts it at the end of a line. Also called a **discretionary hyphen** or **ghost hyphen**.

spread — two facing pages, especially if treated for design as a single unit. A spread that crosses the gutter (divider between the pages) is called a "double truck."

stem — the main vertical stroke (or one of the main vertical strokes) making up a character. For example, the central vertical stroke in the letter "T".

surprint — printing over previously-printed graphics or text, or a design in which lettering or other darker elements appear over a halftone or lighter element.

swash letters — an ornamental letterform used particularly at the beginning of chapters or sections. Strictly speaking, it is a type of italic character with some characteristic extra flourishes.

tail — a downward-sloping part of a letter, such as the lower arm of the "K" or "R".

text-style types — type styles patterned after the hand-lettered ornamental styles of the middle ages. Old English is the most well-known. These type styles are rarely used for actual text, because they are hard to read.

text type — type styles and sizes used for the main text of written material. Generally, this means type of 14 points or less in size, and in one of the more readable typefaces.

thin space — the thinnest space normally used to separate words or other typographic elements (not counting the **hair space**, which is normally used within elements or in combinations). It is usually the same width as the period.

tight — said of lines that do not have much space between words (or other elements). Good typography requires lines that are neither too tight nor too loose.

tombstoning — the unwanted horizontal alignment of unrelated elements on a page.

typeface — a complete set of characters in a particular design or style. Typefaces come in families of different weights (light, medium and bold), different point sizes, and different slants (roman, italic, or other oblique).

u & lc — a common abbreviation for *upper and lower case*, the format often used for titles and headlines that starts each significant word with an uppercase letter but otherwise uses lowercase.

vertex — a point at which two strokes in a character meet to form a point, particularly one at the bottom (such as in the letter "V").

video layout terminal (VLT) — what people in the typesetting industry call terminals that allow the user to arrange type on the page.

weight — the boldness or thickness of a letter or font. Many type styles have been designed with special light, medium and bold forms, but on many electronic typesetting systems the other weights are created as variations on the normal medium.

X — a symbol for line length or column width used in marking copy for typesetting. Unless otherwise specified, the number following the X is the desired width in picas (the printer's measure approximately equal to ⅙ of an inch).

x-height — the size of a small letter "x", which is also normally the height of the main body of the lowercase letters excluding ascenders and descenders.

APPENDIX A:
COMPANY LIST

Addison-Wesley Publishing Co.
Reading, MA 01867
Phone: (617) 944-3700
MicroTeX
Price: $495

Adobe Systems Inc.
1870 Embarcadero Road
Palo Alto, CA 94303
Phone: (415) 852-0271
PostScript

Aldus Corporation
411 First Avenue South,
Suite 200
Seattle, WA 98104
Phone: (206) 622-5500
PageMaker
Price: $495

Allied Linotype Company
425 Oser Ave.
Hauppauge, NY 11788
Phone: (516) 434-2000
Linotronic 100
Price: $30,000
Linotronic 300
Price: $40,000

Altsys Corp.
PO Box 865410
Plano, TX 75086
Phone: (214) 596-4970
PostScript Fonts
Price: $450
FONTastic
Price: $50

Ann Arbor Softworks, Inc.
308 1/2 South State Street
Ann Arbor, MI 48104

Phone: (313) 996-3838
InMotion
Price: $140

Apple Computer Inc.
20525 Mariani Ave.
Cupertino, CA 95014
Phone: (408) 973-3317
Appletalk cables
Price: $50 ea.
HD-20
Price: $1499
LaserWriter
Price: $6000
LaserWriter Plus
Price: $6800
Macintosh Plus
Price: $2599
Macintosh 512K
Price: $1995
MacPaint,
MacWrite &
MacDraw
Price: $125 ea.
MacTerminal
Price: $99

Ashton-Tate
10150 West Jefferson Blvd.
Culver City, CA 90230
Phone: (213) 204-5570
dBASE II
Price: $695

Assimilation Inc.
485 Alberto Way
Los Gatos, CA 95030
Phone: (408) 356-6241
Mac Spell Right
Price: $89

Bestinfo
33 Chester Pike
Ridley Park, PA 19078
Phone: (215) 521-0757
Superpage
Price: $7000

Borland International
4585 Scotts Valley Drive
Scotts Valley, CA 95066
Phone: 800-255-8008/800-742-1133
SideKick w/PhoneLink
Price: $100 Mac
Turbo Lightning
Price: $99.95
SideKick
Price: $50 IBM PC
SuperKey
Price: $69.95 PC

Boston Computer Society
One Center Plaza
Boston, MA 02108
Phone: (617) 367-8080
Desktop Publishing User Gp
Price: $28/yr

Boston Software Publishers Inc.
1260 Boylston Street
Boston, MA 02215
Phone: 617-267-4747/800-556-0027
MacPublisher II
Price: $150

Broderbund Software
17 Paul Drive
San Rafael, CA 94903
The Print Shop
Price: $49.95

Canon USA Printer Division
One Canon Plaza
Lake Success, NY 11042
Phone: (516) 488-6700
LBP-8A1 and LBP-8A2
Price: $3495

Centram Systems West, Inc.
2372 Ellsworth Ave.
Berkeley, CA 94704
Phone: (415) 644-8244
TOPS PC AppleTalk Board
Price: $349

Century Software
2306 Cotner Ave.
Los Angeles, CA 90064
Phone: (213) 829-4436

LaserFonts Microfonts
Price: $30
LaserFonts Willamette
Price: $30

CompuCRAFT
PO Box 3155
Englewood, CO 80155
Phone: (303) 850-7472
Mac-Art Library
Price: $200, or $30 per disk

CompuServe
5000 Arlington Centre Blvd.
Columbus, OH 43220
Phone: 614-457-0802/800-848-8199
On-Line Information
Price: $6-15/hr

Control-C Software Inc.
6441 S.W. Canyon Ct.
Portland, OR 97221
Phone: (503) 292-8842
StarJet
Price: $150

Cordata
275 East Hillcrest Drive
Thousand Oaks, CA 91360
Phone: (805) 495-5800
Cordata LP300
Price: $3395

Creighton Development
16 Hughes Street, Suite C-106
Irvine, CA 92718
Phone: (714) 472-0488
MacSpell+
Price: $99

Creighton Development Inc.
4931 Birch
Newport Beach, CA 92660
Phone: (714) 476-1973
ProPrint
Price: $74-225

Cricket Software
3508 Market Street, Suite 206
Philadelphia, PA 19104
Phone: (215) 387-7955
Cricket Graph
Price: $195-495

Data Transforms Inc.
616 Washington Street
Denver, CO 80203
Phone: (303) 832-1501

Fontrix
Price: $150

Datacopy Corp.
1215 Terra Bella Ave.
Mountain View, CA 94043
Phone: (415) 965-7900
Model 730
Price: $4950

Datalogica USA
Matrix Plz, 1964 Westwood Bld325
Los Angeles, CA 90025
Phone: 213-474-0068/265-7596
dMacIII

Dataproducts Corp.
6200 Canoga Ave.
Woodland Hills, CA 91365
Phone: (818) 887-8000
LZR-2665
Price: $22,900

Dest Corporation
1202 Cadillac Court
Milpitas, CA 95035
Phone: (408) 946-7100
PC Scan
Price: $1995
Text Pac Software
Price: $595

Digital Marketing
2363 Boulevard Circle Suite 8
Walnut Creek, CA 94595
Phone: (415) 947-1000
Index (formerly DocuMate Plus)
Price: $99
Milestone
Price: $99

Digital Research Inc.
60 Garden Court
Monterey, CA 93942
Phone: 408-646-6218/408-646-6220
GEM Collection
Price: $199

Enterset
410 Townsend Street
San Francisco, CA 94107
Phone: 415-543-7644/800-556-2283
QuickPaint
Price: $50

Epson Corporation
2780 Lomita Blvd.
Torrance, CA 90505

Phone: (213) 533-8277
Epson FX/MX Printers
Price: $400-$800

FTL Systems Inc.
234 Eglinton Ave. E. #205
Toronto, Ontario,
M4P1KS   Canada
Phone: (416) 487-2142
MacT$_E$X
Price: $750

Forethought, Inc.
1973 Landings Drive
Mountain View, CA 94043
Phone: 415-961-4720
800-622-9273
Factfinder
Price: $150

Fuji
350 Fifth Ave.
New York, NY 10118
Ink Jet Printer

Genicom Corporation
509 West Grace St.
Richmond, VA 23220
Phone: 800-437-7468
703-949-1170
5010 Laser Printer
Price: $2995

Good Ideas
175 Lowell Street
Andover, MA 10810
Phone: (617) 475-7238
Type-Set-It
Price: $395

Graphics Communications Inc.
200 Fifth Avenue
Waltham, MA 02254
Phone: (617) 890-8778
Graphwriter
Price: $595

Hayden Software Company Inc.
650 Suffolk Street
Lowell, MA 01854
Phone: (800) 343-1218
(617) 937-0200
Hayden:Speller
Price: $79.95
Art Grabber+
Price: $50
VideoWorks
Price: $100

Hayes Microcomputer Products Inc.
5923 Peachtree Industrial Blvd.
Norcross, GA 30092
Phone: (404) 441-1617
SmartModem 1200 w/Mac cabl
Price: $649

Heizer Software
5120 Coral Street
Concord, CA 94521
Phone: (415) 827-9013
Font Explorer
Price: $25

Hercules
2550 Ninth Street
Berkeley, CA 94710
Phone: 415-540-6000/800-532-0600
Hercules Color Card
Price: $245
**Hercules Monochrome
Graphics Card**
Price: $499

Hewlett-Packard
11000 Wolfe Rd.
Cupertino, CA 95014
Phone: 800-367-4772
PCLPak
Price: $79, free w/Font purchase

IOMEGA Corporation
1821 West 4000 South
Roy, UT 84067
Phone: 800-556-1234
800-441-2345
Bernoulli Box

IQ Technologies
11811 N E 1st Street, Suite 308
Bellevue, WA 98005
Phone: 800-232-8324/206-451-0232
SmartCable SC817
Price: $49.95

ImageSet Corporation
555 19th Street
San Francisco, CA 94107
Phone: (415) 626-8366
IMCAP/IMSHOW
Price: Free

ImageWorld Inc.
PO Box 10415
Eugene, OR 97440
Phone: (503) 485-0395
MacMemories
Price: $40/disk-$400/13 disk set

Innovative Data Design Inc.
1975 Willow Pass Rd. #8
Concord, CA 94520
Phone: (415) 680-6818
MacDraft
Price: $239

Insight Development Corp.
2005 Vine Street #4
Berkeley, CA 94709
Phone: (415) 527-8646
LaserControl
Price: $150-100/$499-200/$749-30

Interleaf Inc.
1100 Massachusetts Ave.
Cambridge, MA 02138
Phone: (800)241-7700
Interleaf Publishing Sys
Price: $46,000 system

Kensington Microware Ltd.
251 Park Ave. South
New York, NY 10010
Phone: (212)475-5200
Maccessories Graphic Accen
Price: $50

Knowledge Engineering
GPO Box 2139
New York, NY 10116
Phone: (212) 473-0095
JustText
Price: $195

Koala Technologies
2065 Junction Ave.
San Jose, CA 95131
Phone: (800) 562-2327
MacVision
Price: $400

Lexisoft
706 5th Street
Davis, CA 95616
Phone: (916) 758-3630
Spellbinder
Price: $495

Lifetree Software Inc.
411 Pacific St, Suite 315
Monterey, CA 93940
Phone: (408) 373-4718
Volkswriter 3
Price: $295

Linguists Software
137 Linden St.

South Hamilton, MA 01982
Phone: (617)468-3037
foreign language fonts
Price: $100-180

Lotus Development Corp.
55 Cambridge Pkwy.
Cambridge, MA 02142
Phone: (617) 577-8500
Jazz
Price: $595

Macadam Publishing Inc.
4700 SW Macadam Ave.
Portland, OR 97201
Phone: (503) 241-8060
Famous People
Price: $30

Magna Computer Systems Inc.
14724 Ventura Blvd.
Sherman Oaks, CA 91403
Phone: (818) 986-9233
MagnaType
Price: $8500

Magnum Software
21115 Devonshire St. #337
Chatsworth, CA 91311
Phone: (818) 700-0510
McPic!
Price: $50

Manhattan Graphics Corporation
163 Varick Street
New York, NY 10013
Phone: (212) 924-2778
ReadySetGo 2.0/1.0
Price: $195/$125

Micro Planning Software
235 Montgomery St, Suite 840
San Francisco, CA 94104
Phone: (415) 788-3324
Micro Planner
Price: $349

MICROGRAFIX Inc.
1820 Greenville Ave.
Richardson, TX 75081
Phone: 214-234-1769/800-272-3729
Windows DRAW!
Price: $199

MicroPro Intl.
33 San Pablo Ave.
San Rafael, CA 94903
Phone: (415) 499-4022

WordStar
Price: $495

Microtek Lab, Inc.
16901 South Western Ave.
Gardena, CA 90247
Phone: (213) 321-2121
MS-300 Scanner

Microvision Company
38 Montvale Ave.
Stoneham, MA 02180
Phone: (617) 438-5520
MacViz
Price: $299

Miles Computing Inc.
21018 Osborne St. Bldg.5
Canoga Park, CA 91304
Phone: (818)994-7901
Mac the Knife Vol.1
Price: $40
Vol 3: Mac the Ripper
Price: $60

Mouse Systems Corp.
2600 San Tomas Expressway
Santa Clara, CA 95051
Phone: 408-988-0211/800-547-4000
PC Paint Plus
Price: $99, $220 w/PC Mouse

Multimate International Corp.
52 Oakland Ave North
East Hartford, CT 06108
Phone: (203) 522-2116
Multimate Advantage
Price: $595

Mycroft Labs, Inc.
2615 North Monroe Street
Tallahassee, FL 32303
Phone: (904) 385-1141
MITE
Price: $195

New Image Technology Inc.
10300 Greenbelt Rd. #104
Seabrook, MD 20706
Phone: (301) 464-3100
Magic
Price: $399/without camera

Oasis Systems
4909 Ostrow St., Suite F
San Diego, CA 92103
Phone: (619)279-5711
Word Plus

Price: $150
Punctuation & Style
Price: $125

Paradise Systems Inc.
217 East Grand Ave.
South San Francisco, CA 94080
Phone: (415)588-6000
Mac 10
Price: $999

Peripherals Computers & Supplies
2232 Perkiomen Ave.
Mt. Penn, PA 19606
Phone: (215) 779-0522
VersaTerm
Price: $99

Personal Computer Peripherals Inc
6204 Benjamin Rd.
Tampa, FL 33614
Phone: 813-884-3092/800-MACBUTT
MacBottom
Price: $1595-10MB

Personal TeX Inc.
20 Sunyside, Suite H
Mill Valley, CA 94941
Phone: (415) 388-8853
PCTeX
Price: $379-579

Polaris Software
310 S. Via Vera Cruz #205
San Marcos, CA 92069
Phone: (619) 489-8243
PrintMerge
Price: $99

ProSoft
7248 Bellaire Ave.
No. Hollywood, CA 91605
Phone: (818)765-4444
Fontasy
Price: $49.95

QMS
PO Box 81250
Mobile, AL 36689
Phone: (205) 633-4300
Lasergrafix 2400 (PS)
Price: $29995

Quadram
One Meca Way
Norcross, GA 30093
Phone: (404) 923-6666
QuadLaser

Price: $3795
Imageware
Price: $295

Queue Inc.
562 Boston Ave.
Bridgeport, CT 06610
Phone: 800-232-2224/203-335-0908
Q-Art
Price: $30

Qume/Hitachi
2350 Qume Drive
San Jose, CA 95131
Phone: (800) 223-2479
LaserTEN
Price: $2895

Rabar Systems
PO Box 306
Westport, CT 06881
Phone: (203) 227-4415
CtlLaser
Price: $65

RoseSoft Inc.
4710 University Way NE, Suite 601
P.O. Box 45808
Seattle, WA 98105
Phone: (206) 524-2350
ProKey
Price: $130

RoZet
1400 Shelbyville St.
Center, TX 75935
Phone: (409) 598-5378
Pattern Collection Vol. 1
Price: $13

ScenicSoft Inc.
12314 Scenic Drive
Edmonds, WA 98020
Phone: (206) 742-6677
ScenicWriter
Price: $995

Silicon Beach Software
PO Box 261430
San Diego, CA 92126
Phone: (619) 695-6956
Paint Cutter
Price: $39

Simon & Schuster Computer SW
1230 Avenue of the Americas
New York, NY 10020
Phone: (212) 245-6400

Paper Airplane Construction
Price: $40
The Mac Art Department
Price: $39.95

Soft Wares Inc.
19 Monroe Drive
Williamsville, NY 14221
Phone: 800-848-5500/800-447-5500
GRIDS
Price: $38

SoftCraft
222 State Street
Madison, WI
Phone: 800-351-0500/608-257-3300
Fancy Word
Price: $140
Fancy Word Fonts
Price: $15 per disk
Fancy Font
Price: $180

SoftStyle Inc.
7192 Kalanianaole Hwy #205
Honolulu, HI 96825
Phone: (800) 367-5600
Laserstart
Price: $95
Printworks for Lasers
Price: $125

SpectraFAX Corp.
2000 Palm St. S.
Naples, FL 33962
Phone: (813) 775-2737
SpectraFAX 200
Price: $3995

Springboard Software Inc.
7807 Creekridge Circle
Minneapolis, MN 55435
Phone: (612) 944-3912
The Newsroom
Price: $59.95
Graphics Expander
Price: $39.95

Studio Software
17862-C Fitch
Irvine, CA 92714
Phone: 800-821-7816/800-221-3806
Do-It
Price: $2500

Summagraphics Corp.
777 State Street Extension
Fairfield, CT 06430

Phone: (203)384-1344
MM1812 Digitizing Tablet
Price: $995
MacTablet
Price: $495

T/Maker Company
2115 Landings Drive
Mtn. View, CA 94043
Phone: (415) 962-0195
ClickArt
Price: $50
ClickArt Effects
Price: $50
Personal Publisher
Price: $185 (dot matrix), $335 (laser)

Tangent Technologies Ltd.
5720 Peachtree Pkwy #100
Norcross, GA 30092
Phone: (404) 662-0366
PC MacBridge
Price: $650

Tech Knowledge
2615 11th Ave. West
Seattle, WA 98119
Phone: (206) 285-2146
WX
Price: $35

Tegra Inc.
900 Middlesex Turnpike
Billerica, MA 01821
Phone: (617) 663-7435
Genesis

Telos Software Products
3420 Ocean Park Blvd #3050
Santa Monica, CA 90405
Phone: (213) 450-2424
Filevision
Price: $195

The Model Office Co.
49 Wellington St East, Flatiron
Bldg, Toronto, ONT
M5E 1C9, CANADA
Phone: 416-860-1033/800-268-8181
Document Compare
Price: $99

The Software Store
706 Chippewa Square
Marquette, MI 49855
Phone: (906) 228-7622
Mastercom
Price: $49

Thunderware, Inc.
21 Orinda Way
Orinda, CA 94563
Phone: (415) 254-6581
ThunderScan
Price: $229

Ventura Software
675 Jarvis Drive, Suite C
Morgan Hill, CA 95037
Phone: (408) 779-5000
Ventura Publisher
Price: $695

Writing Consultants
300 Main Street
Rochester, NY 14445
Phone: (716) 377-0130
Word Finder
Price: $79.95

Xerox Corp.
101 Continental Blvd.
El Segundo, CA 90245

Phone: (213) 536-7000
4045 Laser CP
Price: $4995

XyQuest, Inc.
PO Box 372
Bedford, MA 01730
Phone: (617)275-7194
XyWrite III
Price: $195

ZSoft Corporation
1950 Spectrum Circle Suite A495
Marietta, GA 30067
Phone: (404) 980-1950
PC Paintbrush

ZyLAB Corporation
233 East Erie Street
Chicago, IL 60611
Phone: 312-642-2201
800-54INDEX
ZyINDEX
Price: $145

APPENDIX B:
PRODUCT LIST

4045 Laser CP — Xerox Corp.
5010 Laser Printer — Genicom Corporation
Art Grabber — Hayden Software Company
Bernoulli Box — IOMEGA Corporation
ClickArt — T/Maker Company
ClickArt Effects — T/Maker Company
Color Graphics Adapter — IBM
Cordata LP300 — Cordata
Çricket Graph — Cricket Software
CtlLaser — Rabar Systems
dBASE II — Ashton-Tate
dMacIII — Datalogica USA
Do-It — Studio Software
Document Compare—The Model Office Co
Epson FX/MX Printers — Epson Corp.
Factfinder — Forethought, Inc.
Famous People — Macadam Publishing Inc.
Fancy Font — Softcraft Inc.
Fancy Word — Softcraft Inc.
Filevision — Telos Software Products
FONTastic — Altsys Corp.
Font Explorer — Heizer Software
Fontasy — ProSoft
Fontrix — Data Transforms Inc.
FTLTEX — FTL Systems Inc.
GEM Collection — Digital Research Inc.
Genesis — Tegra Inc.
Graphics Expander — Springboard Software
Graphwriter — Graphics Communications
GRIDS — Soft Wares Inc.
Hayden:Speller — Hayden Software
Hercules Color Card — Hercules
Hercules Graphics Card — Hercules
Imageware — Quadram
IMCAP/IMSHOW — ImageSet Corporation
InMotion — Ann Arbor Softworks, Inc.
Index — Digital Marketing
Interleaf — Interleaf Inc.
Jazz — Lotus Development
JustText — Knowledge Engineering
LaserControl — Insight Development Corp.

Lasergrafix 2400 (PS) — QMS
LaserJet & LaserJet Plus — Hewlett-Packard
LaserFonts Microfonts — Century Software
LaserFonts Willamette — Century Software
LaserStart — SoftStyle Inc.
LaserTEN — Qume/Hitachi
LaserWriter & LaserWriter Plus — Apple Computer, Inc.
LBP-8A1 and LBP-8A2 — Canon USA Printer Division
Linotronic 100 — Allied Linotype Company
Linotronic 300 — Allied Linotype Company
LZR-2665 — Dataproducts Corp.
Mac 10 — Paradise Systems Inc.
Mac Art Department — Simon & Schuster, Computer Div.
Mac-Art Library — CompuCRAFT
MacBottom — Personal Computer Peripherals Inc.
Maccessories Graphic Accen — Kensington Microware Ltd.
MacDraft — Innovative Data Design Inc.
MacDraw — Apple Computer, Inc.
Macintosh — Apple Computer, Inc.
MacMemories — ImageWorld Inc.
MacPaint — Apple Computer, Inc.
MacProject — Apple Computer, Inc.
MacPublisher II — Boston Software Publishers Inc.
MacSpell+ — Creighton Development
Mac Spell Right — Assimilation Inc.
MacTablet — Summagraphics Corp.
MacTerminal — Apple Computer Inc.
Mac the Knife — Miles Computing Inc.
Mac the Ripper — Miles Computing Inc.
MacVision — Koala Technologies
MacViz — Microvision Company
MacWrite — Apple Computer, Inc.
Magic — New Image Technology Inc.
MagnaType — Magna Computer Systems

285

Mastercom — The Software Store
McPic! — Magnum Software
Micro Planner — Micro Planning Software
MicroTeX — Addison-Wesley Publishing
Milestone — Digital Marketing
MITE — Mycroft Labs, Inc.
MM1812 Digitizing Tablet — Summagraphics
Model 730 — Datacopy Corp.
MS-300 Scanner — Microtek Lab, Inc.
Multimate Advantage — Multimate Intl. Corp.
Newsroom — Springboard Software Inc.
On-Line Information — CompuServe
PageMaker — Aldus Corporation
Paint Cutter — Silicon Beach Software
Paper Airplane Constructio — Simon & Schuster, Computer Div.
Pattern Collection Vol. 1 — RoZet
PC MacBridge — Tangent Technologies Ltd.
PC Paint Plus — Mouse Systems Corp.
PC Paintbrush — ZSoft Corporation
PC Scan — DEST Corp.
PC Scan — Dest Corporation
PCLPak — Hewlett-Packard
PCTeX — Personal TeX Inc.
PostScript — Adobe Systems Inc.
PostScript Fonts — Altsys Corp.
PrintMerge — Polaris Software
Print Shop — Broderbund Software
PrintWorks for Lasers — SoftStyle Inc.
ProPrint — Creighton Development Inc.

Punctuation & Style — Oasis Systems
Q-Art — Queue Inc.
QuadLaser — Quadram
QuickPaint — Enterset
ReadySetGo — Manhattan Graphics Corp.
ScenicWriter — ScenicSoft Inc.
SideKick — Borland International
SmartCable SC817 — IQ Technologies
SmartModem 1200 — Hayes Microcomputer Products Inc.
SpectraFAX 200 — SpectraFAX Corp.
Spellbinder — Lexisoft
StarJet — Control-C Software Inc.
Superpage — Bestinfo
Text Pac Software — Dest Corporation
ThunderScan — Thunderware, Inc.
TOPS PC AppleTalk Board — Centram Systems West, Inc.
Turbo Lightning — Borland International
Type-Set-It — Good Ideas
Ventura Publisher — Ventura Software Inc.
VersaTerm — Peripherals Computers & Supplies
VideoWorks — Hayden Software
Volkswriter 3 — Lifetree Software Inc.
Windows DRAW! — MICROGRAFX Inc.
Word Finder — Writing Consultants
Word Plus — Oasis Systems
WordStar — MicroPro Intl.
WX — Tech Knowledge
XyWrite III — XyQuest, Inc.
ZyINDEX — ZyLAB Corporation

APPENDIX C:
BIBLIOGRAPHY

Books

Adobe Systems, Inc., *PostScript Language Reference Manual* and *PostScript Language Tutorial and Cookbook* (2 volume set), Addison-Wesley Publishing Company, Reading, MA. 1985.

Holt, Robert Lawrence, *How to Publish, Promote, and Sell Your Own Book*, St. Martin's Press, New York, NY. 1985.

International Paper Company, *Pocket Pal, A graphics arts production handbook*, International Paper Company, New York, NY. 1983.

Laing, John, *Do-It-Yourself Graphic Design*, Macmillan Publishing Company, New York, NY. 1984.

Labuz, Ronald, *How to Typeset From a Word Processor*, R. R. Bowker, New York, NY. 1984.

Lem, Dean Phillip, *Graphics Master 3*, Dean Lem Associates, Inc., Los Angeles, CA. 1985.

Poynter, Dan, *The Self-Publishing Manual*, Para Publishing, Santa Barbara, CA. 1984.

Sikonowiz, Walter, *The Complete Book of Word Processing and Business Graphics*, Prentice-Hall/Micro Text, Reading, MA. 1982.

Strunk, William and White, E. B., *The Elements of Style*, Macmillan Publishing Company, New York, NY. 1972.

University of Chicago Press, *A Manual of Style*, University of Chicago Press, Chicago, IL. 1979.

Magazines, Journals, Newspapers

American Printer, 300 West Adams Street, Chicago IL 60606. $35 per year.

Desktop Publishing, P. O. Box 5245, Redwood City CA 94063. (415) 364-0108. $24 per year.

Folio, the Magazine for Magazine Management, P. O. Box 4006, 125 Elm Street, New Canaan CT 06840. (203) 972-0761. $58 per year.

The Futurist, World Future Society, 4916 St. Elmo Avenue, Bethesda MD 20814. (301) 656-8274. $25 per year.

Graphics Arts Monthly and The Printing Industry, Technical Publishing, 875 Third Avenue, New York NY 10022. (212) 605-9548. $50 per year.

Inside Print (formerly *Magazine Age*), MPE Inc., 125 Elm Street, New Canaan CT 06840. (203) 972-0761. $36 per year.

Magazine Design and Production, Globecom Publishing Ltd., 4551 West 107th Street #343, Overland KS 66207. $36 per year.

Personal Publishing, Renegade Publications, Box 390, Itasca IL 60143. $36 per year.

Printing Impressions, 401 North Broad Street, Philadelphia PA 19108. $50 per year.

Printing Journal, 2401 Charleston Road, Mountain View CA 94943. $16 per year.

Publisher's Weekly R. R. Bowker, 205 East 42nd Street, New York NY 10017. $52 per year.

Small Press, the Magazine of Independent Publishing, R. R. Bowker, 205 East 42nd Street, New York NY 10017. $18 per year.

TypeWorld, 15 Oakridge Circle, Wilmington MA 01887. $20 per year.

Newsletters

Brilliant Ideas for Publishers, Creative Brilliance Associates, 4709 Sherwood Road, Box 4237, Madison WI 53711. (608) 271-6867. Free to publishers.

CAP (Computer Aided Publishing) Report, InfoVision Inc., 52 Dragon Court, Woburn MA 01801. (617) 935-5186. $195 per year.

The Desktop Publisher, Aldus Corporation, 616 First Avenue, Suite 400, Seattle WA 98104. (206) 441-8666. Free to registered users of Aldus software.

microPublishing Report, 2004 Curtis Avenue #A, Redondo Beach CA 90278. (213) 376-5724. $175 per year.

Quick Printer's Guide, Lambda Company, 3655 Frontier Avenue, Boulder CO 80301. (303) 449-4827. $75 per year.

Seybold Report on Publishing Systems, Seybold Publications, Box 644, Media PA 19063. (215) 565-2480. $240 per year.

WYSIWYG, Ramos Publishing Company, 127 Columbia Avenue, Redwood City CA 94063. (415) 364-4867. $195 per year.

INDEX